ma

WEST AFRICAN
RELIGION

WEST AFRICAN RELIGION

A Study of the Beliefs and Practices of Akan, Ewe,
Yoruba, Ibo, and Kindred Peoples

Edward
GEOFFREY PARRINDER

With a Foreword by the
REV. DR EDWIN SMITH
Late Editor of *Africa*, Author of *The Ila-
speaking Peoples of Northern Rhodesia*, etc.

BARNES & NOBLE, Inc.
NEW YORK
PUBLISHERS & BOOKSELLERS SINCE 1873

Reproduced and Printed in Great Britain by
Redwood Press Limited
Trowbridge & London

Preface to the Second Edition

THE DEMAND for a second edition of this book made me turn back and look critically at what was my first publication. It was eighteen years since, living in Dahomey in 1943, I had begun work on this comparative study, which was completed in 1946 and published in 1949. Since then much has changed. Colonies have become independent States, Gold Coast has changed to Ghana, I hope I have grown in knowledge and some viewpoints needed alteration.

The readers I had originally in mind were mainly European students of comparative religion, and prospective missionaries and Government officials. Some of these have read it, but even more has it been used in West Africa, both by African students of religion and by general readers. In 1949 I was appointed to be the first lecturer in the new Department of Religious Studies in the University College of Ibadan, Nigeria. I worked out and for nine years taught a syllabus for a London University examination paper, on the Indigenous Religious Beliefs of West Africa, using this book as one of the text-books. This was the first time that such a syllabus had been taught in any university, though since then courses on African religions have become less rare. I owe a great debt to my students. It was strange for a foreigner to teach them the outlines of the religion of their own fathers. We learnt many things together, and I want to thank them for their forbearance, and also to express the hope that they learnt something of the value of systematic study and of the proper place of their ancestral religion in the context of the world's religions.

My years in Nigeria enabled me to continue research, and in particular to gain closer acquaintance with the beliefs of Yoruba and Ibo, and related peoples of Western and Eastern Nigeria. When it was clear to me that a complete rewriting of this book was the only possible course, in view of the many changed circumstances, then I felt that Ibo beliefs must be included, and reference made wherever possible to Bini, Ibibio, Nupe, and Gã, so as to make the work useful to a wider range of students. Comparative studies are still scarce and go rapidly out of print. To include these further notes I have drawn on research work done with the help of some of my students, and on books published since the first edition. As it was required that the book should be kept to about the same length, some of the paragraphs about migrations and origins have been omitted, and some of the minor details that have special reference to Dahomey but which are of little interest to other readers. To help students I have changed the order in some chapters, so that the comparison usually proceeds from Akan to Ewe, Yoruba and Ibo, in that order. The last two chapters have been combined, and cut down in detail, and a new one has been added to soften the abrupt ending and bring it up to date. A bibliography has been added to help those who want to do further reading.

I look back on twenty years in different parts of West Africa with happy memories, and I hope that the new edition of this book may be widely used in Nigeria, Ghana, Dahomey, and many other countries, in Africa and elsewhere. To the many friends who have helped me I express my deepest thanks.

KING'S COLLEGE   GEOFFREY PARRINDER
LONDON
April 1961

Contents

Foreword

IN MANY books and papers various phases of the religion of individual African tribes have been described. The time is ripe now for synthetic studies bringing together the beliefs and practices over wider fields and comparing them so that we may discern the principles which underlie them. It is such a synthetic study that Dr Parrinder offers in this book. He has wisely limited his field. He has not attempted the difficult—and indeed, in the present state of our knowledge, the impossible—task of covering all West African peoples, but has selected one very important group—the group that includes as its most prominent members the Yoruba, Ewe, and Akan, culturally among the most advanced of the Negroes.

The day has gone by when the indigenous faith of these and other Africans could be labelled 'fetishism', for we now know more about it than did those who invented this term. I agree with Dr Parrinder that this misleading label should be completely relegated to the museum of outworn categories. He correctly classifies the religion as Polytheism and this immediately puts a new face upon it. 'Fetishism' we think of as something brutal, credulous, irrational. We have advanced beyond polytheism, but it is not, I think, inherently absurd; it corresponds to a stage of human thinking when the universe is seen as the arena wherein many spiritual forces are operating and men have not yet discerned a unity amid the diversity. The polytheism has many features in common with that with which we are familiar in the history of Rome, Greece, Egypt, and other parts of the earth. The no less striking divergencies are, I suppose, accountable by differences in climatic conditions and ethnical character. The African gods are personal, supernatural, perhaps ubiquitous. Many of them, maybe the majority, are associated with phenomena of nature —sky and sun, rain and thunder—or with particular human activities. As Europeans and Asiatics had their Great Mother, De-meter, so Africans have their Mother Goddess—Asase Yaa, 'Old Mother Earth' of the Akan; and Abassi Isu Ma, 'the Goddess of the Face of Love', of 'the Face of the Mother' of the Ibibio; both givers of fertility. Among the scores or even hundreds of gods one may be exalted, as in Europe so also in Africa, to a rela-tively high or to a supreme position above others—as Jupiter was and Olorun is: exalted so high indeed as to be remote from men, if not inaccessible, like some great African potentate who is to be approached only through intermediaries. In Africa as in Europe religion has inspired art; but African artists have lavished their skill upon temples and drums and masks and not upon representa-tions of the gods in human form as the Greeks did. Dr Parrinder notes the exceptional instance of an image of Mawu, the deity of the Ewe—this may be of foreign origin; he also makes reference to the Madonna-like figures of the Earth Mother made by the Ibo. Besides the high and lesser beings who may be dignified by the title 'gods', there is a multitude of other spirits which, if taken alone, might warrant us in speaking of polydemonism rather than polytheism. Here again we are in an atmosphere familiar to readers of Roman and Greek literature. What W. Warde Fowler said of the Romans might be said also of West Africans: 'The early Roman seems to have looked upon all life and force and action, human or other, as in some sense associated with, and the result of, divine or spiritual agency.'

As if these were not enough, there are the divinized ancestors. The relation between these human and those non-human spirits is not always easy to determine; it is quite likely that some of the gods were once men. But certainly among West African negroes as among the Bantu-speaking peoples of other parts of Africa, the forefathers are very prominent in religious belief and practice. Some of the gods at least are remote but the ancestors are always near and normally attentive. 'Every pious West African,' says Dr Parrinder, 'before drinking will pour out a little wine from his gourd on to the floor, for the fathers.' Every religion has its higher and lower strata—our popular Christianity is no exception. So in West Africa there is what I call Dynamism—the belief in, and the practices associated with the belief in, impersonal, pervasive, mysterious forces acting through charms and amulets, words, spells, divinations. This sort of thing is universal and we ourselves have not completely grown out of it—witness our mascots and superstitions about 'luck'.

Dr Parrinder weaves his way courageously through this dense tangled jungle of belief and practice; and under his masterly guidance we can discern some order therein. His study is admirably objective, with a minimum of speculation as to origins and provenances. It is based, as synthetic studies must of necessity be, largely upon the researches of others, but Dr Parrinder has the enormous advantage of having lived among and studied at first hand the peoples whose religion he describes. Quite evidently he enjoyed the confidence of pagan priests and others who talked to him about matters not commonly the subject of conversation between black men and white. Every chapter shows how deeply the author has lived into his theme. I would single out for special mention the sections in which he describes the training of priests and devotees.

When such a rich feast is spread before us it would be churlish to ask for more. It is always stupid to complain that an author does not tell things he never planned to tell. I hope that some day Dr Parrinder, or someone equally competent, will follow up this study of the pagan religion with a study of the actual religion of those Africans who in various degrees of reality have accepted Christianity. It is not to be expected that they have made, or can make, a complete break with the past, however much they profess to do so. What in Christianity most attracted these polytheists and how precisely did they react to it? Do preachers and teachers deliberately set themselves to relate the new religion to the old? The Church has adopted African names for translating 'God'; but how far is the popular theology coloured by the old beliefs? Aggrey, we know, always thought of God as Father-Mother, or rather Mother-Father; and I doubt not this sense of the motherhood of God lingered on from his early training in a pagan family. Christianity may thus be enriched from pagan sources. On the other hand, it may be debased when the lower elements of paganism are perpetuated. West African polytheism will follow European polytheism into oblivion. One could wish that some at least of its best features were sublimated: on the credal side by recognition in daily life of ubiquitous spiritual forces working in the universe; on the practical side by the transference to the new religion on a higher level of something of the symbolism, the colour, the artistry, the gaiety that marked the old.

15th September 1947   EDWIN W. SMITH

Note on Pronunciation

g   is always hard
j   is voiced as in English (instead of dj or dz)
r   is the rolled lingual, tongue-tip
sh is used instead of ṣ, *orisha* in place of *oriṣa*
y   is consonantal as in *you*
a,e,i,o,u,   have the Italian values
ɛ   is used for the open e, instead of the old ẹ, as *Lɛgba*
ọ   is used for the open o, as in *Ọlọrũn*

Nasalized vowels are represented by the sign ~ placed over the vowel letter, thus *vodũ* instead of the common French rendering *vodoun*. But the *n* has been retained where it is usually printed, in well-known words like Ọlọrũn and Fõn.

    Tones have not been marked.

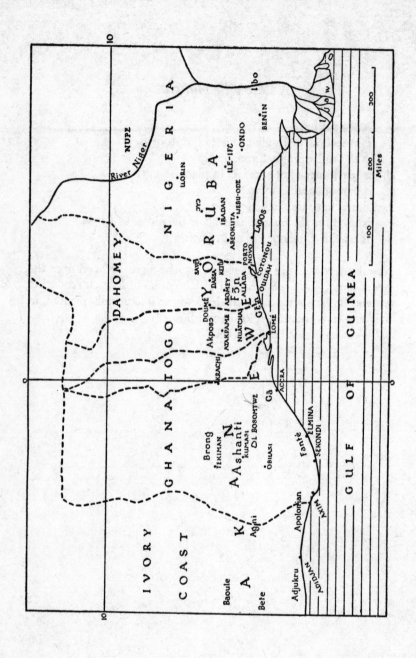

CHAPTER ONE

Introduction

T HE RELIGIOUS beliefs and practices of the peoples of West Africa have long been of interest, although careful investigation into concepts of deity and observation of rituals was hardly begun by trained scholars before the present century.

Systematic and critical studies have greatly developed during recent years, particularly between and after the two World Wars. The growth of the sciences of anthropology and the comparative study of religion has sent serious workers into special fields, and numbers of authoritative volumes have appeared, covering a considerable part of West Africa.

These investigations contain material unobtainable apart from long periods of research on the spot, and they have usually involved more than a passing acquaintance with the languages of the regions studied. Most of them are invaluable mines of reference. Often, however, the very detail of such works is a handicap to those who wish to become informed of the chief principles of African religion, and have neither the time nor the inclination to read about each group of peoples individually.

Lord Hailey, in his *African Survey*, writing of anthropology, pointed out the necessity for grouping the results of research, so that practical use might be made of the material by governments and other interested bodies. 'From the scientific, as well as from the practical, point of view there may be doubt whether the existing organization of field inquiries now being undertaken in Africa is such as to secure the best results from the available sources. . . . The selection of problems for study has largely been left to different investigators, who have published their results mainly in the form of monographs on a restricted area. . . . In consequence, there appears to be a dispersion of energy. It is clear that a complete investigation of every African tribe is impossible; but if an intensive study, arranged on a concerted plan, were made of three or four important tribes in every territory, the results would have a value extending beyond the immediate field of study, and would compensate more amply for the cost of research.'[1]

Such a concerted study is just as necessary in the religious field as elsewhere. Religion is a fundamental, perhaps the most important, influence in the life of most West Africans; yet its essential principles are too often unknown to educated Africans and Europeans, who thus make themselves constantly liable to misunderstand the people among whom they live.

In the study of West African religion it is necessary to exercise that comparative and critical analysis that some particularist investigators (for example, R. S. Rattray) have felt to be the essential corollary to their work of collecting first-hand data. Many obscure groups, and even villages, may have some practice stamped with their own special emphasis; but they certainly have much more that is common with their neighbours. These common elements need drawing out and collating, so that the student may have presented to him the nature of the chief beliefs and practices of these deeply religious peoples.

It is my aim to attempt such a comparative survey, and to indicate an approach to the understanding of the religion that has so often been miscalled 'fetishism'. While a certain detachment from the field is valuable, and a knowledge of general comparative religion is a great help, yet it could scarcely be hoped that the attempt would be successful without some first-hand knowledge of the field itself, a privilege that I have had in living in some places and visiting most parts of the area to be defined.

This task was begun by P. A. Talbot, for the peoples of Southern Nigeria. He collated the beliefs of Yoruba, Bini, Ibo, Ijaw, and the semi-Bantu tribes. His books gave an excellent survey, although some references are now out of date.[2]

I have tried to continue this study farther west. A wider field has been chosen, that which crosses the boundaries of Nigeria, Dahomey, Togo, Ghana and the Ivory Coast. It is necessary, as far

---

[1] *An African Survey* (1938), pp. 56–7.
[2] *The Peoples of Southern Nigeria* (4 vols., 1926). He says that the whole of his information was personally obtained, 'except for some details about the Yoruba'.

2

as possible in scientific works, to disregard the artificial political frontiers which carve up West Africa, divide its peoples, and isolate anthropological studies.

In this wide area I have selected four outstanding groups for fullest comparison and study, and have referred to sub-tribes and smaller divisions when some interesting point arises on which they have special importance. The four chief groups are the Ibo, Yoruba, Ewe, and Akan peoples, and within the two latter in particular the kingdoms of the Fõn of Abomey and Porto Novo, and the Ashanti of Kumasi. These great stocks divide most of the Guinea Coast linguistically between them; they and their sub-groups are the chief constituents of the Kwa group of the coastal Sudanic languages.[3]

The Akan group is found in Ghana and the eastern Ivory Coast. Of the Akan, the Ashanti came into special prominence in religious studies through the researches of the great anthropologist R. S. Rattray.[4] I have drawn on the works of Rattray and other writers, and some private information. I have worked among part of the Akan group in the Ivory Coast and refer occasionally to these little-known branches.

The Fõn (Fõ, nasalized) of Dahomey had the greatest kingdom, and most highly organized religion, of the loosely related Ewe peoples. Although they are not so well known to English readers as they deserve to be, or were formerly, yet Fõn priests and medicines are renowned among the neighbouring countries of Ghana and Nigeria and men come from far to learn their secrets. They are still one of the most highly organized indigenous religions, and most resistant to Christianity and Islam.

The American scholar, Melville Herskovits, made the standard work on the Fõn of Abomey.[5] I myself lived among the Fõn and Gũ for years, in and near the centres of Porto Novo and Abomey, and collected original material there. The Dahomean and Togolese divinities are very similar: Mawu, Da, So, Ifa, Lɛgba, Vudu, and Yɛhwe, are common to both.

---

[3] D. Westermann, *A Study of the Ewe Language* (1930), pp. 199–200.

[4] *Ashanti* (1923); *Religion and Art in Ashanti* (1927); *The Tribes of the Ashanti Hinterland* (1932).

[5] *Dahomey, An Ancient West African Kingdom* (New York, 1938).

3

I have also had the good fortune of living among the great Yoruba people, both among those branches that are in central Dahomey and in Nigeria. Although there is diversity among the different traditional kingdoms of this people, particularly if Benin is included, much is common in their religious life. I have also visited many parts of Ibo country and neighbouring regions in the Cameroons. In addition to my own observations and inquiries, I have referred to such scholars as S. S. Farrow, E. B. Idowu, P. A. Talbot, C. K. Meek, and S. F. Nadel for comparisons among different sections and neighbouring tribes.[6]

It may be noticed that the main groups chosen almost correspond to those studied by Sir A. B. Ellis at the end of the last century, in his series of books: *The Tshi-speaking Peoples of the Gold Coast, The Ewe-speaking Peoples of the Slave Coast, The Yoruba-speaking Peoples of the Slave Coast.*[7]

Ellis's works were useful in their day, but they are now outmoded. Especially are some of the writings of Ellis vitiated by theories, such as that which held the idea of a Supreme Being to be a recent European importation, and the characterization of West Africa as 'the land of Fetish'.

Ellis did, however, spread a large canvas before earlier readers. Later divisions of colonial and national rule tended to split up ethnological studies. The Yoruba, for example, while cradled in Nigeria, spread right across Dahomey and into Togoland; the Akan continue from Ghana into the Ivory Coast; and Ewe groups occupy much of the seaboard of Ghana, Togo, Dahomey, and even spread into Nigeria.

A further advantage in the choice of four main groups is that not only are they prominent in the religious sphere, but they are fairly compact in culture. The tribes of the western Ivory Coast and Liberia present an appalling confusion of languages and systems of government. The same applies in the Niger delta and in the Cameroons. Then to the north, not only are there many more backward tribes, but also Islam has come to rule and in many places to replace the ancient religion.

[6] S. S. Farrow, *Faith, Fancies and Fetich* (1926), E. B. Idowu, Olodumare, *God in Yoruba Belief* (1961), C. K. Meek, *Law and Authority in a Nigerian Tribe* (1937), S. F. Nadel, *Nupe Religion* (1954).   [7] 1887, 1890, 1894 respectively.

4

Some of the groups in which religion has reached its greatest development were also advanced in political structure and general culture. Ile-Ife was the religious home of the Yoruba and the centre of the fine brass heads and stone sculptures that have become renowned; Benin, not far away, was also famous for its bronzes. The kingdom of Old Oyo, at its greatest peak, had stretched from Benin to Togo.

The Ewe clans lacked coherence, but the kingdom of Dahomey gathered strength from the time of King Hwegbaja (died about 1680), and finally shook off the yoke of Oyo to which it had long paid tribute. The old palaces of Abomey with their coloured bas-reliefs, which are still preserved, give some idea of the culture of this kingdom.

The Ashanti also drew together from among the other Akan, some two hundred years ago, when King Osai Tutu finally freed his people from the domination of Denkira. The renown of the kingdom, and of its carved stools and coloured cloths, came to be known far beyond its frontiers. Other Akan groups migrated to the south and became the Fante of today, while the Brong remained to the north of Ashanti. Further clans, Agni (Anyi), Baule, Adjukru, and other Akans, migrated westwards to the Ivory Coast.

The Gã of Accra seem to belong to the Ewe group, though but few of their gods resemble those of Togo and Dahomey. A tradition holds that the Gã came from Benin far to the east; other groups that migrated later to Togo and Dahomey are called Gɛ̃ (or Popo and Mina), but they are of the same family. Some of the Gã religious concepts resemble those of Ashanti, perhaps picked up through close contacts.

The Ibo people of Eastern Nigeria had no central organization, but they were and have remained an active and progressive people with a high population which led them into the delta among the Ijaw people and into contacts with the outer world. Over the whole of Iboland and beyond, some of their religious beliefs became widely known, for example the great Earth Mother and the Aro Chuku oracle.[8]

The growth and development of the large kingdoms favoured a

[8] See K. O. Dike, *Trade and Politics in the Niger Delta* (1956), pp. 19ff.

development of religion beyond the local to a stage of 'generalization'. The cult of Shãngo seems to have been spread over all the Yoruba domains, and 'Nyame was known far beyond the Akan. Each tended to develop its own special emphasis, however. The warlike Ashanti concentrated upon ancestor cults of warrior heroes; the Fõn worked out a highly trained and controlled priesthood; the Yoruba cherish the intricate system of divining by the Ifa oracle.

As already stated, this book is a combination of original research together with references from the works of modern and well-qualified observers. In every chapter I have some new matter to add. I have been fortunate, in particular, in obtaining first-hand information upon the recruiting and 'convent' training of mediums and priests, to an extent hitherto unpublished.

In addition to comparison of religious practices in the four groups of our field, reference is also made to the comparative study of religion in general. The aim here is twofold: firstly, to show the relationship of West African religion to other religions, instead of treating it as an isolated phenomenon; secondly, to bring out some of the points which show clearly, over a large part of West Africa, an advance beyond the early stages of religious life.

CHAPTER TWO

The Nature of West African Religion

'PRIMITIVE RELIGION'?

THE RELIGION of West Africans often used to be referred to as 'primitive', but this is an inaccurate term. 'Primitive religion' means either religion as it appeared in its earliest forms among mankind, or else religion that has remained in the lowliest stages even in modern times. Neither of these is true of the West African groups that we have selected for study.[1]

Some of the older anthropologists were in the habit of collecting material from all over the world and putting it all together as 'primitive' or 'savage'. This was quite unscientific and all serious modern writers have abandoned this method. The famous French writer Lévy-Bruhl, although he held that many races were 'pre-logical', yet recognized that the Ashanti possessed 'a real religion' above the primitive level. The same could be said of the intricacies of Ewe, Yoruba, or Ibo belief.

Even in the most refined religions some lower features, magic and superstition, may linger, though these are frowned upon by purer worshippers. Similarly, in West Africa some totemistic ideas remain, and human sacrifice occurred not so long ago in some places, but by their gradual disappearance these religions show a development and a purification.

Instead of being confounded with a universal substratum of 'primitive religion', it may be claimed that these central and important groups of West Africans have had traditional religious beliefs which deserve consideration in comparison with some of the races of Europe and Asia. Though there are no scriptures and little known history, the subtlety of many religious beliefs shows them to be developed well beyond the primitive. There is room

---

[1] For a study of what remains of really primitive religion, see E. O. James, *Prehistoric Religion* (1957).

for comparison of methods of divination with European horoscopes, and of beliefs in rebirth with those of India.

'FETISHISM'

One would have thought that the use of the word 'fetishism', as vaguely descriptive of West African religion had been so thoroughly trounced by scholars that it would by now be altogether abandoned. Unhappily this is still not so (even at the time of this second edition). Not only does 'fetishism' remain in the popular mind as a handy, but undefined and therefore practically useless, description of queer practices in Africa, but it still appears in some works on religion and anthropology. The term is still often used by missionaries and many other Europeans and Africans. I have heard it applied to gods, shrines, ancestors, charms, and amulets.

This unhappy word was introduced by the Portuguese, the first European traders along the West Coast. They called the African charms and cult objects '*feitiço*', with the meaning of magical, like the talismans they themselves wore, the word deriving from the Latin '*factitius*', for a thing made by art. But anything could be called 'fetish' and the first reference to it in English says that 'the chief fetiche is the snake', which is hardly a magical object made by art.

Because of the many confusing ways in which the word was used, attempts have been made to limit its usage. So E. B. Tylor tried to 'confine the word "Fetishism" to that subordinate department which it properly belongs to, namely, the doctrine of spirits, embodied in, or attached to, or conveying influence through, certain material objects. Fetishism will be taken as including the worship of "stocks and stones" and thence it passes by an imperceptible gradation into idolatry'.[2]

This definition would need careful handling, for well beyond Africa spirits are believed to be 'embodied in, or attached to, or conveying influence through' material objects. The theory of sacramentalism rests upon this. Tylor, working on unreliable evidence, soon also confused with his supposed 'stock and stone worship' the worship of gods and the veneration of ancestors. But it is generally held today that no 'heathen in his blindness bows

[2] *Primitive Culture* (4th edn), II.143-4.

down to wood and stone', and the accusation of idolatry is denied not only by Africans themselves.

Later an anthropological committee suggested that the word 'fetish' might be retained for 'a limited class of magical objects in West Africa': that is, the charms, amulets, and talismans which form a subordinate part of the religious complex. Rattray used the word in this way. He objects to speaking of the worship of God or the gods as 'fetishism', or the cult of dead kings as 'fetish' worship. But he thought 'fetishism' might be used of magical objects in West Africa. But why isolate West Africa from the rest of the world? This has been one of the most harmful effects of speaking about 'fetishism'. For there is not a single religious or magical practice in West Africa that cannot be paralleled in some other continent. Magical objects abound in Asia and in Europe, and for a scientific comparative study of religions it is quite useless to talk about 'fetishism' any longer.

A further point which cannot be overlooked without peril, in view of the French- and English-speaking countries of West Africa, is the difference between French and English usage. The French *'fétiche'* is often represented in English by 'juju', apparently to denote the image or symbol of a god. The French-speaking peoples say *'gris-gris'* (gree-gree) for those charms which Rattray wanted to call 'fetishes'. The English word 'juju' is said by the dictionary to come from the French *'jou-jou'*, a toy; but the French do not use it of any religious or magical objects, and it occurs in English as long ago as 1699 when James Barbot spoke of an idol-house as 'Jou-Jou'. Professor Christophersen suggests that the word is a corruption and reduplication of the Portuguese *'Deus'* for God.[3]

It is best to drop this confusing and unfair word 'fetish' altogether, along with 'juju' and 'gree-gree'. They need to be relegated to the museum of the writings of early explorers.

After all, English is not so poor that it lacks suitable terms to describe many West African religious phenomena: spirits, gods, shrines. It is true that the meaning may vary by slight shades with

---

[3] *Some Special West African English Words* (Ibadan University Press, 1954), p. 7. As examples of different usage, Talbot calls minor divinities 'jujus', but J. U Egharevba equates 'juju' with 'black magic'.

the environment, but that is so in most countries of the world. If there are unique phenomena in African religions, it would be better to adopt the names used by the people themselves. The lower graded objects may normally be called charms (probably the most suitable word), amulets, or talismans; mascots would not convey the magico-religious attitude involved.

FROM ANIMISM TO POLYTHEISM

The word 'animism' is often used nowadays of African religion, because it looks more scientific, though people seem to be uncertain what is meant by it. Tylor regarded animism as a 'minimum definition of religion' and thought that 'the theory of souls is a fundamental concept of primitive belief'. Animism comes from the Latin word for the soul, '*anima*', and is the belief that objects and natural phenomena are inhabited by souls or spiritual beings. So hills, trees, rocks, streams, oceans, all have their resident soul. But some have objected that it is not a personal soul but an impersonal force that animates these objects, and so Marett in 1899 coined a word 'animatism' for this more impersonal notion. It must be said however that his word has not become popular.

There is no doubt that in many parts of West Africa, as in other lands, souls or spirits are believed to inhabit what the scientist would call 'inanimate' objects, and so they are 'animists' in that sense. But it goes beyond this, for the spirits are not merely local souls, each tied to a special place—some are found in many places and have a highly developed and widespread worship.

Tylor suggested the process of development from animism when, commenting on the popular notion of 'fetishism', he said: 'When the similar vegetation of the different oaks of a forest led to a theological generalization from their common phenomena, the abstract being thus produced was no longer the fetish of a single tree, but became the god of the forest; here, then, is the intellectual passage from fetishism to polytheism reduced to the inevitable preponderance of specific over individual ideas.'[4] So Tylor spoke of 'species-deities', the spirit common to all oaks or snakes, which become gods worshipped in many places under the same name.

In West Africa the process of development from the particular

[4] *Primitive Culture*, II.242–3.

to the general has long been going on. The iroko or African oak (*chlorophora excelsa*) is a sacred species all along the coast and is a god, Loko, in Dahomey. Silk-cotton and baobab trees, and several shrubs, are sacred species. The python is generally a sacred snake, and it has a temple and priests in many places. There are generic gods of the storm, mountain, wind, and sea. Special stones are associated with the thunder god, and granite and laterite rocks are sacred to the spirit of the earth. Most rivers are sacred, many rule over a pantheon of gods, like Tano of the Ashanti.

In our field, indeed, we find widely worshipped spirits that have passed beyond the stage of being merely local dryads, and they have become gods worshipped at many temples and served by trained and dedicated priests and acolytes.

The religion of this part of West Africa, then, may be best understood by the student, and not inaccurately described, if it is roundly called 'polytheism'. While in the past there may have been reluctance to honour these divinities even by the term 'false gods', 'fetishism' seeming better to imply the unintelligible and primitive, yet these gods are just as truly conceived as personal, supernatural, and ubiquitous beings as were the gods of ancient Egypt and many of modern India. To speak of West African polytheism immediately puts a better light and a clearer understanding upon the great variety of religious practices of this region. For polytheism can be taken as including a number of different facets of religion, as we shall see below.

As in most polytheistic religions, there is little reluctance to accept new gods or cults, no narrow doctrinal walls, or jealous gods that forbid the addition of new beliefs, provided that the traditional deities are not attacked. Migration, conquest, and intermarriage alone would suffice to explain the adoption of strange gods, to those who are familiar with the story of the mingling of the Israelite desert religion with the agricultural 'baalim' or lords of the soil of Canaan.

A FOURFOLD CLASSIFICATION

It has been discovered that there exist, in many West African languages, convenient categories for the consideration of the types of religious belief.

Briefly, we may distinguish: (1) a supreme God or creator, some-times above the other gods, sometimes first among equals—Onyame in Twi-Ashanti, Mawu in Ewe-Fǫn, Ọlọrŭn in Yoruba, Chuku in Ibo; (2) the chief divinities, generally non-human spirits, often associated with natural forces (called *abosõm, vodŭ, orisha, chi*); (3) the cult of the human but divinized ancestors of the clan (*samãnfo, nɛsuhwe, babanla, ndichie*); (4) the charms and amulets, which some have called 'fetishes' or 'juju' (*sumãn, gbo, ogŭn, ǫgwu*).

This is a workable classification. It represents well-known distinctions used by polytheists, as shown by the separate terms, equivalents of which exist in other African languages. Dr Edwin Smith, the greatest expert on African religion, used to say that a pyramid or triangle was an apt illustration of the order of the spiritual forces. At the apex was the supreme God, on one side of the triangle were the nature gods, and on the other side the ancestors, while at the base were the lower magical powers.

It is true that distinctions should not be made too rigidly. Imposing a logical order may sometimes be foreign to the subject, but it is important to seize upon the broad differences that do exist between the main classes of spiritual force. There is bound to be some overlapping between these categories. In some places the supreme God is quite separate from the other gods, elsewhere he is one of them. Some of the ancestors merge into the divine non-human category; Shãngo of the Yoruba is both the god of the storm and the fourth king of Oyo; the water-spirits of the Fǫn are closely related to some departed souls. Some charms grow beyond a local importance, and by acquiring a regular worship, a temple, and a priest, they rise to the rank of gods. Other kinds of religious belief, such as totemism and taboos, will be considered separately.

CHAPTER THREE

The Supreme God

EXISTENCE AND WORSHIP

SOME DISCUSSION has ranged round the question whether the idea of a 'Supreme Being', a 'high God', is native to West Africa. An even more important issue is whether such a God is worshipped, and to what extent.

Sir A. B. Ellis at first thought that the Supreme Being was a 'loan-god', introduced by missionaries. He said that the people of Ghana 'added to their system a new deity, whom they termed "Nana Nyankupon". This was the God of the Christians, borrowed from them, and adapted under a new designation, meaning "Lord of the Sky".'[1] Later Ellis modified this opinion, and writing of Mawu of the Ewe, he said: 'While upon the subject of this God, I may as well say that, from additional evidence I have since collected, I now think that the view I expressed concerning the origin of Nyankupon, the parallel god of the Tshi-speaking peoples, was incorrect; and that instead of his being the Christian God borrowed and thinly disguised, I now hold he is like Mawu, the sky-god, or indwelling spirit of the sky; and that, also like Mawu, he has been to a certain extent confounded with Jehovah.'[2] Later still he wrote about Yoruba religion: 'Just as the missionaries have caused Nyankupon, Nyonmo, and Mawu to be confused with the Jehovah of the Christians, by translating these names as "God", so have they done with Olorun.'[3]

It might be objected not only that Jehovah is a Jewish rather than a Christian term, but also that to use the word 'God' for West African Supreme Beings was not inappropriate and can be paralleled with similar names adapted to Christian usage from paganism in other parts of the world. But while Ellis varied his

---

[1] *Tshi-speaking Peoples of the Gold Coast*, p. 24.
[2] *The Ewe-speaking Peoples of the Slave Coast*, p. 36.
[3] *The Yoruba-speaking Peoples of the Slave Coast*, p. 35.

13

opinions, other people began to take it for granted that there was no idea of God in Africa before the arrival of Europeans. Yet two hundred and sixty years ago William Bosman observed that West Africans believed in a high God, though they did not worship him. 'They have a faint idea of the true God, and ascribe to Him the attributes of Almighty and Omnipresent; they believe He created the Universe, and therefore vastly prefer Him before their idol-gods; but they do not pray to Him, or offer any sacrifices to Him.'[4] This was written long before any missionaries, except travelling padres, began settled work in West Africa. Apart from the kingdom of Benin there is little Christian work of more than a century old in our area.

There is no doubt that Christian and Muslim ideas have modified some religious beliefs, in the coastal areas, in recent years. But even today much of the interior is little affected, where pagans are in the majority. Ellis himself admitted that the Twi-speaking peoples had been little changed in other things by centuries of trade with Europeans on the seaboard, and that their inland kingdoms were 'mere specks in a vast track of impenetrable forest', which therefore would only with difficulty change a fundamental religious belief.

On the other hand some writers have maintained the theory of a general primitive monotheism in Africa; this was the thesis of Father Schmidt who thought that all peoples had once believed in one God from the time of Adam though many of them later fell into polytheism. There is no solid evidence to support this in West Africa, though both S. Farrow and R. E. Dennett suggested that Yoruba religion was a degeneration from a purer mono-theistic faith, and J. B. Danquah considers that Akan religion is fundamentally monotheistic despite the lesser gods.

The peoples we are now studying all believe in a supreme Deity, yet different attitudes are taken towards his worship, and to this important matter we must now turn.

GENERAL WORSHIP

R. S. Rattray showed conclusively that not only was a supreme God believed in throughout Ashanti, but that there were countless

---

[4] *A New and Accurate Description of the Coasts of Guinea, Divided into the Gold, the Slave, and the Ivory Coasts* (1705), p. 348.

small altars to him, as well as some dedicated priests and temples. 'It is hardly an exaggeration to say that every compound in Ashanti contains an altar to the Sky God, in the shape of a forked branch cut from a certain tree which the Ashanti call "'*Nyame dua*", lit. "God's tree".'[5] This forked branch holds a brass or earthenware pot containing ancient stones (neolithic celts). People put daily offerings in these pots, or on the roofs of their huts, for 'the Great God of the Sky'.

Rattray also gave photographs of finely decorated temples of 'Nyame, some of which were in the old Ashanti palaces. Priests wore gold or silver ornaments suspended from their necks, like enlarged crescents, with embossed motifs suggesting sun, moon, and stars. Priests had peculiar styles of hairdressing; white clay lines were drawn in the centre of the forehead, and on shoulders, arms, and chest. They were dedicated for life service to the god.

The Ashanti are unique in West Africa not in honouring a Supreme Being, but in having temples, priests, and altars to Him. In fact, over the whole of tropical Africa the only other people who seem to give similar attention to God are the Kikuyu of Kenya. But it must be said that since Rattray wrote forty years ago much has changed, many of the household forked branches are no longer to be seen and old temples have crumbled away. The new towns have modern houses, in different style and without the old adornments. Many people have drifted away from the old ways, or have become Christian. On the other hand the faith in the old Supreme God is preserved in the God of the new religion.

That 'Nyame has long been known is shown by many references to the Sky God in proverbs and traditional pieces of drummers: 'Of all the wide earth the Supreme Being is the elder', 'When God gave sickness He also gave medicine', 'God needs no pointing out to a child', 'There is no short cut to God's destiny', 'It was none but Ǫdomankoma who made death eat poison'.[6]

There are a number of names for God. The principal name is ''Nyame' or 'Nana Nyãnkopǫn'. 'Nana' is a title given to chiefs and head of families. 'Nyãnkopǫn' is said to mean the 'Nyame

[5] *Ashanti*, pp. 142–3.
[6] See R. S. Rattray, *Ashanti Proverbs*, and J. G. Christaller, *A Dictionary of the Ashanti and Fanti Languages.*

who alone is great. Akan gods are worshipped on special days and have their day-names; that of Nyănkopǒn is 'Kwaame', 'He of Saturday', and He is addressed in prayer and rite as 'Nana Nyănkopǒn Kwame'.

Other names are 'Qdomankoma', said to mean He who is full of abundance or mercy and so connected with creation; 'Tweaduampon', 'the One on whom men lean and do not fall'; and praise-names such as Creator, Giver of Rain, Giver of Sunshine, Elder, Grandfather, God of Comfort, Mighty, He who is beyond all thanks, Enduring from ancient time, the Great Spider.

There is little mythology about creation which connects it with God, but it is said that all men are His offspring, that He sends the soul to the embryo and gives it a destiny, and that God also made death. Mrs Meyerowitz in her books on the Akan has made much of the symbolism of gold and the sun in the worship of 'Nyame, possibly as an ancient sun-god, and also of the dual male-female nature of 'Nyame in which the female side is represented by the moon. Her interpretations are very different from those of Rattray.[7]

The name 'Nyam', the shortest form, and its variants, occurs widely throughout West Africa. This does not mean that it originated in Ghana as against the Sudan, or vice versa; it is probably a very ancient word, and may originally have been connected with a root *nyama* for power, or supernatural force, which is still used by semi-Islamized tribes in the Sudan; this is an essence or potency which fills all living creatures, is uncanny, and may be dangerous.

Akan tribes in the Ivory Coast say 'Nyam' or 'Nyanke'. I have often heard Adjukru say *'Nyam am o'* (God is coming) when rain approached. Among the Gã of Accra, Dr Field wrote: 'The word "Nyoñmọ" means rain. The only way of saying it is raining is to say that Nyoñmọ is falling. . . . Certainly he was a sky-god, for the sky is the home of rain, but I doubt if he was ever a supreme god except in so far as the rain-god is always supreme in any Gã group of gods. As we have learnt, from the old religious songs, there has been indeed a long succession of supreme gods, each a giver of rain and all good things, but most of them now forgotten. . . .

[7] See her *Sacred State of the Akan* (1951). Her later books on parallels with Egypt have been heavily criticized by Egyptologists.

If it were imperative to translate the word "Nyoñmǫ" and to translate it as other than rain it could probably always be rendered fairly with the word "Nature". For instance, in the burial speech at Nungwa we find the dead man bidden to rest in peace if his death was in the course of nature—"Nyoñmǫ's death".[8]

This should not be allowed to suggest that because a god may have been closely associated with nature in his origins he cannot later be a true Supreme Being detached from natural processes. In Ashanti both the person and the worship of 'Nyame were prominent. At the same time other gods were worshipped and ancestral cults held a prominent place.

PARTIAL WORSHIP

In other parts of our field a Supreme Deity is recognized by everybody, but He is not worshipped by all who take His name on their lips.

Among the Ewe of Togo and Dahomey the name Mawu is given to the Creator. The origin and meaning of the word are obscure; 'none greater' or 'overstretching' have been suggested as possible meanings. Praise-names are: almighty, creating spirit, saving spirit, God full of pity.

Mawu has not the general worship that is accorded to 'Nyame. But in some areas, particularly at Abomey, there is an organized cult, with temples and priests, and He is regarded as one of the gods albeit supreme. Because of this, Protestant Christians made up a compound term for God, 'sky-house-spirit' (*Ji-hwe-yɛhwe*); but Roman Catholics use Mawu.

Most Ewe offer no regular worship to Mawu, and many are ignorant of the fact that temples are dedicated to Him in some places. Even at Abomey the number of temples of Mawu is much less than those of the thunder and smallpox gods which are the most popular today. This may be because Mawu does not combine the attributes of Sky and Thunder as 'Nyame does.

Also at Abomey, in the centre of the old Dahomean kingdom, is found the belief that Mawu is female, and has a male consort Lisa. Mawu is the elder, a woman and usually a mother too, and

[8] *Religion and Medicine of the Gã People* (1937), pp. 61–2.

is gentle and forgiving as the night is cool after a fierce day, Mawu being the moon and Lisa the sun. A proverb says: 'When Lisa punishes, Mawu forgives.'

Yet the name 'Mawu' is on the lips of every Ewe, in the various clans. The other gods are subordinate to Mawu: 'Mawu owns the gods.' And if there is no regular temple worship still people may and do utter prayers, especially in times of distress: 'Mawu look into my belly and help me.' Prayer is worship, even if not regular or in a fixed place.

There are many myths that connect Mawu with creation. He (or she) created the earth and then retired to the sky because of the trouble or over-familiarity of men. Then he saw that all was not going well on earth so he sent his only son, Lisa (!), giving him a sword to clear the forests and make tools. Another version gives Gu, the iron god who taught men the use of metals. Mawu divided the world among his children, and gave Lisa the sun to watch over all things.

Mawu created all souls. The soul is *sɛ*, or *Mawusɛ*, the 'Mawu who lives in everyone's body', like a guardian spirit or genius. Mawu made the first human beings of clay and water, but the clay ran short and so he used the bodies of dead men to make other bodies, and so there are resemblances in families. Mawu gives and upholds the moral law, and after death souls go to him to be rewarded or punished.

The priests of Mawu wear white, and on great occasions rams and bulls are sacrificed at his temples. It is of Mawu that occurs the only image of a Supreme God that we have seen. It is in the ancient royal collection at Abomey, and is in the form of a wooden statue, coloured the red of dawn, with large breasts and a crescent in one hand (so female and the moon).

It is said that the cult of Mawu, and Lisa, was introduced to Dahomey from the region of Togo, by the mother of King Tegbesu (1732–74). But that the Lisa cult at least is a century or so older, and probably more, is proved by the adoption of the name Lisa by a brief and abortive mission of Spanish Capuchins in 1660. They translated *vodŭ* for God, and Lisa for Jesus. Their *Doctrina Christiana* was translated into Fɔ̃n as *Pranvi elisa (kplã vi ne Lisa)*. Jesus is translated throughout as Lisa, no doubt due to an

18

interpretation of local myth wherein Lisa was understood as son of the Supreme God.[9]

There are other aspirants to the title of Supreme God in Ewe country: Nana Buku in central Dahomey, and Bruku in Togo. It has been claimed that these are true high gods. I have some original matter on this subject, but it has been deferred to the next chapter, as today, among the Fǒn and most Ewe, Mawu is generally recognized as the Supreme Being.

The folklore of most of West Africa shows traces of earlier deities than those now recognized or worshipped (as Dr Field said above of Gã belief). For example, there is a widespread fable of Father Spider as Creator of all things ('Nyame is called the Great Spider). In Fǒn fables it is often Sɛ or Dada Sɛgbo, and not Mawu, who is father of gods and ruler of the destinies of men, and no doubt he was an earlier god. The following song is often heard: 'Whatever Dada Sɛgbo has left undone, even the king cannot do. Nothing in the world can be done without Sɛmɛvo; I use the same drumstick as my father had, The firefly knows that the fire is given to his own head (i.e. is not of his own making), Nothing in the world can be done without Sɛmɛvo.'

BELIEF WITHOUT WORSHIP

A further variation upon the attitude adopted towards the Supreme Being is found when we turn to the Yoruba and Ibo peoples. The Yoruba call God 'Olọrũn', and the Ibo, 'Chuku'. No cult is offered to him, and there are no temples or priests. He is not called an *orisha*, a god; he is above and beyond all gods.

The Yoruba title 'Ọl-ọrũn' is a simple compound meaning 'owner of the sky' (*ọrũn*), the prefix *Ol* is used in many other words with similar meaning of ownership. Its clear meaning may seem suspicious, as if it were made up for the purpose, and this has been suggested. Farrow strongly disputed both the suggestion that the idea of God was introduced to the Yoruba from outside and the name Ọlọrũn was foreign to them, and quoted myths and proverbs in support of his case. But recently Dr Idowu has argued persuasively that the older name for God is the title Olodumare,

[9] H. Labouret and P. Rivet, *Le Royaume d'Arda et son Evangélisation au xviie siècle* (Paris, 1929).

still widely used, and rather mysterious in meaning, perhaps 'almighty' or 'omnipotent ruler'. He quotes many hitherto un-recorded songs and proverbs to show the antiquity of Olodumare, and suggests that the popularity of the name Ọlọrũn grew with Christian and Muslim influence because of its clear and monotheistic sense.[10]

Other names of God are Creator, Owner of breath or spirit, Benefactor, Merciful, Living, Lord of glory, Silent but active judge, King in the heavens, King of great majesty, The owner of this day, He whose being spreads over the whole earth, The owner of the mat that is never folded up, The immovable rock that never dies. Of Olodumare it is said, 'You do not know the father or mother of Olodumare', and 'the old ones never hear the death of Olodumare'.

There are many sayings and proverbs that use the name of God. The regular morning salutation is, 'Have you risen well?' and the answer, 'I thank God'; and at night again: 'May God awake us well.' Proverbs say: 'God alone is wise', 'If man does not see you, does not God see you?', 'No one but God can put a crown on a lion', 'God drives away flies from the tailless cow.'

God is creator, either directly or through the intermediary of the chief of the gods, Orisha-nla (the great god), who was sent down from heaven to bring earth out of the watery waste below; this was done in four days, hence the Yoruba four-day week, and afterwards human beings were made. God is judge, 'no wicked man will escape the judgement of God', 'when we die we shall have to state our case in the hall of heaven'. So God gives the moral law now, and judges men after death, sending the good to the 'good heaven' and the wicked to the 'heaven of potsherds', a sort of celestial rubbish heap. So God has perfect knowledge, 'only God is wise', He sees all things and the sky is 'the face of God', and when it lightens, men say 'God is winking'. God is pure, a 'king without blemish', and 'One clothed in white robes who dwells above'.[11]

---

[10] E. B. Idowu, *Olodumare, God in Yoruba Belief* (1961). I am grateful to Dr Idowu for much information, and for being allowed to use the proofs of his book before publication for reference in the revised edition of this book.

[11] E. B. Idowu, ibid. chapter 4.

Yet there are no temples of Ọlọrũn (or Olodumare) in Yoruba country, and no priests dedicated to his service. Only in the worship of lesser gods may a concluding phrase ask, 'May God accept it', 'May God send a blessing upon it'. It is held, therefore, that God receives the sacrifices which are made through the intermediary of lesser deities. Similarly during the masquerades of the Egũngũn dancers God is invoked in prayers before the ceremonies. But some older people break kola nuts and pour water on the ground in the name of God. And anybody can call upon God in time of need, at any place, and without the intermediary of a priest. So that extemporary prayer is made to God.

Similar beliefs are held by the Bini in their conception of a creator God, Osa or Osanobua. But while anybody can pray to him at irregular times, there are some people who make a heap of sand in which they put a stick with a strip of white cloth and offer kola nuts, chalk, and a gourd to him. And there are three shrines in Benin City to Osanobua which are said to be on the places where the Portuguese missionaries built churches in the sixteenth century.[12] The Nupe belief in Soko, the word that is used both for God and the heavens, seems to be more remote—'God is far away' they say. But there is a song which says: 'God is in the front, he is in the back.' Yet with the strong rule of Islam over Nupe country the beliefs of this people are becoming assimilated to Muslim teachings.[13]

The Ibo name for the Supreme Being is Chuku or Chukwu, perhaps a combination of *chi*, spirit, and *uku*, great. Other names are: God who creates (Chineke), God of grace, The great God who has the power, God who controls life, He that makes and controls the world, Chi in heaven, Our father in the heavens, The most high who does not bow (the name Obasi is used in Ibibio areas).

God is creator (Chi-na-eke), The author of heaven and earth, The one who sends rain, The maker of the growing crops, and The source of the human soul. The soul (*chi*) is given to every human being from the time of conception and Chuku entrusts it with its destiny. So proverbs say, 'God makes up good parcels,

---

[12] R. E. Bradbury, *The Benin Kingdom* (1957), p. 52.
[13] S. F. Nadel, *Nupe Religion* (1954), pp. 10–11.

but *chi* adds the bad things'; but on the other hand 'a bad *chi* can have a good child', and in time of misfortune a man may say: 'I do not know what I have done to my *chi*'.

There are no temples or priests of Chuku, yet it is said that he is the final recipient of sacrifices offered through the intermediary of other gods. Especially the sun (Anyanwŭ) is regarded as close to God and he is asked to take sacrifices made to him and offer them to God. Simple prayers may be addressed direct to God, and the elder of a house in the morning may take a kola nut in his right hand and lay it on the ground saying: 'Our father in heaven eat kola.' Similarly the Ibibio who call God 'Obassi' may invoke Him in the morning: 'Obassi watch over me and my children today.'

The people of Aro Chuku, whose famous oracle was renowned and feared throughout Ibo country in the last century (the 'Long Juju'), are still called 'Sons of God' (Umu-Chukwu). They held their oracle to be the supreme deity and offered slaves to him with prayers for the aversion of sickness.

There are popular myths which explain the distance of the sky and of God in it. In the beginning, it is said, God lived quite near the earth and the sky could be touched by man's hand. The blame for the removal of the sky is laid on a woman, probably because the story was told by men. One day a woman was pounding yam in a mortar, at each stroke she lifted the long wooden pestle higher into the air, to bring it down with greater force. Each time she did this she hit the sky. God called out to her to stop, but she paid no heed, and finally God moved away in anger to the distant heights where the sky has been ever since.

Other versions of the myth abound. Some told in Togo say that people got into the bad habit of wiping their hands on the sky after eating, cut bits off it for soup, took too much food from heaven, or sent smoke into God's eyes so that he moved farther away. In Dahomey it is said that a woman threw dirty water into the air out of the door of her hut, and thus annoyed the sky so that it moved far away into the air. Some people have seen in these stories reflections of myths of a Golden Age when God was nearer to men.

Many West African stories suggest that man was originally

22

immortal, or was meant to be so. How death came, visiting the town of death, or struggles with death, are the theme of myths. A careless messenger from God is said to have mixed up the message to man, so that instead of living for ever he now dies. Various animals are blamed for this mistake, the dog, or the chameleon.

God is not much identified with the sun in West Africa, although symbols of the sun occur in connexion with 'Nyame and Mawu or Lisa. The sun is oppressively present in West Africa, and its appearance in springtime varies little from the winter (which is a hot, dry season anyway), and so has not the importance that was given to it by people in the cold northern countries of Europe and Asia. Neither has the moon the importance that it has for desert people who are on the move on moonlit nights. In the tropics full moon is a time for dancing, but not for many religious ceremonies. God is closely connected with the sky or heaven, and is creator and father in heaven.

Polytheists who justify their worship of the many lesser gods, when pressed, may refer to the remoteness of the sky or at least to the more pressing demands of the other gods. These are nearer to him, more likely to intervene in his life, and easier of access. They might be annoyed if they were neglected in favour of one sole deity. Any priest will say that his god is a son of the supreme God, and that God speaks through his sons. But he will argue that he must obtain the favour of all the spirits, and not please one alone, lest the others withdraw their favour and power.

THE SIGNIFICANCE OF THE SUPREME GOD

From the above sketch we have seen that there is a generally recognized head of gods and men, among the peoples of West Africa. He is the Supreme God, though differing attitudes are taken up towards his worship, and he is thought to be more remote from human affairs and needs than the gods which are his sons.

It needs to be considered in what sense God is held to be 'supreme'. Is it so merely in myth, or in practice and worship? It may be quite misleading to transfer ideas and categories from European to African theology. God the Father is supreme in Christian theology, and Allah in Islam. He could not be removed from the faith without undermining the whole structure; belief, worship, and morals are all finally dependent upon him, and he could not be relegated to an inferior station. Does this hold good of all West African views of the Supreme God?

On the whole worship is irregular, and apart from Ashanti there are no temples or priests of God. Even the small offerings which in Ashanti are put in the forked branch altar or thrown on the roof are similar to daily libations of maize and water which Ewe and Yoruba offer in front of their protector Eshu-Lɛgba (see later chapter). The few temples of 'Nyame are old and hidden away. There are no frequent and splendid gatherings, with parades, dance and sacrifice, such as occur twice every seven weeks for the Ashanti ancestors and many other gods elsewhere.

Apart from occasional ejaculations, made before a journey or an undertaking, many people do not seem to give God much place in their life. He does not have the great attention given to him that is devoted to the thunder, tree, snake or smallpox gods; these have every fifth day sacred to their worship, when no land must be tilled, no loads carried, and sacrifices are offered. They also have their great seasonal festivals, which the Supreme God has not.

On the moral side also, though God is generally regarded as upholding the moral law, and judging men after death in accordance with their actions, many practices seem to have little to do with him. A man's taboos are hereditary, or else declared in infancy by the oracle, or those of the god to whose service he is dedicated; few concern the Sky God directly. Marriage and inheritance are determined by the tutelary deity. Funeral and ancestral rites refer to former human or divine beings, but not to the great God. Social and political arrangements are blessed by the ancestors or gods of the tribe.

It is true that 'Nyame, Mawu, Ọlọrũn, and Chuku are called 'father' of the gods. This assertion should be taken at its face value, as a distinguishing mark from other sky and thunder gods. One would think that it is not unnatural to look on the sky as father of all, because it is literally higher than all. 'Father' also often indicates belief in the most ancient god; other members of the pantheon adopted later became 'wives' or 'sons'.

In the first edition of this book I quoted with approval the dictum of Westermann that the African's God is uncertain and remote: 'He is the God of the thoughtful, not of the crowd, of people whose mature observation, personal experience, and primitive philosophy have led them to postulate a central and ultimate power who is the originator of everything and in whose hands the universe is safe.'[14] I have come to think that God is closer to ordinary people than this suggests, and certainly that he is not a new creation of lonely philosophers but has been believed in from time immemorial. And I strongly reject the suggestion (made by J. H. Driberg in East Africa) that God is only an abstract Power, that he is never regarded anthropomorphically (having names and attributes as men), and that the High God idea is not to be found in Africa.[15]

It is quite clear from what has been said above of the various kinds of West African belief in God that God is not merely a power but He is a person. He has a personal name, and many attribute names. He has life and consciousness, and sometimes is credited with a wife or consort; other gods are His children. Generally speaking, however, he is not human and was not an ancestor. He is judge, ruler of morals, and the final tribunal before whom man must appear after death. Many myths speak of his activities in the past, and proverbs tell of his power and presence now—he knows all things and nothing can be hidden from him.

To sum up, there are only a few temples of God, found almost exclusively in Ashanti. Only one image of Him has been traced. Sacrifice is rarely offered to him, though simple gifts of kola nuts and water may be made. Prayers however are offered to him at any time and place, though generally these are individual prayers. But communal prayers may be made for rain, and in sacrifices to other gods worship may be concluded in the name of the Father of all.

---

[14] *Africa and Christianity*, pp. 74–5.
[15] Quoted in *African Ideas of God*, ed. E. W. Smith (1950), p. 21.

CHAPTER FOUR

The Gods: Sky and Thunder

SKY GODS

MANY OF THE divinities worshipped in West Africa seem to have come from the personification of natural forces, since all the universe is thought to be peopled with spirits. Others are deified ancestors. Some may have a double quality, both human and divine combined. The gods are felt to be closely concerned with men and their goodwill is sought by appropriate offerings.

The word 'god' or 'divinity' is the translation of vernacular words used with approximately the same sense through West Africa. *Obosõm* is used in Twi, *vudu* or *vodũ* in Ewe-Fõn, *orisha* in Yoruba, *chi* in Ibo. It may be noted that Mawu is included among the gods (*vodũ*) at Abomey, but Ọlọrũn is never called an *orisha*.

The Fõn make a convenient distinction between sky-spirits, earth-spirits, water-spirits, and forest-spirits. The first two categories are the senior gods; the latter include fairies and certain departed souls.

The Supreme Being may be called without disparagement a Sky God, though senior of all. He is sometimes paired with an earth god or goddess, like the male and female principle, or to use a current simile like the upper and lower halves of a calabash.

We have already noticed that 'Nyame of Ashanti is sometimes said to be both male and female; the female element is symbolized by the moon, by silver ornaments, and her power to invest the Queen Mother who is a great influence in the State. The male element is seen in the sun, fiery, golden, and in the king. The female element created men with water, and the male sun shot its life-giving fire into human veins where it fused with the blood, as the blood of a man is said to come from his mother and the fiery semen from his father. But another most important female deity in Ashanti is Asase Yaa, the great earth mother, and to her we shall come in the next chapter.

The most important of the Yoruba *orishas* is Orishala (Orisha-nla, great god). He is also called Ọbatala, 'king who is great' or 'king in white clothing'. We have seen that Orisha-nla was sent down by God to bring the first earth, and he spread it abroad with the help of a hen and a pigeon and then planted the first trees. Later he created human bodies into which God placed breath. Orisha-nla likes white—albinos are sacred to him and his priests wear white clothes. His temples are whitewashed, chalk and white beads are placed there as symbols, and snails rather than blood sacrifices should be offered to him. Clean water should always be in his shrine, drawn by a virgin or an old woman past menstruation.

Akin to and sometimes consort of Orisha-nla is Oduduwa. There has been a great deal of discussion about the sex of this deity, and it is complicated by the modern national society of the 'Sons of Oduduwa', which look back to this god as ancestor of the Yorubas. But as far as religious worship goes it seems that the god is male in some places and female in others, possibly because of the pre-dominance of a matriarchal family system in some places, though this is by no means certain. The name Oduduwa seems to mean 'chief who created us' or 'chief who created being', and credits this deity with original creating powers. In some of the complex creation myths it is said that Orisha-nla neglected the creating duty that he had received from God, and so this was given to Oduduwa, but other versions contradict this. In some places Oduduwa is mother of seven gods, of which Orisha-nla was first; elsewhere she is the lower half of the calabash of which Orisha-nla is the upper half.

The Ibo cult of the sun, Anyanwũ, varies from place to place. Sometimes a simple prayer is made with a request to bear it to God, or a white fowl is hung on a bamboo at sunrise or sunset with a like prayer. At Nsukka many houses have a shrine of Anyanwũ, a tree or branch outside the house with a bowl at its foot and a gong; here white fowls are offered, with kola nuts and wine. At Owerri special sacrifices were offered in times of sickness to bring down the soul of the man which was thought to be rising up to heaven prematurely. Anyanwũ is a god of good fortune, and is prayed to

27

for profit in the market and for good harvests. There is no corresponding moon cult, though men may lift up their hands to the new moon and say: 'New moon protect me as the last moon protected me.' But the great Ibo deity is Mother Earth, leader of all the rest, of whom we shall speak in the next chapter.

Of the Ewe gods it is said that the supreme Mawu-Lisa, themselves twins, had fourteen children, seven pairs of twins, which were the major gods. Mawu and Lisa themselves are the principal sky gods, others are concerned with thunder, iron, and the earth. Like Orisha-nla (a name his own resembles) Lisa favours white. His worshippers and priests wear white clothes, albinos are sacred to him, no blood or oil may be poured on his altar, bloodless white snails and white kola nuts are his favourite offerings, and a whitened calabash is kept in his temple or in the priest's house. Lisa is associated with the west and the setting sun; his chief emblem is the chameleon, often to be seen painted on the outer walls of temples.

An important sky god in Dahomey and Togo is Buku, or Bruku. 'Some of the gods enjoy such great fame and are so widely known that they almost attain to the rank of high-gods, as, for instance, the god Buruku who is known and worshipped in Nigeria, Dahomey, Togoland, and on the Gold Coast.'[1] When I lived at Dassa I got to know the temple and priestess of Nana Buku there, for this is one of the most important centres of the deity, the other chief ones being at Doumé and Banté.

The compound, or 'convent', for mediums and priests who are trained here, is half-way up the hill that dominates the village of Dassa Zoumé. In front of it there is a fine natural platform of solid granite, which only initiates may cross, overlooking the village from a height of about three hundred feet. Passing three long huts for the neophytes, one comes to a fourth containing several small drums, each with a dozen cowrie shell bands, and one with a modelled human figure attached. Beyond this hut is an open place, the site of the shrine. A large baobab tree to the right has its trunk blackened in parts with blood and oil. A collection of diviner's rods, iron staffs, and 'standards' (*asɛn, ɔsanyin*), is also to the right of the shrine. All Buku shrines or altars are in the

[1] D. Westermann, *Africa and Christianity*, p. 91.

open air, and are easily recognizable by a typical plaited thatch crown and straw sheath or robe that encloses a clay mound in which are embedded two or three earthenware inverted pots; the latter are normally veiled from profane eyes by the thatch covering, but sometimes they fall into neglect, when the constituent parts are seen. The cover is taken off for sacrificial ceremonies.

The priestess wears a white headcloth, and a single cowrie shell bracelet as sole ornament. She told me that Nana Buku is creatress, and head of the other gods. She is female, and lives in the sky (emphatically), but this is one of her earthly temples. The priestess prays, sitting or kneeling, facing the straw figure. Prayers are begun and ended with liturgical formulas in Yoruba: 'Nana Buku, owner of the world and sky, known in all lands. . . . What I ask for, if it is not granted, that is your concern.'

On the granite platform outside the temple, a drum is beaten at four every morning and prayer offered at the shrine. On this slab novices must sing all night before ending their probation; they are congratulated if their words are clearly heard in the village below, for unlike other gods who speak in cult dialects Nana Buku uses the tongue of the people, a sign that the cult is indigenous.

Many people in this region use the name of Nana Buku in proverbs, blessings, and curses, and yet offer her no worship. Buku is particularly renowned as an oracle, and people come from far to the various temples with their palavers. She imposes ordeals; perhaps once this was done directly but now it is through the intermediary of fowls which symbolize the suppliants. Messages are sent regularly from these temples, by envoys carrying long red poles and they are obeyed implicitly by all the population. It may be said that market prices are too high, the poor are suffering, and locusts will come if there is no reduction, and so prices drop at once.

THUNDER AND IRON GODS

Thunder gods are found almost everywhere in West Africa, as in many other parts of the world. The powerful tornadoes, which yet bring the longed-for rain, make the spirits of the storm important

29

in the life of the people: thunder, lightning, thunderbolt, and rainbow.

In the forests of the Ivory Coast there are many storm spirits which have different names. Here, as in many other places, it is held that the thunder god brandishes an axe which he casts to the earth on occasion. An Agni legend recounts that during their last struggle with Denkira there were violent thunderclaps, a tree was struck, and a cutlass with a golden handle fell from the sky. The Agni seized the handle and the Denkira the blade and they then separated. This is probably a variant of the thunder-axe myth.

There are many pointed and polished stones which, throughout West Africa, are associated with the thunder. These were probably prehistoric axes, or 'celts', used before the coming of metals to the forest regions. Piles of these stones are still to be found in parts of the Sudan and travelling traders do a good business in selling them to priests of the storm gods. For it is widely believed that whenever there is a storm one of these stones falls from heaven, and the priests make a great pretence of searching for them and, of course, usually find one.

At first sight the worship of storm gods might seem to be absent from Ashanti, but there is reason to believe that 'Nyame was a thunder and sky god, and his chief 'son' Tano has some of the characteristics of the thunder, i.e. axe-bearing. The three-pronged tree, God's tree, used in the worship of 'Nyame is like that which occurs in the worship of some other thunder gods. Rattray describes a tornado during which a tree was struck by lightning and had all the appearance of having been cleft by an axe. 'One of the villagers came up, and after looking at it, says that God's axe ('Nyame akuma) had, after splitting the tree, passed underground to the river where no doubt it would some day be found.'[2]

'Nyame also incorporates the emblem of the rainbow, Nyãnko-tǫn, the Sky God's arch; other people associate it with water.

The Gã of the Accra district have a very important thunder god called Gua. He is the god of blacksmiths, and a smith is always his priest. There are two principal types of temple, one at the forge and one in the forest where the blacksmith's hammer and tongs,

[2] *Ashanti*, p. 176.

together with a pot, are laid at the foot of a silk-cotton tree. Prominent in the cult are the chisel-shaped stones, 'God's hoes'. Gua is closely linked with agriculture, and the manufacture of iron tools and hoes by the priest-smith was formerly an important rite. There is an annual feast and dance which lasts several weeks.[3]

The Ewe call their thunder god So, or more frequently Hevioso from the village of Hevié which is a centre of the cult. Near the coastal lagoon of Nokoué it is linked with a strong python cult.

In the coloured clay wall decorations (bas-reliefs) on the palace and museum at Abomey, So is represented as a ram painted red; lightning is coming from his mouth and two axes ending in curves like lightning stand by his side. The ram represents the growling of the thunder, here as also in Togo and Nigeria. The ram is sacred to priests of the thunder god and taboo to them as food. Devotees carry a well-carved 'axe'; the wooden handle is some two feet long, ornamented with brass bands. The blade end is shaped like a ram's head and from its mouth projects an 'axe', six to nine inches long of thin beaten brass, delicately worked and with symbols of fish and lightning. The axe occurs in the Yoruba storm cults also, and Talbot gives samples of five different patterns of a double-headed axe. I have in my possession such a wooden axe, with wooden symbolical double blades, belonging to the Yoruba god Shãngo, and it is decorated with faces looking in four directions and two others looking forwards and backwards like the Roman god Janus.

The god So is believed to strike down the impious and to destroy the trees which witches use for their meetings in the night. Those people who are struck by lightning are not allowed normal burial, 'the god has taken them', and their corpses are appropriated by the priests. They are placed on a rough platform in the temple of So and slowly burnt.

As soon as a storm bursts, the priests of the storm god are heard going round the village with a double gong; they speak in high tones to imitate the voice of their god. It is believed that whenever there is lightning So has claimed a victim, and if the person or tree cannot be found near at hand then the lightning must have

[3] M. J. Field, *Religion and Medicine of the Gã People*, pp. 64, 74. I am indebted to Dr Field for some particulars given to me personally about this god.

struck another village. A house destroyed by lightning may not be repaired until sacrificial and propitiatory rites are made. However, So is not only an angry god, casting down his axes on wicked people; it is also said that he owns the heavens, sends heat and rain, and gives fertility to men and to their crops.

The Ewe god So is akin to the Yoruba storm god Shāngo, but the Yoruba cult is complicated by the identification of Shāngo with the fourth king of Oyo. Another name for the thunder god is Jakuta, 'one who hurls stones', or fights with stones. This seems to be a more ancient cult, indicating the activity of the god in hurling stones from heaven, and one of the four sacred days is called by Jakuta's name and used by the priests of Shāngo for their god.

There are various legends about king Shāngo, who reigned over a kingdom stretching from Benin to Dahomey. He was a tyrannical and powerful man, and so fiery that he is said to have sent out clouds of fire and smoke from his mouth. One version of the legend says that Shāngo discovered a charm by means of which he could call down lightning from heaven, and he went up a hill near the city to try its effect. The charm worked only too well; a storm blew up at once, but the lightning descended on Shāngo's own palace and destroyed it. Most of his wives and children perished in the fire, and Shāngo was so broken in spirit that he hanged himself on an *ayan* tree of which wood the axes (*oshe-Shāngo*) are made. Another version says that Shāngo ascended to heaven during a storm, or that he disappeared into the earth on a long chain. But it is interesting to note that priests of Shāngo still say that it is dangerous to invoke the storm, for lightning will fall upon the house of the very person who calls upon it.

That Shāngo hanged himself is deeply enrooted in several stories, but the priests deny it, and say 'the king did not hang' (*Oba ko so*). The place of his assumed death is called Koso, but it is said that his very name proves that the king did not hang— *ko so*. Whatever happened, people believe that Shāngo eventually went to heaven and became controller of thunder and lightning.

Shāngo's consort is Oya, the river Niger. In one story he is said to have chased her across the sky, rising like the sun and following her all day till he reached the place where heaven and

earth meet and she hid in the sea. Qya has some storm characteristics; she is fierce and bearded, her face is so terrible that no one
can look at it, and her anger is greatly feared. She is said to strike
down trees and houses, and is often identified with the wind that
blows when no rain follows.

Shãngo was of great importance in Yoruba religious and national
ceremonies, and it is said that he was the principal national god
whose worship was imposed wherever the rule of Qyq stretched.
Like the king, a flash of lightning or a peal of thunder would be
greeted with the cry, 'Welcome to your majesty', 'Long live the
king'. The Alafin of Oyo, head of all the Yoruba in ancient
days, claimed Shãngo as his ancestor and was crowned in his
shrine; previously he had to spend a night with the head priest of
Shãngo and be initiated into some of the cult mysteries. A ram
sacred to Shãngo belonged to the Alafin and wandered freely
round the market, and among the stone sculptures of Ile-Ife there
is a large stone ram's head.

Some of the Yoruba have altars to the thunder god outside their
houses. This 'altar' is a simple three-pronged stake, in the fork of
which is a hollowed-out log or bowl containing 'axes' and other
stones; it is the 'thunder tree' of Shãngo, and is like the God's
tree of Ashanti.

The Ibo storm god is Amadi-Qha or in some places Kamalo.
He is one of the most important gods and most villages have a
shrine dedicated to him where the symbols are peeled forked sticks
or a tree with two pots in front of it. Amadi-Qha is seen in the
lightning and heard in thunder, and punishes sorcerers, witches,
and those who break his laws. But since he sends rain he is also a
giver of fertility and prayers are made to him both for increase of
crops and for children in the home. Before the yams are dug
offerings are waved before his shrine, a fowl may be sacrificed and
prayers made for the household.

Gua, the Gã thunder god who is served by blacksmiths, may be
related to Gu and Ogũn the blacksmith's god of the Ewe and Yoruba. Akin to him may be the deified Igue-igha of Benin, who according to tradition took brass-casting to that country from Ile-Ife in
the thirteenth century; he is worshipped today by Bini brass-
smiths. But the Bini also share Ogũn, the god of iron, with the

Yoruba, and at every forge there is an altar where smiths present offerings to ensure success in their work. Hunters and warriors also put the skulls of their victims on Ogŭn shrines and most Bini houses have a small Ogŭn altar where bits of iron are put. Oaths are sworn over metal objects because the curse of Ogŭn is feared.

The iron god is one of the most popular deities and myths tell of his early doings. He was the earliest hunter and used to come down from heaven on a spider's web. When the other gods were unable to get through the bush Ogŭn cleared a way with his magic tool. Hailed as chief of the gods he preferred the solitary life of a hunter to ruling over his fellows. But at most temples a small symbol of Ogŭn indicates his power and also serves to ensure truth-speaking for those who recognize his influence in oaths. He is the protector of blacksmiths, and his symbols, pieces of iron and a dog's skull, are hung up in blacksmiths' huts. Dogs are sacrificed to him. The silk-cotton tree, and other trees from which bows are made, are sacred to him. The shrine of Ogŭn is in the open air, near a tree, and may or may not have a roof over it.

The importance of the introduction of metals explains the popularity of Ogŭn. As maker of tools Ogŭn was naturally a god of war, hunting, and smiths. Thus he had a triple claim on men's attention. His invocation for war has, of course, gone out of fashion in more peaceful modern times; but especially north of the coast, where hunting is the great occupation of many of the young and active men during the dry season, Ogŭn is constantly called upon. Before every hunting expedition, especially if it is an elephant hunt, sacrifices are offered to him. On return with a good bag the lower jaws of animals killed are laid at the foot of Ogŭn's tree; sometimes the whole skull is painted with stripes of different colours. Ogŭn is believed to protect hunters in their lonely and dangerous pursuits, and to make them invisible when attacked.

The popularity of Ogŭn continues in modern times and in changed conditions. There is no warfare, and if a god is out of work he soon loses his claim to men's attentions. But Ogŭn has 'beaten his swords into plowshares'. He has become the deity of many lorry drivers and cyclists, who hang his favours on their vehicles and hope that the god of metal will still protect them from accidents. His importance in swearing oaths has been mentioned: kissing a piece of iron ensures that a pagan speaks the truth in a court of law, and private people also cement pacts of friendship at a smithy or share pieces of kola nut which have been placed on a metal object.

The Ashanti smith's god is Ta Yao (Yao is his day-name, he is worshipped on a Thursday). He was closely connected with war in the olden days and he still has an attribute name by which he is addressed in rites and on the talking drums: Preko, 'the Aggressor' or 'Eager for war'. Symbols of the war gods were carried into battle in the olden days, clay objects in calabashes which are still borne in annual processions.

Stools were also used to help in war in Ashanti and neighbouring countries, like the ark in Israel. The Gã town chief was set apart to accompany the stool to war. He was 'medicined' by being held over the stool three times (the only time he ever sat over it), naked and blindfold, so that its power might pass into him and make him invincible. This was done vicariously, on behalf of the rest of the town. Then this military father proceeded to 'cook the war' and bathe the soldiers in holy water. He went with them to battle, but stood apart from the fighting, with a bodyguard to protect him. He was not a chief but a spiritual official. The stools of the Gã are not thrones of chiefs like those of Ashanti, but 'war-medicines'.[4] But the Golden Stool of Ashanti was a national emblem, and not a seat to be used.

Ashanti and Gã war gods have naturally lost much of their purpose, though ancient military titles may be retained. The gods survive if they take on other functions. Thus the Fante war god Aflim gives blessings with holy water and is becoming fishing god of coastal peoples. Other gods fill new religious and magical needs with only part of their ancient warlike ritual and accoutrement.

NOTE ON VODŪ (VUDU, VOODOO)

The Fǫn word vodū for a god may be derived from vo, 'apart', like the original sense of the word 'sacred'. The Togolese form is vudu, which is undoubtedly the origin of the American term

[4] M. J. Field, *Social Organization of the Gã People*, pp. 73-4, 89-90.

Voodoo. Slaves from Dahomey and Togo seem to have been sent mainly to Haiti and San Domingo, and those from the ancient Gold Coast went to Jamaica and Cuba. Yorubas went to Brazil. The Jamaican practice of Obeah may take its name from Twi *obayifo*, 'witchcraft'. Much work has been done in recent years in tracing out the survival of African cults, and often of dialects, in the Americas.[5]

[5] Cf. R. Verger, *Dieux d'Afrique*, with its many illustrations (and titles in English) of Yoruba cults in Brazil; and A. Métraux, *Voodoo in Haiti*.

CHAPTER FIVE

The Gods: Earth, Smallpox, Water

MOTHER EARTH

SPIRITS of the earth figure prominently in West African religious life. The givers of fertility in family and crops receive great honour, as did De-meter, the Earth Mother, and similar goddesses in ancient Europe and the East, like the Great Goddess in India today.

Among the Ibo, earth 'is the great Mother Goddess, the spirit of fertility, the nearest and dearest of all the deities. Some of her statues in the Ibo Mbari temples . . . with a child in her arms or on her knees and a halo round her head and with the crescent moon often depicted on or near her, are reminiscent of some Italian Madonnas and still more of Ast or Isis with her son Horus.'[1]

This Ibo earth goddess is called Ala (or Ale or Ane) and is the most important of all the gods. She is both the spirit of the earth and also queen of the underworld, ruling the ancestors who are buried in the earth. In addition she is the giver and administrator of moral laws, and priests are guardians of public morality on her behalf. Oaths are sworn in her name and she is invoked in law-making. Crimes such as murder, theft, adultery and poisoning, and mishaps such as giving birth to abnormal children, cripples and twins are offences against Ala and must be purged by sacrifice to her. 'Ala is, in fact, the unseen president of the community, and no group is complete without a shrine of Ala. The common possession of a shrine of Ala is, indeed, one of the strongest integrating forces in Ibo society.'[2]

Every Ibo village has a shrine of Ala and this shrine is senior to all others in the village. This is usually a tree with a pot for offerings, and in some places iron rods, stones, and wooden gongs are also found there. The *mbari* ('decorated') houses of the region

[1] P. A. Talbot, *Life in Southern Nigeria*, II.43.
[2] C. K. Meek, *Law and Authority in a Nigerian Tribe*, p. 25.

of Owerri are extraordinary buildings with highly decorated walls, and filled with numbers of painted clay figures which may represent any being from gods to travellers in sun helmets. But the central figure in the *mbari* house is invariably Ala and they are set up in her honour, to invoke the blessings of prosperity and offspring.

As goddess of the earth and of fertility Ala receives special sacrifices at the time of planting, at the first fruits, and at full harvest. Palm wine is poured into the pot at the foot of her tree and prayers made for protection in planting, against the accidents of falling trees and cutting with hoes. At the yam harvest wine and yams are offered to Ala, with the gift of a fowl waved before her tree. On special occasions public sacrifice may be made if a diviner has declared that the goddess needs special propitiation. In these ceremonies the priests of Ala take the lead, and they are potent forces in many aspects of village life. Even with changing times the importance of the earth spirit is great to farmers and in connexion with burial and the ancestral rites.

It used sometimes to be said that the Ibibio Sky God, Obasi, was of dual nature, Father God and Mother God (Ete Obasi and Eka Obasi), and weekly sacrifices were made before the Face of Obasi (Isu Obasi). Nowadays the earth goddess, Isong, is more prominent, symbolized by a tortoise shell and responsible for the fertility of the crops, The Ekoi call her Obasi Nsi, the earth goddess, in distinction from the Sky God.

The earth spirit is the second great deity revered by the Ashanti and is sometimes regarded as the consort of 'Nyame of the sky. She is called Asase Yaa, or Aberewa (old mother; Asase Efua in Fante). Yaa is a widely used term for an old woman, and is also the personal name for women born on a Thursday. Thursday is the day set apart for Mother Earth. No Ashanti farmer would till the ground on this day, and the penalty for breaking the taboo was formerly severe. Conflict over this point caused a deadlock between pagans and Christians, because the latter only wanted to rest on a Sunday, and it seems that only time will resolve this impasse.

Asase Yaa has no temples or priests, nor is she consulted for divination; the Ashanti say: 'The Earth does not divine.' Yet she is a most potent principle, with powerful taboos. Like Ala she is called creator of the underworld, and she is mother of the dead 'who lie buried in her pocket'. Mankind is thought to have emerged first from the bowels of the earth, and thither the spirits of the departed return, as to Hades. All along the West Coast, many pagans when they drink palm wine pour out a little from the gourd on to the ground so that the ancestors may drink first.

No Ashanti farmer would till the ground without first asking permission. When the season for cultivation comes round, at the beginning of the rains in March and April, the farmer kills a fowl and pours its blood on the ground, then the corpse is cut up and mixed with cooked plantain or yam, and scattered to the four points of the compass. Meanwhile he prays to his grandparent who had cultivated the land, and to Asase Yaa, to give help in cultivation, preserve from accidents and snake-bites, and give fruitful increase. The real owners of the land, here and elsewhere, are the ancestors who have laboured there, who watch over the land still, and who have to be consulted before it can be leased or even disposed of by a conquering race.

Asase Yaa is addressed in the three-weekly ancestral Adae ceremonies:

> *Earth, when I am about to die*
> *I lean upon you.*
> *Earth, while I am alive*
> *I depend upon you.*
> *Earth that receives dead bodies.*[3]

Similarly when a grave is to be dug the permission of the earth must first be asked: 'We have come to beg you for this spot, so that we may dig a hole.' So that although there is no temple or other cult object for the Asase Yaa, and though some writers prefer to speak of an Earth power or principle rather than a Goddess, yet the influence of this power is felt at many points. Farmers of course have a special reverence for Asase Yaa, but the ancestors are connected with her and chiefs who rule over the land are bound to respect her.

[3] K. A. Busia, *The Position of the Chief in the Modern Political System of Ashanti*, pp. 41-2.

The connexion of earth and smallpox in Ewe and Yoruba belief will be mentioned in the next section. Some of the Yoruba used to invoke the spirit of the earth with kola nuts and the sacrifice of pigeons and fowls, and with this kind of prayer:

> *O Earth, I call thee,*
> *Thou who shavest thy head with hoes;*
> *O God of heaven, O God of earth,*
> *I pray thee uphold my hand;*
> *My ancestors and ancestresses*
> *Please lean on earth and succour me.*[4]

Still today many people (including Christians) will pour a little wine or rum on the ground at the naming ceremony of a child on the eighth day after birth.

An important Yoruba earth and agricultural deity is Orisha Oko, the Farm God or Goddess. This has some of the commonest temples, in which strings of cowrie shells are the chief decoration and small images of twins (*ibeji*) show the importance of the cult for fertility. The principal worshippers are women who decorate themselves with the cowrie necklaces in worship and dances. The chief festival is at the beginning of the yam season in June and yams must not be eaten before then. It is said that in olden days there was considerable licence at this festival, which showed the fertility of human beings linked with that of the soil.

The Ewe revere the earth under the names Ayi and Li. Li is often connected with the popular snake spirit Dã, and the chief priestly family of the royal shrine of the python at Porto Novo is 'chief of Li', Ligan. In each market there is a shrine to the earth god (*ayi-zã*), and there is a clan of 'sons of the earth' who worship the iroko tree. We shall refer to these snake and tree cults in the next chapter.

In many towns and villages there is a chief or 'owner of the soil' (*balɛ*, *ayi-nõn*). He is the representative of the original occupants of the place; he may receive tribute from the reigning chief of the later invaders, and play a prominent part in investiture ceremonies, having alone the power of inviting the chief to take his throne.

[4] A. K. Ajisafe, *History of Abeokuta* (1924), p. 33.

The licence that is often to be found, or still remaining in traces, in connexion with earth gods, gods of town or village, and agricultural deities, is a clear expression of the desire for increase of the family as well as of the land. In Nupe the Navŭ festival at the beginning of the Muslim New Year has become such a time of lax conduct between the sexes as is never seen at other times of the year. In Ibadan, the Oke'badãn festival of the presiding hill spirit is a day when work and fires are forbidden and bands of youths roam the streets shouting forbidden words and making suggestive gestures; but assaults upon persons may be punished with speedy court justice.[5] Similarly at the Apo ceremony in Ashanti there is sexual freedom, bandying of insults and free drinking. 'Custom enjoins that no redress for seduction or adultery may be claimed, or any complaint lodged, during the eight days the ceremony is in progress. Once this period has expired, all such cases are liable to trial before the customary native courts, and are liable to the sanctions of native customary law.'[6] There were similar occasions of licence in the ancient world of which the Roman Saturnalia are the best known, but modern carnivals often still have traces of this.

EARTH AND SMALLPOX

A cult that used to be very widespread in Nigeria, and still is in Dahomey, is that of the so-called smallpox god, Shǫpǫna and Sapata, in Yoruba and Ewe, and closely associated with the earth. In Dahomey, Sapata still counts the greatest number of devotees of any god, but in Nigeria the cult was forbidden in 1917 though still found in places.

Shǫpǫna is regarded as one of the four principal deities, with his own sacred day. He is commonly hailed as Lord or King of the Earth, and one of his titles is Olode, Lord of the Open. In songs sung in his honour Olode is said to bring pleasure to the farmer by preserving the seed. Yet Shǫpǫna is feared as the god who sends the scourge of smallpox. A time of the smallpox epidemic is called 'hot earth' and it is said that victims have been afflicted by hot earth, or struck by his arrow, or under bondage to the king; for

[5] See my *Religion in an African City*, pp. 11ff
[6] R. S. Rattray, *Ashanti*, p. 154.

smallpox is called king and of one who dies of the disease it is said that 'Hot-earth has carried him away'. As a king Shọpọna must be respected and thanks given to him even when he has taken a victim away; no mourning must be worn, lest the anger of the god be even more aroused. There is no doubt that Shọpọna is feared, for he is thought of as dressed in red and prowling about during the dry season to vent his anger on the offending, therefore people avoid wearing red or anything that might seem to imitate him.

The shrine of Shọpọna was usually outside the village, where it might be less dangerous, though possibly also to defend the village against other evils. Sometimes, however, symbols of Shọpọna are seen at other shrines, for example that of Shãngo. Many shrines must have disappeared since the prohibition of the cult, and those that remain are not prominent.

The Ewe-Fọ̃n give the place of honour to Sapata as first in the earth pantheon (*ayi-vodũ*). There is a myth which places Sapata as the lower half of the calabash, of which the ancient sky god Dada Sɛgbo is the upper half. While earlier writers were puzzled by this cult the general opinion now is that earth and smallpox are the same.

Sapata, like Shọpọna, was called 'king of the earth', and this was given as one of the reasons for the occasional banishment of the cult by some Dahomean kings, as two kings cannot reign in the same city. The real reason was probably the anger of the kings when the priests failed to check an epidemic of smallpox which ravaged their army and ruined the summer campaigns against the Yoruba.

One of the chief titles of Sapata is 'king of pearls' (*jɛhọlu*); this is much used at Porto Novo. It is never said that a man has smallpox, but a euphemism is substituted: 'He salutes the chief,' 'He has the king,' or 'It is the king makes him suffer.' Some of the Akan tribes also call smallpox 'king' and speak in roundabout ways of his devastations.

One of the days of the ancient Dahomean four-day week is sacred to Sapata. No earth should be tilled on that day, and so it is usually market-day; or it is Thursday where there is now a seven-day week.

The shrine of Sapata is a low mound, crowned with a block of ironstone (laterite), darkened with oil and sacrificial blood, with a large cactus plant growing beside it. This mound is to be seen at the entrance of most Dahomean villages. One is told today that Sapata is outside the village because he kills, but the reason may be that as an earth god he is put nearer the fields.

The followers of this god in Dahomey shave the right half of the head and on special occasions, in addition to bracelets of cowries and black grains, they wear white skirts and a band round the head decorated with red parrot feathers. Men and women wear a small wire earring.

The priests of the cult, at its best, appear to have tried to prevent the spread of smallpox and other contagious diseases by removing the corpse of one who died of the sickness, as well as all his belongings. The hygienic value of this will be realized when it is known that corpses were normally buried under the floors of huts which were still used as living-rooms.

The priests seem to have gained some knowledge of the cause and treatment of smallpox, leprosy, and tuberculosis. The roots and leaves of a shrub (*newbouldia laevis*), whose leaves resemble the smallpox rash, are found in most temple compounds in West Africa and are used by priests in treatment of this and other diseases. No doubt other preparations were used whose ingredients they kept secret.

People sick of smallpox were removed by priests to their convents or retreats in the forest, before the coming of modern hospitals and vaccination. It is said that the pustules were opened to let out the virus, and sand and leaf preparations rubbed in. As with victims of lightning, those who died of smallpox were not allowed to be kept by the family for burial; the priests interred them naked. The family of the deceased must show no signs of mourning; they must not say that their relative is dead, but that he has gone to the good place (*fi dagbe*). Of one who died of tuberculosis or leprosy, which were also under the control of Sapata and whose victims were buried away from the village, it was said: 'The walls have fallen upon him.' Relatives were informed of the death of their family member by the cryptic phrase: 'Let your ears hear, but let your mouth be silent.' All the possessions of the dead person would be put outside his hut for collection by the priests, and also propitiatory offerings to the gods.

Early writers suggested that smallpox was often deliberately spread by the priests of Shǫpǫna and Sapata, but later writers tended to deprecate this suggestion. The protective, as well as the dangerous, nature of the virus seems to have been known and types of inoculation by incision of the skin were practised in some areas.[7]

There are always unscrupulous men who are willing to tyrannize the suffering, or their relatives, in order to extort money. It was no doubt because of this that the cult of Shǫpǫna was forbidden in Nigeria. But abuse may have been less frequent than was imagined. The Dahomean kings, at least, exercised a careful control over the cults, and it would be difficult to imagine that the priests wrecked their wars deliberately, when the penalty of death or banishment hung over them.

As in the invocation of thunder, it is held that Sapata will choose for his first victim the favourite wife in the family of the priest who invokes his action. The general belief is that evilly disposed men make a preparation of leaves of irritating nature, which are mixed with oil and powdered bones of the type sacred to the god. The mixture is poured on the shrine and is believed to be carried by the wind, and to infect those with whom it comes into contact. A similar procedure is followed when sending out a curse against an enemy. But more potent poison may have been used on occasion.

Some of the Ibo gods are specially concerned with smallpox, Igwe or Ojuku, and there is the taboo of burying victims near the village. Epidemics seem to have been rarer among the Ashanti and Gã, and so there are no special smallpox gods. In modern times any popular divinity may be called upon for help in time of epidemic.

RIVER AND SEA DIVINITIES

After the earth gods may come those very popular divinities of river and sea which play such a large part in West African thought,

[7] Compulsory inoculation was practised in northern Ghana, virus taken from a person suffering with the disease being placed in an incision in the wrist and rubbed in. Smallpox is considered a disgrace, corpses are buried in the field or midden, and no mourning is allowed. R. S. Rattray, *Tribes of the Ashanti Hinterland*, p. 55.

especially for fishermen and those who live near rivers and sea. They are the spirits which dwell in the mysterious depths of the water and which make it so important.

All the great rivers of Yoruba country have their presiding spirit. We have referred to Ọya, goddess of the river Niger, wife of Shāngo the thunder god; two other wives of his were the rivers Ọshun east of Ibadan and Ọvia at Benin. One of the most popular river spirits is Yemọja, who is called mother of all deities, and has shrines in many parts of the country, but especially rules over the river Ogūn at Abeokuta. Yemọja is served by priestesses, and women, who come to the temples to pray for children and offer yams and fowls, are her principal worshippers. In the temples the goddess is represented by wooden or clay female images.

Olokūn is the 'owner of the sea' in Yoruba, Bini, and Ibo; he is Hu in Fọn. The sex of the god seems to vary in different places. Naturally, like Ọlọsa the lagoon goddess, he is worshipped chiefly by those who live along the coast. Yet Olokūn is sometimes claimed as the ancestor of the Ọni of the sacred inland city of Ife and his shrine in that town is said to be senior to all others of this god.

Olokūn is believed to live in a palace under the sea, as sea kings do in many other mythologies, and to have his attendants and mermaid wives, lesser divinities, human and fishlike. Rough seas are attributed to the anger of the god, and propitiatory sacrifices were thrown into the sea for him, generally fowls and animals; formerly, human beings were sacrificed on special occasions. He is the protecting god of fishermen.

In Benin, Olokūn is one of the most important of gods, and is identified with the sea and with a river that rises in the south-east of the kingdom and into which all other rivers in the world are believed to flow. In this place there is a large temple where Olokūn is represented by a clay figure with his attendant wives, and is served by a priest and a priestess. Elsewhere the shrines are attached to houses, and women have a small altar of Olokūn which is installed at their marriage, and such women are regarded as priestesses of Olokūn. The god is both a giver of fertility 'bringer of children', and also of wealth, which may both link him with the abundance of fertility and also with the wealth which came over the sea with the coming of European trade from the fifteenth century onwards.[8]

The Fɔ̃n chief priest of the sea god Hu is said in olden days to have gone into the depths of the sea, for seven days each year, riding a bull and seeking to find the god's messages and commands, during which time his attendants danced on the shore. He was accompanied by two virgins—a way of saying that they were sacrificed. Another popular sea-goddess of the Fɔ̃n and Gɛ̃ is the daughter of Hu, Avlekɛtɛ, or according to some a child of the thunder. She is the most prominent modern goddess at the port of Cotonou and the surrounding coastal villages.

The great river god of Ghana and the lower Ivory Coast is Tano or Ta Kora. Kora is a term used in northern regions for the Niger, meaning 'the immense'. The prefix Ta used here and in the names of other Akan gods may derive from *ata*, 'father'.

Tano is credited with creation, as is shown in the extract from the drum pieces, with which all readers of Rattray are familiar from his frequent quotations of the verse:

> *The stream had its origin in the Creator.*
> *He created things,*
> *Pure pure Tano.*

Tano is said, in Ghana, to be the second son of 'Nyame the Supreme God. He cheated the elder son, Bia, of his inheritance, although Bia was 'Nyame's favourite. Bia, also a river god, thus only received the more barren Ivory Coast lands, while Tano had the fertile land west of Ghana; for once 'Nyame had given these lands to the deceitful Tano he was unable to reverse the promise. In the Ivory Coast the Agni people say that Bia cheated Tano of the blessing and then fled to the west. Other myths say that Tano fought with Death, but they had to come to a compromise, so that while Tano was allowed to come to the town of man, Death came also.

Tano is thus a nature god, but has heroic attributes. He was possibly once, in one aspect, a thunder god also. In the olden days his priests used to dance with axes. Blackened axe shafts, without the axe heads which have been lost, are still in existence. Today he

[8] R. E. Bradbury, *The Benin Kingdom*, pp. 52-3.

is a river god but, like other divinities, he was endowed with extra functions as need arose, and was invoked as a war god in time of military need.

Rattray described the principal temple of Tano in Ghana, at a small village near the source of the river, Tano Oboase, 'Tano beneath the rock'. Here is a finely decorated temple, but without charms of any sort such as are found in most temples. There are many minor shrines. By rivers and fords stand altars to the god or one of his 'sons': rough platforms of sticks, bearing a basket or brass pan, or a stone from the river bed.

Tano has widespread worship, far beyond the river that bears his name. Tribes that migrated westwards into the Ivory Coast still sacrificed to the god at the foot of fan-palm trees. Tano was the chief god, after Nyam, of the Adjukru of the Ivory Coast, before their conversion to Christianity. The cult was held at night and the priests were renowned seers. They dressed in white, and performed ritual washings in brass pans, the water then being considered sacred and sprinkled on the followers of the god. Often in the worship of Tano the priests fell into ecstasies, and their words were received as messages from the god. It was Tano whose symbols were destroyed by the famous Liberian prophet Harris and his followers, in the movement that swept the lower Ivory Coast in 1913 and later years.

The sea god is called Opo by the Ashanti. The Fante and Gã think that Bonsu, the whale, incarnates the sea god and they make offerings of corn to his spirit. Other Fante fishing gods, Tantrabu and Abọdinkra, receive gifts of yam, and so do ancient war gods such as Aflim which now have become patrons of fishing.

Any lake or large stretch of water is liable to be thought of as the abode of a spirit. One of the most remarkable lakes is Bosomtwe, some twenty miles from Kumasi. This lake is circular, five miles across in each direction, and surrounded by cliffs about seven hundred feet high. It has no outlet and the water flowing in evaporates in the intense heat. Twe is said to be the name of a spirit (*obosõm*) who came out of the water and made love to an old woman, Aberewa, a name also given to the earth spirit, Asase Yaa. Twe promised to give fish to the old woman whenever she wished, if she would simply knock on the water. To this day no hooks or cast nets are allowed for fishing in the lake, nor can canoes be used. The fishermen who live in the villages round the lake balance on logs, paddle with their hands, and catch the abundant fish in reed baskets. It is said that every Sunday, the day of his worship, Twe used to emerge from the lake to sit among his worshippers. From time to time the vegetable matter that accumulates in the bottom of the lake, brought in by the feeding streams, lets off an accumulation of gases from decomposition. To the lake-dwellers this is a supernatural event, and it is said that the lake spirit 'explodes its gunpowder'.[9]

The Akan gods are mostly tree and water gods. They are children of 'Nyame and contain some of his person and force. There are said to be hundreds of *abosõm*, descended from four original sons of 'Nyame. This origin from 'Nyame, however, is a priestly or sophisticated explanation, an effort to reconcile and grade different cults, and it is not reflected in the rituals performed at the various shrines. Usually the god of the locality takes precedence, and new gods are added on as 'wives' or 'sons'. A pantheon may grow up, because of the tolerant nature of the religion. The new god may enjoy great popularity for a time, but he will tend to sink into subordination to the place-god.

The gods were less important in the Akan group than among the Ewe and Yoruba and there is a tendency nowadays to say that they were non-existent, but the descriptions and photographs given by Rattray and other careful writers disproves this suggestion. Ancestral rites, however, were no doubt more prominent and public than offerings to the gods. In the Ashanti kingdom the cult of the ancestors came to play a predominant part in tribal life during the last two centuries of intense military activity. Warrior ancestors tended to displace the more agricultural gods, and their stools played a great part in practical religion than did some of the older shrines, which began to decline. Agriculture was often neglected, and in any case the vast forest lands never received that intensive cultivation which is a characteristic of Dahomey and Nigeria. The Omãnhene or King owned no land, but he exacted a tithe of gunpowder and money received from traders.

[9] See Rattray's detailed description, *Ashanti,* pp. 54ff. I checked this on a visit to Lake Bosomtwe in 1955.

Religion is a living thing and is changing with the great revolution in life that has taken place during the present century. The impact of new religions, Christianity and Islam, democratic government, education, overseas trade, mining, large-scale farming, and great new towns has been incalculable. A great deal of the old paganism has gone, though a great deal remains either visible or potently under the surface. Quite apart from the new historical religions, there are also new pagan cults that arise. Dr Field, writing of Akim, points out that new gods arise, or ancient ones are revived or are imported from outside, particularly under the ever-present influence of the belief in witchcraft. 'The forest festivals of Afahye and Odzira are now for the most part mere stool festivals, very perfunctorily performed, and most of the people do not bother to stir out of their houses to attend them. A sheep is killed for the stool, a fowl for the river, the young boys dance to the chief's drums, and nobody bestirs himself to take much interest. But when there is a local shrine of, say, Kupo, there is an annual festival which may justly be so-called. The town subscribes to buy a cow which is slaughtered and cooked before the shrine and shared between all who have partaken of the "medicine".'[10]

---

[10] 'Some New Shrines of the Gold Coast and Their Significance', in *Africa*, XIII.138ff.

CHAPTER SIX

The Gods: Other Divinities

THE SNAKE CULT

THE SNAKE is a prominent feature in religious symbolism in many parts of the world. We may recall in the Bible the serpent in Genesis, the brazen snake made by Moses and to which incense was burnt in the time of Hezekiah and the woman with the spirit of a python in Acts.

In some parts of West Africa there is a developed snake worship, the python in particular being admired for its wisdom and gentleness. Some of the inland peoples, however, have little or no snake cults, and it is especially in river and coastal areas that snake worship is more pronounced. Early traders in Ewe country were so struck by what they saw along the coastline that they thought all the inhabitants of the country to be snake-worshippers.

John M'Leod wrote: 'In Whydah, for some unaccountable reason, they worship their Divinity under the form of a particular series of snake, called Daboa, which is not sufficiently large to be terrible to man, and is otherwise tameable and inoffensive. These Daboas are taken care of in the most pious manner, and are well fed on rats, mice, or birds, in their Fetish houses or temples, where the people attend to pay their adoration, and where those who are sick or lame apply to them for assistance.'[1]

It is the python, a non-poisonous snake, that is worshipped at Ouidah (Whydah on English maps). It was the chief god of the ancient Peda tribe, which was originally established in Ouidah but is now scattered along the coast and round Lake Ahemé. The largest python temples are in Ouidah, Porto Novo, and villages along the coast to Badagry, and on rivers such as the Ouémé.

When I visited the principal snake temple at Ouidah it was a small, unrepaired, mud-walled compound, opposite which the large Roman Catholic cathedral has been built (in the building of

[1] *A Voyage to Africa* (1820).

which the snake-worshippers shared at the invitation of the bishop). One enters through a round hut at a corner of the square, and the central shrine is a small house, with an open veranda from which there leads a doorway into the interior, screened with a cloth. The priest willingly fetches out pythons to show to visitors. They are quite tame and harmless, they wander freely about the town; they must never be killed and their flesh is taboo as food. A man who meets a python will salute it by kissing the ground, calling it 'my father', because it is thought to be an ancestor, and asking its blessing. If it threatens his fowls, he will call a priest to take it back to the temple. Behind the temple is a sacred Loko (iroko) tree, with bones of animals at its foot.

The python is called *dãngbe* (M'Leod's *daboa* probably comes from a dialectical form), which means 'snake of the forest', or perhaps 'good snake'. The devotees of the python are *dãngbesi*, 'wives'. There seems to be no foundation for travellers' suggestions, made from the time of Bosman onwards, that python worship was an immoral cult. The conjunction of snake, tree, and 'wives' of the python made them think this; but devotees of all Ewe gods are called 'wives'. (The -*si* suffix indicates a devotee, male or female, of any god.)

The cult of the python is mainly coastal and fluvial, and it is said to have been 'bought' for the inland kingdom of Abomey after the conquest of Ouidah in 1727. There was probably an exodus of coastal slaves after this capture and they took vestiges of the python cult to enter into the Voodoo worship of parts of the West Indies.[2] In Dahomey the python cult is allied to those of the thunder gods, and the python is taboo to servants of the thunder deity So, and the ram to those of the serpent.

In some parts of the interior there are isolated python cults, for example among the Dagomba of central Togo. Elsewhere there is no regular worship but there may be strong taboos. The Ashanti must not kill or eat a python, and if he finds a dead python in the forest he will bury it with funeral honours, like a human being. On the other hand the Yoruba generally have no python cult or taboo, though occasionally people are seen who have tame pythons and pay them honour.

[2] See note at end of Chapter 4 above (p. 35).

Pythons are revered in some parts of Ibo and Ibibio country, and particularly among the Ijaw of the Niger delta. The chief water spirit is Adumu and pythons are his children. Their flesh is taboo of course and at death they are buried with the honour due to a chief. Any house that a python enters is thought to be blessed, though the prudent householder will steer it away from doing any serious damage. Women dedicated to the water spirits are said to be married to the sacred serpents and in periods of long dancing they go into ecstasies, true pythonesses, and their utterances are regarded as oracles. Carved staves, with human heads and snakes twined round them in the wood, represent the snakes. At one of the most important shrines, at Adum'Ana, the water spirit is represented by a large wooden figure with moustache, beard and hat like the early Portuguese traders, and sacred serpents are also carved on the statue.[3]

Apart from the python, the snake in general appears in Dahomean symbolism and art, though little in Yoruba. In the clay wall mouldings (bas-reliefs) and decorated cloths in the palace-museum at Abomey there are striking representations of brightly coloured snakes, red, blue, and white, the most sacred colours. The snake is curled in a circle, with its tail in its mouth; a very ancient and almost universal way of portraying it as a symbol of immortality and eternity. The snake sheds its skin and yet lives on, so illustrating immortality after the death of the body; by swallowing its tail it forms a circle, a symbol of eternity, which goes round and round for ever, 'like a great ring', or like 'first, and last, and midst, and without end'. This motif of the tail-swallowing may be seen in some Benin brass-work. The very popular chain design, seen on clothing, brass trays, wooden plates, and so on, may also be linked to the circular snake design; this is found widely over Africa and in other parts of the world; the ancient Romans frequently made use of it.[4]

The coloured snake is not only called by the name of the principal snake Dǎ, but is also regarded by the Ewe as representing the rainbow, Aido Hwedo. In Yoruba also the rainbow is linked with

[3] P. A. Talbot, *Life in Southern Nigeria*, II. 101ff.
[4] E. G. Waterlot, *Les Bas-Reliefs des Bâtiments royaux d'Abomey* (1926), plate IX.

the boa, which is its messenger. It is popularly said that at the end of the rainbow could be found its dung, like that of a snake, and those who find it get great riches. This compares with European and Asiatic myths and dreams of excreta in a fantasy of wealth.

The Dahomean snake Dã is not worshipped or tamed like the python. Dã is thought to be a spiritual principle, the idea of life and movement, which is represented by snakes, rainbows, curling smoke, running water, waving grasses. Everybody has his own Dã in his belly which is the umbilical cord; this is cut off at birth and buried under a tree, or a tree is planted at the spot. This tree records the growing child's age, and as it may be dangerous to tell his own age a fictitious one is substituted. A secret worship may be offered at the tree, not public, lest somebody mutilate the tree and harm the owner.

Dã is believed always to go in pairs. The rainbow is thought to be always double, as it is sometimes seen like this. Earthen pots representing Dã are always in pairs, and each has a double horn on it because snakes are thought to be horned. Dã is held to live in the heart of the bush, or in the ground. When a doctor is called in to treat a sick man, he may prescribe sacrifices which are taken into the bush for Dã. Those who carry the offerings are daubed with white clay on their faces and arms; the priest himself leads the way, decked with small gourds and cowrie shells, with red and white spots on his body.

NATURE SPIRITS

There are countless other divinities, some of general, others simply of local importance. The greater gods have their pantheon of associated gods. In Ashanti many have the prefix Ta, which may indicate relationship to Tano or their place as 'fathers' (*ata*). The most important is Ta Mensa; then there are Ta Yao, Ta Asubonten, Ta Kofi. Others are associated with rivers, such as Bia and Eholie.

In central Dahomey there is the family of Nana Buku, all the shrines of which have the typical thatched cover. There are Buku Olokpa, 'the owner of wood', a stake that formerly used to impale witches; Buku Aja, 'of the market'; Buku Kataku, 'run-die', a reference to the possession and apparent death of those possessed by this god. A related oracle is Nana Jakpa, 'throw-kill', perhaps related to the Yoruba Jakuta; the devotees of this goddess walk naked for some months after the seclusion of their training is ended and are called 'fools'.

The iroko tree is held to be sacred all along the coast. Called Loko in Dahomey it is one of the most ancient cults and has its special characteristics. Myths tell how men and women descended to earth from the branches of a huge mythical Loko. A number of ancestral-divine shrines at Abomey and Porto Novo bear names compounded of Loko. If a shoot of the iroko tree appears in a compound or street, that is taken as a sure sign that the god wishes for a cult to be founded there. Perhaps it is the grave of an ancestor who has been neglected, and so a shrine is built. On the other hand it is believed that an iroko will not grow if it is planted deliberately. And it is unlucky to plant a tree, for the planter will not live to see it grow.

Some peoples consider that the spirit which inhabits the tree is particularly concerned with the fertility of human beings. The souls of those about to be born may be said to live in trees, or thickets of bamboos. Women often pray to spirits in iroko, baobab, silk-cotton, acacia, mahogany, and palm trees to send them children. Trees are often girdled with a length of cotton material as a mark of respect.

All trees, as well as animals, are believed to have souls, but other and more powerful spirits than the essence of the tree itself may take up abode there. An Ashanti priest who offered sacrifices near an *akata* tree to an indwelling god called Edinkira, declared: 'I do not ever give offerings to the *sunsum* [soul] of the akata.'

Sacrifices are offered to the particular trees from which drums and stools are carved and the trees to be used for canoes and other purposes, before they are cut down. 'Nor does propitiation stop here, for later the wandering spirit whose habitation or body has been destroyed is expected, and in fact is actually enticed, to enter once again the material substance where it dwelt when the tree was yet alive. This explains the subsequent rites of consecration of the completed stool or the completed drums.'[5]

Spirits are worshipped 'on every high hill and under every

[5] R. S. Rattray, *Religion and Art in Ashanti*, pp. 3ff.

green tree'. Many hills are sacred. There is the generic mountain god Oke of the Yoruba and variations on this name such as Nake, 'hill mother'. Many hills have a sacred cave; at Abeokuta (which means 'under the rock') there is the Olumo cave, a shrine where the people hid during the Dahomean slave-raiding. At Ibadan the hill Oke'badãn is not particularly prominent; the town is built on hills but the hill of the first settlement is hidden in the bush. Yet the hill spirit is the ancient tutelary deity of this city, and was represented by a woman with breasts like great pots, and as the giver of fertility women pray to her for children. The priest in charge of the cult, the Ab'oke, 'hill worshipper', performs worship every five days, and leads the annual festival of the town, going from house to house blessing the people and allowing them to rekindle their fires.[6]

The winds may be thought of as representing spirits; the Harmattan sandy wind, Oye, is said to emerge from the Yoruba village Oye, near Ado-Ekiti, and it begins to blow when the chief of that village opens his door. There are many wood-sprites and fairies that hunters believe in, and that are supposed to teach them the secrets of the forest. Then there are the purely local village spirits which are tutelary gods, and often confused with the ancestors.

ESHU OR LƐGBA

Before leaving the subject of supernatural spirits, to pass on to descriptions of shrines and priests, it is necessary to say a few words about a most prominent figure associated with the gods in Dahomey and Nigeria. This is Eshu or Ɛlɛgbara in Yoruba, Lɛgba in Ewe-Fɔ̃n.

The nature of this spirit used to be commonly misunderstood, and the people were sometimes wrongly called 'devil-worshippers'. Farrow roundly called Eshu 'the devil', 'the prince of darkness', 'he is emphatically the supreme evil spirit'. Samuel Johnson, who was a native of Nigeria but a Christian convert, and wrote fifty years ago, attributed to Eshu or Ɛlɛgbara the specific characteristics of Hebrew-Christian mythology, and called him 'Satan, the Evil One, the author of all evil'.[7]

---

[6] E. G. Parrinder, *Religion in an African City*, pp. 11ff.
[7] S. S. Farrow, *Faith, Fancies and Fetich*, pp. 85ff; S. Johnson, *History of the Yorubas*, p. 28.

Dualism of good and evil is otherwise unknown to the peoples of West Africa, and as the terms used here are obviously of European origin, it is clear that care is needed in handling this subject. Since it is admitted by everyone that the favour of Eshu can be successfully invoked on behalf of his worshipper, it is evident that this is quite different from the Jewish-Christian Devil who, in traditional theology, is a purely evil force, can only do evil, and therefore would never be used to protect houses and villages as Eshu is.

Farrow admits that Bishop Crowther in his *Vocabulary* called Eshu 'the god of mischief'. It is this mischievous character that is prominent. Eshu is demoniacal, but not diabolical. He is a tricky, mischievous being, who can bring evil on a house and is sometimes invoked by the vengeful to bring harm upon their enemies.

On the other hand, by daily propitiation, men hope to use Eshu as a protection. The image outside houses and villages may perhaps be compared to a savage dog, that will rarely bite the hand that feeds it but, it is hoped, may be relied upon to attack any evil that approaches and that naturally, to the pagan mind, will follow the high road by which the shrine of Eshu stands. For this reason, as a protector, and not only because of his dangerous character, Eshu is not usually found inside the house but at the door, facing outwards.

This idea is not peculiar to West Africa, it is indeed very ancient. 'There were snakes and dogs and gryphons,' wrote Sir Leonard Woolley of Ur, 'human figures and figures of men with the heads of lions and bulls, with bulls' legs or fishes' bodies, every sort of kindly demon that might guard the house and keep off sickness or ill-luck.'[8]

Eshu plays a great part in Yoruba mythology, and often in relationship to the oracle deity Ifa or Ọrunmila. It is said that Eshu is the messenger of the oracle, taking sacrifices to him and bringing his commands to men, acting under his orders and punishing the wicked for him. It is said that in a battle with Death Eshu lost his club but Ọrunmila recovered it for him and that created a pact between these two divinities. But Eshu is also important in his own right, and he is greatly feared for the evil that he can do;

[8] *Ur of the Chaldees* (Pelican edition), p. 109.

because of this fear, it is said, a portion of every sacrifice offered to other divinities is set aside for Eshu. Eshu is said to impel men to evildoing, and wicked men are often called 'Sons of Eshu', while the weak blame him for moving them to do wrong.

The evil character of Eshu can be used, it is hoped, against one's enemies. By feeding him with his favourite dish of palm oil, and then offering him his great taboo of palm-kernel oil in the name of an enemy, it is expected that Eshu will fly off and avenge himself on this insulting enemy. In this character he is Elɛgbara or Shigidi, the avenger.

On the other hand Eshu is looked upon as protective and even benevolent, if he is well fed and respected. He is called 'father', and some people even take his name or a compound of it. He is said to have two hundred names, which indicates that he is a many-sided character, and perhaps too diverse to grasp.

The shrines of Eshu and Lɛgba are everywhere, and to the superficial observer they are the very characteristic of 'fetishism'. The shrines are at the entrance to the village and the compound, in the market, at cross-roads and groves, outside or in the house. They may be simple mounds of earth, or a piece of laterite rock, or an earthenware pot upside down with a hole in the middle. Sometimes the mound is decorated with cowrie shells, blackened with oil and blood, and daubed with feathers. Often the mound is crudely shaped into human form, it may have horns on its head, and a knife or club in its hand. The Lɛgba images very often have a prominent phallus, when they are said to be 'crowned'. Some of them are large and fantastic, and I have seen one as a life-size clay image of a man, wearing a sun-helmet and wrist-watch, with phallus.

The phallic side is strong in the cult of Lɛgba and accounts for some of his popularity. Dances in his honour are often accompanied by gross sexual imitations, because it is hoped that he will give fertility. Associated with the image are his wives and children, small mounds in front of which are little dishes and iron rods, to receive libations.

Every morning the householder stands in front of Eshu or Lɛgba, shuffles his feet, rubs his hands together, and asks for evil to be turned away from himself and his family during the day. A few beans or corn grains are offered, or a child takes a bleeding fowl to the low hut of the market or village shrine. If a dog eats these offerings it is a sign of favour, for the dog is sacred to this spirit.

A man setting up his house will have a personal Lɛgba made, but this may be delayed until his father's death, when the father's Lɛgba is destroyed; for it is thought to be unlucky to have a new one made and thus hasten the father's death.

A priest making the shrine sacrifices first a goat to the spirit of the earth, where a hole is dug. Fowls are also sacrificed and put into the hole over which a mound is raised. A second goat is sacrificed when the mound is complete, and a third goat is given to the priest. One or two phalli are put in the mound; if there are two, one will be of metal and one of wood, if one it will be of wood. A piece of white cloth, or a palm frond, is fastened round the mound as a garment.

Unlike most of the other Dahomean gods, Lɛgba has no priesthood and no convent for training devotees. But he is associated with all the gods and serves as intermediary between them and men. As with Eshu, in every offering to a god part is first given to Lɛbga; and the same obtains in every consultation of the Fa oracle. This character of a divine messenger is brought out clearly in the corresponding Bini cult of Esu, the messenger of the gods, by whom alone man can approach the immortals.

Similar but inferior to the Eshu protecting spirit are the clay images which are placed outside every town and village in the Gã plain of Ghana. Dr M. J. Field says: 'These are not gods, nor representatives of gods, nor the abode of gods; they are mere medicines placed there to keep away, by taking upon themselves diseases and other evils entering the town.' She gives one exceptional example of such an image bearing the name of a god, and fashioned like a dog.[9] While the mythology of these objects may not be so developed in Ghana as in Dahomey and Nigeria, yet for practical purposes they seem to serve much the same ends. They are village guardians; some have wooden phalli, or wooden rods placed in front, as chalk cones are put at some shrines in Ibo country. Offerings are laid in front of these images by people coming from the farms.

[9] *Religion and Medicine of the Gã People*, pp. 77–8.

In Akan theology every god has its own messenger, whom it sends to warn its adherents or a village of impending danger or to protect them from evil. Te Bekue is the messenger of Tano, and Bogyaago is the messenger of the god Kobi. Whereas Christian Yoruba and Ewe use the words Eshu and Lɛgba for the Devil, the Akan have adopted for this the name Obonsam, a forest monster (*sasabonsam*, perhaps once meaning the gorilla).

Discussion of the great oracle-god Ifa or Qrunmila is left for separate consideration in Chapter 13. Ifa is closely associated with Eshu, for both are intermediaries between the gods and men, and Ifa declares the will of the divinities. According to myths it was Eshu who first taught Ifa the use of palm nuts for divining. Sacrifices may be offered to both when consulting a god.

CHAPTER SEVEN

Temples and Worship

TEMPLES AND SHRINES

W E TURN NOW from the consideration of the supernatural gods to some description of the sacred places and persons devoted to their service. Temples dedicated to the gods, for sacrificial and ceremonial purposes, are both public and private. All are sacred, and not to be entered or touched by the unbelieving.

Something must be said of the use of the words 'temple' and 'shrine'. In the first edition of this book the word 'shrine' was largely used, with the purpose of indicating that the temples are usually small and often not entered by the laity. But the word 'shrine' can also be used of an inner sanctuary, a shrine within a temple, and so it is ambiguous. Here we shall use the word temple, if it is a building like a house, and shrine to mean either an inner sanctuary or a temple so small that it is only a small shelter or a tiny wayside altar. In all cases, however, it must be understood that African temples are small constructions, and are not meant for large gatherings of people. In this they are like many Hindu and Buddhist temples and pagodas, which are primarily shrines to enclose a relic or sacred object, and not made to enclose large congregations. Christian churches or Muslim mosques are always made to provide for a congregation at communal worship, which is regular and weekly. But in other religions worship may be much less regular, not communal, and little place given to the laity. Priests enter or stand in front of the temple or shrine, and lay worshippers generally stand or kneel in the courtyard outside.

The principal divinities have their priesthood and altars, with the exceptions we have noted. There may be a number of temples of the same god within the radius of a few miles, especially in cities like Ibadan or Porto Novo. There are some fine temples, like large houses, on which all the care and artistry of which the worshippers are capable have been bestowed. There are carefully polished with moulded pillars and walls, that are marvels when one considers that the sole material is unbaked clay; bright decorations in colour, red, white, and blue or black dyes, represent animal and human forms, or geometrical patterns. These make a striking contrast to the houses of ordinary folk, which are usually undecorated except for chiefs' dwellings. Most art seems to have had a religious origin and certainly it draws its inspiration therefrom.

The Ibo *mbari* houses are only temporary temples, since though they are built at some specific command of a god, they are never repaired and soon fall into ruins. The commonest design is a central square shrine, in which sits the image of the god, surrounded by a veranda on all sides which is filled with clay and painted images of human beings and animals of all kinds: chiefs, policemen, traders, Madonnas, women, goats, and crude sexual representations of things that are normally forbidden. They serve as an act of propitiation to the offended spirit, a representation of any old or new people and objects, and an expression of the taboo.

Images in human form do occur in temples of Yoruba and Ewe people, but apart from Eshu which is very often represented in this way, many of the temples use symbols of the gods rather than anthropomorphic images: closed calabashes, stones, posts or trees, pots, axe heads, metal snakes, and so on.

The shrines may be small altars in the fields, forked posts in compounds, or large buildings in villages. There are temples in clearings in the bush, commonly called 'groves'. Here there may be a square surrounded by a mud wall, or by characteristic shrubs which make a hedge, particularly the long-leafed *dracaena scoparia* or *terminalis*, and the jagged-leafed *newbouldia laevis*. If it is a temple of Loko there is a tall iroko tree to one side, several small thatched huts near the tree, and earthenware unglazed pots at its base. The romantic imagination of the inquisitive and uninformed visitor may connect such quiet and shady spots with 'dark deeds'. He will often be exaggerating.

In some regions the people use many religious objects. I have seen a dozen or twenty separate pots and shrines at the house of a pious layman. Most family compounds have small mounds for one or more of the gods, some dishes by the house door for the twin cult and for Eshu, some iron rods (*asεn, ǫsanyin*) in a little hut for the ancestors, charms over the doorway and in the corners of the rooms, and a roughly carved 'guardian' post at the door fastened with a chain, to drive away and chain down evil.

In addition to personal shrines there are the market and village Eshu, larger public temples, and perhaps a convent for training priests and mediums. Outside the village there is often a large cactus with a laterite rock and a pot on a raised mound, for the earth and smallpox god.

The symbolism of the objects in the shrines and temples may not always be clear even to the worshipper. But posts and snakes are usually male, and water and pots female. Cowrie shells are used in various rites but particularly in female ones. Strings of nuts painted on the walls represent the instruments of divination. A spotted image may indicate the god of smallpox, or be simple decoration. Paintings or images of chameleons, leopards, and the like may indicate sacred animals or attendants on the gods.

Many of the temples and shrines have an air of neglect and the objects in them may be dusty and dirty. But every so often there is a spring-cleaning—a donation from a rich visitor or grateful suppliant or the annual festival of the god impels the priest to get the place cleaned up and painted. Of course nowadays with the decline of the ancient religion, and the spread of Christianity and Islam, many of the old temples fall into complete ruin; only a few old people are left faithful to the cult and they are unable to make the necessary repairs. But collectors of antiques make a great mistake if they procure old images and keep them in their dusty condition under the impression that this is original; the real owners and users of these images would always clean and paint them if they could afford it.

None of these symbols or shrines is worshipped in or for itself. They are the dwelling-places, permanent or temporary, of spiritual beings and express some of their attributes. Therefore they are not 'fetishes', though the ignorant may call them such. Nor are they ill-treated if the prayers of the worshippers are not granted. Some early writers thought that this was often practised, but the only instance I have met with in life, or in the works of serious modern observers, was that of a man who abused a 'charm', not connected with a god, which he found among the ruins after his hut had been burnt, and which had not afforded him protection. A magical charm is supposed to protect automatically, if it has been properly prepared. 'Magic commands, religion implores.' A man does not abuse his god if his prayer is not granted, for the constant word of religion in which man deals with a higher power is 'Thy will be done'.

All the temples, shrines, and altars, great and small, public and private, are made and dedicated by priests and properly qualified persons. The ceremonies of consecration are not fully open to the general public, and the average layman has but a vague idea of what constitutes his shrine and how it was made. All he knows is that the god may be invoked there, after consecration.

Research workers are rarely successful in witnessing the hallowing of a shrine themselves. But the following accounts are based on first-hand information, given by priests who knew precisely what was done and who communicated details unknown to many laymen.

A widely known priest, now a Christian, whose services used to be sought over an area more than a hundred miles in length, described to me the procedure he had followed in making shrines. First of all, for a village Sapata (smallpox god), he required for sacrificial purposes and personal fees the following: eight goats, forty fowls, ten four-gallon cans of palm oil, many gourds of millet or maize beer, several bottles of gin, rum or other spirits, three pieces of cloth, white, red, and black. Having received these offerings the priest then collected the indispensable ingredients for a shrine of Sapata: the head of a boa, and the skulls of a lion and a crocodile or cayman. Most priests have stocks of bones in reserve.

Next he collected five hundred leaves, which must include a number of those which are peculiar to Sapata, probably with obvious or imagined resemblances to the symptoms and pustules of the disease; the rest may be made up of any variety. During the night the priest takes a handful of sand or soil from the road, another from the refuse of the market-place, and a third from the village stream or well. This is added to the leaves, and pounded or mixed together in an earthen pot.

Next day, the priest with his attendants and novices resorts with the above preparation to the spot chosen for the shrine, usually just outside the village. Half the gift of goats, fowls and drinks are set aside as fees for the priest and his associates. The village chief also claims a large part of the fees.

Laymen are required to keep at a distance and cannot follow the ceremony in detail. The priest and his companions gather round the chosen place. They make a hole in the ground, having first killed a goat and let its blood drop on the ground to ask permission of the earth to dig in it. Into this hole are placed, in great secrecy, the heads of the boa, lion, and cayman, and the mixture of leaves and soil is added to them. Earth is then taken and mixed with some of the fermented beer, not with water as would normally be done in building a house; on some great occasions a mixture may be made with the blood of sacrifices. With the clay thus made, a mound is raised over the hole where the bones and leaves are buried, which may be up to two feet high.

The remaining goats and fowls are sacrificed, their blood being poured on the mound. Half of these are given to the lay spectators, the other half being eaten at once, after cooking, by the priest and his acolytes. A cactus is planted on the mound, and a laterite stone and pot of water put in front of it. By these tokens the shrine will ever be recognizable at a glance as dedicated to the smallpox god. The priest then prays, beseeching the god to come into the shrine. He asks for divine protection for the village: may there be no disease or epidemic, no sudden deaths, no difficulties of childbirth, no destruction by fire, no accidents with guns; may there be in-crease of money and abundant harvests.

The procedure followed in making a shrine for the thunder god (So, Shãngo) is similar to the above, but some of the ingredients are different. Two hundred and fifty leaves are gathered: special to this god are the silk-cotton, a medicinal herb, and a bush with four-sided shoots. Seven stone axe-heads ('thunderbolts') are taken from the priest's store, though a lesser number may be used. A hole is made, as for Sapata, but the leaves are first put in a pot with the stones on top of them and the mound built up.

For public temples a hut is built and in the thunder cult it is often round (old style) and may have as distinguishing mark a pointed roof with a piece of wood in the middle. A piece of cloth or a leather pouch is hung inside the hut; the arms of the thunder god, an axe, some polished stones, a gong, and perhaps a metal fish are placed before the shrine. The whole may be surrounded by *dracaena* shrubs or a compound wall. A small private altar may simply consist of the three-pronged stake, with bowl and stones.

The principal elements in the shrine of the snake Dã are more simple. A plant is chosen from a stream, one that floats with the motion of the water, together with leaves of trees that bend before the wind. These, with a few leaves of the earth and thunder gods, are buried as in the previous ceremonies. The shrine may be sheltered or exposed to the elements, and may be at the foot of a tree such as a baobab. It is recognizable by two earthen pots, male and female Dã, put on the mound for offerings. The lid of each pot has two knobs or blunt points which are meant to represent the horns of a snake. Shrines of Dã have several metal models of a snake, each about a foot long, stuck in the mound or pot.

Shrines of other gods vary according to their symbols: the observer may be able to pick these out, or they may be hidden or secret. Ogũn, the god of metals, has iron buried in the ground, but also often a collection of assorted iron objects at the foot of a stake or tree. The shrine is often uncovered and has pots for offerings.

M. J. Herskovits gave the following details of the making of a shrine in a 'convent'. Here three holes were dug in a triangle in the ground, after water mixed with corn meal had been poured on the earth at these spots to obtain authorization to dig. Ingredients included a special god jar, pebbles from the bottom of a lake, earth used by the toucan, earth from a mushroom-shaped ant-hill (the dwelling of fairies), three other pots, and four types of leaves. To these were added the head of an amphibious animal called *djagbwa*, in Fõn, the jaw of which is said to move even after it is dead.[1]

The pots are put into holes in the ground, the ingredients distributed between them, and the head of the *djagbwa* placed in the middle of the triangle. Sea-water, palm-oil and alcohol are

[1] *Dahomey, An Ancient West African Kingdom*, II.172–3.

poured into each of the three pots in turn, the *djagbwa* head being then washed with a leaf. Then formulas are uttered over the shrine, calling down the power of the god into it, and specifying what he is asked to do and what not to do. The large jar is now placed over the three smaller ones and left uncovered. Alcohol, palm wine, and corn-meal mixed with gunpowder are sprinkled on top of the jar. Beans cooked in oil, and chickens and goats may also be sacrificed, these forming the basis of the usual offerings made later by regular worshippers. The water in which the head of the *djagbwa* was washed is reserved for calling up the god on special occasions, when the liquid will be sprinkled on the jar and the god called by name into action.

The shrines in use in Ashanti are usually brass bowls, or baskets, containing various ingredients. These shrines are kept in temples, upon stools, or on rough platforms by rivers or wherever the god resides. On great occasions they are paraded publicly on the head of their priests, covered over with silk cloths. When set down they are rested on their stools which have been carried by attendants; alternatively they are placed on the attendants' head-pads.

While these portable shrines are different from what we have described above, in other parts of our field, yet there are not dissimilar objects in the cultus of Dahomey. These are sacred packages that are kept in the cult-house and paraded on special festivals. Then they are carried on the head or shoulders of priests or fully fledged acolytes; on the head for the greater gods, such as So, Sapata, Loko, and Gu. They are packets of brightly coloured silk and velvet clothes (white for So), about eighteen inches long and decorated with sacred red parrot feathers. The average layman or even devotee is quite ignorant of the contents of these packages. I was told by a trustworthy informant that some contain carved wooden images, about the length of the forearm, with a human head sculptured at each end. This would be made at a distant village, so that the maker is unknown to the public. When not in use these packets are put on stools or hung from the rafters of temples.

I was told by the Ashantihene that the brass basins of the Ashanti gods contain sacred objects that had fallen from the skies (stone axes) or that had been hidden somewhere by a creature employed by the god. The object is put into the receptacle and smeared with the blood of sacrificed sheep and fowls. Eggs, cowries, and the legs, teeth, and horns of certain animals are also placed in the basins. Then the god is implored to dwell in the shrine and a priest or priestess devotes himself to its service.

Rattray made great efforts to obtain for himself, or to witness the making of, an Ashanti shrine, but he was unsuccessful just when he seemed to be on the verge of triumph. From the information he gathered it seems that such preparation is more spontaneous in Ghana than in Dahomey. This is what we should expect, in view of the fact that the training and activity of the priesthood is much less organized and disciplined in Akan country than among their neighbours to the east (see following chapter).

After an Ashanti man has become 'possessed' by a god, he is advised by a priest to prepare a brass pan for the god's worship and to collect the ingredients. 'The possessed one will dance, for sometimes two days, with short intervals for rest, to the accompaniment of drums and singing. Quite suddenly he will leap into the air and catch something in both his hands (or he may plunge into the river and emerge holding something he has brought up). He will in either case fold this thing to his breast, and water will at once be sprinkled upon it to cool it, when it will be thrust into the brass pan and quickly covered up.'[2]

After this the other ingredients are collected and after being pounded together are put into the pan. These are not unlike the materials which have been observed elsewhere, and are objects that are known or believed to have special virtue: medicinal leaves, or those that are striking to the imagination, or that are traditionally associated with the cult, perhaps for reasons long since forgotten. There may be clay from a sacred river, medicinal plants, leaves, bark and creepers of certain trees, notably of one called 'the wizard's tree'. Then there are roots that cross the path or stumps over which one might trip, underwater roots, and leaves that quiver when there is no wind, a nugget of gold that has never been in circulation, and various beads (Aggrey beads) that are prized all along the coast.

These things having been placed in the brass pan all mixed up

[2] R. S. Rattray, *Ashanti*, pp. 147ff.

together, with the object previously thrust in during the frenzy, prayer is offered over them. The Sky God, Earth Goddess, leopard, and animals and plants of the forest, in addition to the particular god now called upon, are invoked. The god is asked to prosper his worshippers, to give guidance and speak the truth in wars and sickness. The blood of a sheep or fowl is poured upon the pan and it is put in a temple.

When the priest wishes to find out the will of the god he puts on his sacerdotal robes and charms, applies some 'medicine' to his eyes and other parts of his body, and carries the *obosõm* on his head. Then the god, when invoked, is believed to speak through the priest. While he is under the spell the priest's whole body shakes and his head turns round and round.

Throughout West Africa the temple or shrine, however prepared, is a dwelling-place of the spirit, where he may be consulted and worshipped. The shrine only becomes his home after consecration and need not be a permanent residence. Moreover, except in the case of local spirits and family gods, the god is known to have other temples. There may be hundreds throughout the country, and the worship of the god is generalized and ubiquitous.

WORSHIP AND SACRIFICE

The worship of the divinities is varied and no fixed pattern can be set down. Nevertheless there are broad lines that can be observed and it is possible to follow it through in a less mysterious way than is sometimes imagined. Generally the performance of worship may be described as daily, weekly, and annual.

The daily worship of Eshu has been described earlier, and such simple ritual is followed for any of the gods. It is a salutation of the god, in which he is called upon by his name and praise-names, his blessing is requested and an attempt is often made to get some idea of the nature of the coming day. For this the worshipper, who is usually the head of the household, takes a kola nut which is split and cast on the ground, and according to the rounded or flat surfaces that fall upwards so the day will be lucky or unlucky; this may be done several times and finally one piece of the kola is put on the shrine and the other eaten by the worshipper. The worshipper usually stands, but he may kneel and ring a bell or rattle to attract the god's attention.

There is an attitude of respect and reverence at the shrine, though at public altars and temples on great festivals the pushing crowds may hide this. The male worshipper bares his head, sometimes the right shoulder, and sometimes is bare to the waist. Women bare their heads and tie their cloths above their breasts, leaving the shoulders bare. If a number of people are present the leader stands, breaks the kola and gives pieces to the assistants who kneel behind him. Most shrines are too small for any number to enter them; the crowd stays outside and only the family elder or priest enters the temple.

Weekly worship is usually more communal than the daily invocation of the god. Each god has a special time for worship, generally one sacred day of the week, on which the worshippers do no heavy manual work. The Akan observe a seven-day week and gods are called by their day-names. The Togo Ewe have adopted the days and names of the seven-day week from the Akan, though indigenous reckoning is still often based on the days of markets held four days apart, but the seven week-days shift about as special feast days of the gods are added on to them. The Fǫn have a basis of four days but are tending to adopt the seven days. Similarly with the Yoruba, whose four days are known by the names of gods, but who are now undergoing Christian and Muslim pressure for many customs.

The pattern of the weekly worship is similar to the daily one, but is more elaborate if there are a number of worshippers gathered. The priest presents each worshipper in turn at the altar, makes him state his petitions and repeats them to the god, then casts kola nuts for each worshipper in order to get a reply and favourable omen for him.

Each god has his annual festival, which may be regarded as his birthday or the occasion of some event in his mythology. These annual festivals are spaced out over the course of the year so that normally they do not clash, and a divinity that does not attract many people at weekly worship may still be able to draw crowds at its yearly festivity. For the annual festival does not merely belong to a small group but is the concern of the whole community or village. The temple has its priest, but the village or town chief is finally responsible for all the temples. The kings of Dahomey strictly controlled all the temples in their kingdom. The chief is supposed to be present, or to send a deputy, to all great festivals. The Oni of Ife should attend at the two hundred and one shrines in his sacred town, and though he is a Christian yet should send a proxy. It is said that 'all festivals belong to the king'.

While each god has his festival, yet on annual occasions other divinities may share in the glory and receive special attention. Offerings may also be made to the ancestors at this time, especially in places like Nigeria where there are no great regular ancestral ceremonies as there are in Ghana. The first person to be presented to the god whose festival is being celebrated is the chief, or his deputy, and kola nuts are first split on his behalf. Then come the elders in order, and visits to other shrines of the same god, of which there may be half a dozen in the town. These are occasions of holiday, of much drumming and dancing, and of sacrifice.

The making of sacrifice, or the offering of some gift even of the smallest kind, is fundamental to worship. Kola nuts are offered to nearly all the gods, though there are a few which prefer the bitter variety of kola. Since the nuts are broken and eaten between human beings as a sign of friendship, so being shared with the god they form a bond of communion. The communion sacrifice is one of the oldest and most universal forms of offering.

The gift sacrifice is another fundamental form. There are daily offerings of food or drink at the shrine: libations of water, oil or alcohol, and gifts of food, beans, maize, snails, fowls, dogs, and so on. Then there is the occasional votive offering, in thanks for some favour received or prayer answered; then vegetables, animals, money, or ornaments may be taken to the shrine.

If the god is angry, or there is an epidemic, a famine or drought, thunderstorm or illness, then a propitiatory sacrifice is offered. This will be given on behalf of the stricken family, or in public concerns by the whole community, and may involve an expensive offering.

Most gods have kinds of offering and food that they like and others that are taboo or 'things hateful' to them. The sky gods usually like snails, the thunder gods rams, and Eshu fowls. To offer a sacrifice that is disliked would be a grave offence and bring certain trouble, so the priest is consulted as to the appropriate offering.

The blood sacrifice is of great importance, for this sheds life and by taking the essence of the animal makes a bond with the god. As in the Old Testament it is believed that 'the life (or soul) of the flesh is in the blood'. Often the blood is poured out to the god and the flesh is eaten by the worshippers. Certain divinities, for example Ogūn and Gu, the Yoruba and Ewe metal gods, like blood sacrifice, and in their worship dogs are killed by having the head sliced off at one blow and the shrine is then rubbed with the blood. But other gods, like many sky deities, do not like blood and receive only bloodless snails on their altars. Dente, a famous god of central Togo, disliked all bloodshed, and wars and murders were hateful to him so that his followers tried to avoid warfare. Many gods receive simple gifts of fowls and vegetables which are laid on their shrine, especially at harvest time.

Human sacrifice used to be practised occasionally, as the highest and most potent form of offering. This was done at the annual festivals of certain gods, especially sea and river divinities, and in times of special need, at the foundations of towns or on outbreaks of epidemics or to avert the threat of war. It should be recognized that this was a phenomenon common to many of the world's religions in ancient times, and though strongly condemned by the prophets is to be found a few times in the Old Testament. The most notorious human sacrifices were those offered at royal funeral rites, in Africa as in Egypt and Mesopotamia, but these are in a special category and will be discussed in Chapter 11.

Sometimes a human victim was chosen as a scapegoat to remove some great evil from the people. The last in Abeokuta occurred in 1891 when Dr Farrow was there.[3] The scapegoat was usually a slave, chosen after the Ifa oracle had declared that unless one was offered great calamities would occur: warfare, death of chiefs, slavery, drought, a plague of locusts. The victim was called Oluwo by the Yoruba, an honourable name reserved for chiefs, and as it was thought that he would be reborn in a high position women would pray that he might be born to them. He would be paraded

[3] *Faith, Fancies and Fetich*, pp. 98-9.

through the streets and people placed their hands on him to transfer the evil from themselves. Finally he would be led into a hut, where only a priest and assistant could enter, and be beheaded or clubbed.

Human beings were killed to strengthen the foundation of a town or protect it from enemies, to accompany chiefs at their death, and for magical purposes to provide the ingredients for a potent charm. Sometimes victims were selected at random from anyone who happened to be in the streets at night when the executioners were on the warpath, but at other times families were told to provide one of their own members who were often household slaves. They might be buried alive, or with the head just showing and the blood then drained away. There is no doubt that this was a very cruel practice, and while we seek to understand the motives which prompted men to sacrifice their fellow human beings, yet nothing must be allowed to hide the fact that the victims died in agony. Such deeds must belong to the past and the strength of Christianity and Islam is that they have never countenanced such offerings of man's early religious history nor indeed any blood sacrifice.

Private people offer sheep or goats as scapegoats, which may be afterwards killed or set free. In a Fǫn village I witnessed a mother of twins that had died, transferring to a goat the evil that she thought prevented her from conceiving again. The diviner cast the Ifa on a tray and told the woman to bring a fowl and a goat. Bare to the waist she then knelt in front of the diviner, who dusted her brow, chest, knees and feet with the fowl. Then, following his instructions, she took the goat by the horns and placed her forehead three times against that of the goat, to transfer her evil. Powdered clay from the tray was then put on her forehead and hands, and she blew it away praying that the evil might not return. The diviner then gave her a pot of leaves and water to wash her head. Before washing she took a small plate of bamboo bearing a cassava cake and placed it at the nearest cross-roads. The fowl was set loose and the goat was sent away to wander outside the village (as the Hebrews sent the scapegoat into the desert).

Music, singing and dancing play an important role in worship. Dr Field made an interesting classification of the gods of the Gã, based on the types of dance used in the festivals of the various divinities.[4]

In the daily morning worship there is usually no music, other than a bell or gong. But in weekly communal worship, and even more on the annual festivals, there is much sound and singing. Many instruments are used: the chief ones are drums of various kinds, then gongs, bells, calabashes with beads tied to them, horns and triangles or pieces of metal. The drums of Ashanti are famous and the books of Rattray include many translations of pieces from the talking drums.

Often singing is unaccompanied, or time is simply kept by clapping and stamping. Each god has hymns of his own, which are connected with his mythology and include many of his praise-names. These may be sung partly as solos, and partly taken up in refrain. In addition, spontaneous hymns of praise may be invented on the spot as a tribute of thanksgiving and happiness. The books of Verger and Idowu give examples of such songs.

Dances take place during the weekly and annual festivals. Some of these are simple accompaniments to the music of the drums, but others are traditional and re-enact some event in the mythology and history of the cult. Dancing is done singly and in procession, and dancers do not normally hold each other. Frequently a spontaneous dance piece may occur under the inspiration of the moment, and the possessed medium gives a message from the god.

In these many ways worship enters into the lives of the people. Although there is no obligation to attend weekly worship, yet the attraction of the arts of music and dance draws people to the temple. The role of the laity in worship is to join in the repetitions, singing in chorus, responding and applauding. The layman is not a priest or medium; in Yoruba he is 'not of the society', in Ewe he is a 'not-wife' in contrast to the devotee who is a 'god-wife'. Nevertheless the layman makes his acts of devotion and can enter the inner circle if he or she is prepared to undergo the training.

It is said sometimes that African worship is only communal, and that 'never does the worshipper face his god in solitude'.[5] It

---

[4] *Religion and Medicine of the Gã People*, pp. 5–6.
[5] S. F. Nadel, *Nupe Religion*, p. 273.

is to be hoped that the above descriptions will have disproved this notion. The ordinary West African is a pious person and performs regular daily devotions. Before speaking to anyone in the morning he worships at the shrine of his god, addresses the god directly, seeking his protection and giving thanks for past help.

In addition to this some people give longer time to private devotion. Priests and diviners use additional rituals, and cast kolas or divining nuts in elaborate ways. They pray to the god on behalf of themselves and their friends. Then there are the priests and mediums of the old religion, and the prophets of the new religions, who retire to solitary places to meditate and find out the will of their god.

There are some people, however, who do not appear to be very religious, rarely join in the worship of the gods and may even work on a sacred day. But just the same they generally use magical charms, consult the Ifa oracle, and seek divine protection from witchcraft. The numbers of the irreligious grow under the impact of modern education and secularism, and the true inheritors of the old religion are the new faiths which give equal attention to prayer and worship.

CHAPTER EIGHT

Priests and Devotees

TYPES OF RELIGIOUS PERSONS

THROUGHOUT the whole of this part of West Africa priests and devotees, mediums devoted to the gods, are set apart for divine service and receive some kind of initiation and training for it. There are different methods of training, from very simple to highly elaborate, but the priesthood as a class is distinct and developed.

These religious persons give themselves to the service of the god, either spontaneously or by the choice of their superiors. They dedicate themselves to the god for life, though they generally have a secular occupation as well so that they do not live wholly from gifts brought to the temples. Many priests are hunters or smiths. They honour other gods as well and mingle charitably with their devotees. Their training may comprise seclusion from the world, instruction in the laws, and sometimes 'possession' by the divinity. The vocation of priest and devotee is highly honoured; it is generally open to both men and women.

There is a great deal of confusion over the words used for sacred persons. Words such as fetish-priest, witch-doctor, medicine-man, sorcerer, magician are often used for a variety of priests and diviners and seem to imply that they are disreputable or evil-working people. They may, however, be distinguished by the following terms: Priests, those who are attached to temples and offer sacrifice; Devotees or Mediums, those connected with the temples and who give messages from the gods; Diviners, those concerned with oracles and divination; and Doctors or Medicine-men, those concerned with healing the sick and preparing magical medicines.

A fuller account of the activities of diviners will be found in Chapter 13, and of doctors and herbalists in Chapter 14. Here we may note that while most priests may be also diviners and herbalists

75

yet the converse does not necessarily hold. There are many diviners who are not qualified to officiate in a temple, even though they may, and sometimes must, assist and advise at important religious ceremonies.

Something of a parallel may be drawn from the later Old Testament, where the priest was usually distinct from the prophet; though Samuel and others combined both functions. The priest was occupied with the service of the temple or high place; the prophet was a seer, sometimes in conflict with the priests, and was believed to foresee at least the 'shape' of things to come.

That these different functions can be readily distinguished is proved by the fact that there are different names for them in West African languages. The priest of a god is Obosõmfo, Vodunõ, Olorisha, and Atama—in Twi, Fõn, Yoruba, and Ibo respectively. The seer is Okõmfo, Bokonõ, Babalawo, and Amǫma; and medicine-man is Sumãnkwafo, Amawato, Onishegũn and Dibia.

To avoid confusion the word witch-doctor is not used here. He is not a witch, of course, but serves to hunt out witches and cure witchcraft. Witches are feared as anti-social beings, whereas priests seers and good medicine-men are publicly recognized and respected.

There is a further difference between the true priests, the sacrificers and leaders of a cultus, and the subordinate ranks of devotees, acolytes, servants, mediums, or 'wives' of a god. The priest is the 'owner' of the god or his cultus (ol-orisha, vodun-õn); the devotee or medium is the 'wife' (iya-orisha, vodũ-si).

The system of training priests and devotees has reached its highest point of complexity and development among the Fõn of Dahomey, where it is still widely practised. The length and complexity of training depends partly upon the grade of the god; that of the devotees of ancestral rites is short.

The choice and office of a priest is rather complicated. In small household shrines the head of the house is the priest and generally needs no other helper. In the worship of the ancestors it is still the householder or the oldest man of the family who remains the priest, since he is closest to the dead and is senior of the living. But in village and communal cults special priests are needed and the head of all those in the town is a special official who acts on

behalf of the town chief who is 'head of all the priests'. Further-
more, new cults are introduced into the house or the village,
especially by women who marry into the family from outside,
and who may remain priestesses of their own god; in time their
heirs will have the right to be priests of that cult.

Choice of a priest is in the hands of the traditional owners of the
cult. The elders meet together and decide who shall take charge
after the death or retirement of the last priest. If the latter is still
alive then he transfers his powers to the new priest, or 'removes his
hands' from the cult. In any case the priest-makers inform the
man of their choice that the office is vacant, hand over to him the
emblems of the god, consult the oracle to gain its consent, and
pray that the blessing of the god may be upon him.

The person chosen may have no other 'vocation' than this
formal appointment. But sometimes he is called to belong to the
god by 'possession' during an ecstatic trance, either when he is
alone or during a public ceremony. A chief priest normally
inherits his office from his father, or one of his family, or through
public appointment. He may undergo a long process of initiation
and training by an older priest into occult knowledge and the
proper performance of public rituals.

After his consecration the priest will marry, if he is not already
married, and his wife will preferably be a medium who can bring
messages from the god. Celibacy is very rare. The priest may take
up his old occupation again, but he often has wives, servants, and
novices to do his manual labour. Gifts and sacrifices supplement
his food, and at a popular temple much of his time is spent in
propitiating the god, finding out his will for inquirers, divining,
settling disputes, healing the sick, and meditation. His god feeds
him, as I have heard a chief priest say: 'Today I shall eat this gift
that you have brought (to the god), but tomorrow I shall have
nothing, and my god will feed me.'

The high priest is generally distinguishable by a white turban,
a straw conical hat, or a pointed cap. Often he wears none of the
magical charms that load inferior persons. Dahomey has given the
greatest attention to the training of priests and mediums, and in
consequence has the most powerfully organized priesthood which
has enabled it so far to resist the appeal of Christianity and Islam.

There were dangers of a powerful clericalism here, but the kings exercised a restraining hand, and confined the priests to their religious offices. An official, the Aplogăn, was appointed to be secular representative of all cults.

PRIVATE TRAINING

In Ashanti 'possession' by a god appears to be a more spontaneous phenomenon than among the Ewe, for the latter control and even induce it among devotees. In the convents great efforts are made to bring about a return of the possessed state, and then the priests check its manifestations. Many Dahomean priests are never subject to possession themselves, but have mediums attached to their temples who enter into trance at will.

Possession, whether due to some physical abnormality or to suggestion, generally occurs for the first time when the person is attending a public religious ceremony. At the movement of the dance and the example of some inspired devotees, the new person falls down in a fit or leaps into the ring and dances in an extravagant fashion. The presiding priests interpret this as a divine call, and persuade the inspired one to begin training for the service of a god.

In Dahomey and Ghana the training may last two or three years, and during this period the novice may have no sexual relationships, whether he or she is married or not. This temporary chastity is surrounded by strong taboos, and if it is broken punishment is inflicted, sacrifices must be offered to appease the offended god, and the whole training may have to be begun over again. This is because the novice is consecrated and 'married' to the god. At the end of his instruction he offers a sacrifice and says to the god: 'Today you have completed marriage with me.'[1] But he will then marry or return to his wife. Suggestions of immorality among priests and devotees are therefore the very opposite of the truth. In all cults and at the simplest act of worship the priest or lay worshipper must be chaste, and a menstruating woman must not draw near.

[1] R. S. Rattray, *Religion and Art in Ashanti*, pp. 47ff. Similar abstinence is often observed with regard to alcohol, priests being forbidden to drink when they go to serve the god.

In Ashanti the novice has private training, and goes to live with an older priest, as learners do with diviners in Nigeria. The first year of training is mostly taken up with ceremonial ablutions. These consist of washing with various mixtures of which the chief components are leaves sacred to the god. Some leaves are to strengthen the ankles for dancing, others are rubbed on the eyes so 'that he may see his god daily', yet others aim at arousing the spirit of possession again if it is slow in recurring. Further plants are plucked that grow near graves, so that the novice may make contact with departed spirits. Then he bathes for seven nights in the 'thicket of the ghosts', and must persevere even if the spirits belabour him till he screams. By these means the state of possession gradually returns to him and he begins to quake.[2]

No special secrets are imparted in the first year until the trustworthiness of the novice becomes quite apparent. He sits by the shrine and tries to listen for the voice of his god. His hair is always left uncut and he looks a wild character; but hair has sacred significance.

The second year continues with further instructions and with revelation of the laws and taboos of the god. He is decorated with charms and informed of the special taboo, the 'thing hateful', to each charm. The laws given by Rattray's informant may be compared with those of a Fŏn novice, in the next chapter.[3] The Ashanti neophyte is told: (1) Not to drink any spirits; (2) Not to gossip; (3) Not to quarrel or fight; (4) To salute his elders by bending the right knee and touching the ground with the right hand; (5) Never to adjure his god to kill anyone; (6) Never to attend the chief's court (unless summoned); (7) Never to go out at night and join other young men. These commandments are meant to emphasize the separateness of the novice, which is an essential part of the sacred life, and the absolute claims of his god.

In the third year the novice learns water-divining, incantations for charms, how to hear and salute trees, streams, and forest spirits. The final ceremony of induction into the priesthood resembles somewhat the concluding rites for the initiates of the thunder gods in other countries. Logs are collected for a fire which is kindled after dark, after drumming and singing have begun. The new

[2] Ibid. pp. 38–47, here and below.   [3] See p. 91 below.

priest, dressed in a palm-fibre kilt and decorated with all his charms, kneels before his instructor. His hair is shaved off and any (spiritually) bad matter which is found is put in a pot. This pot is taken away into the bush by a young boy and left there upside down. The new priest dances all night to the drums and singing of the crowd, and ends in the morning by offering a sheep to his god.

On the Ghana seaboard Gã priests are accompanied by female devotees who are mediums charged with messages from the gods. Some mediums are appointed officially by priests or village elders; others are free-lances who are taken to be called by a god if they are subject to hysterical fits in private life, or are possessed during the excitement of dancing at religious feasts.

These mediums are trained by the priests. They must leave their family if they are married, and they marry again after the end of their training and this time only to a male medium or priest. While the official devotee (woyo) has only a week's training, with initiation into her duties, and gets possessed about once a year, the spontaneous mediums have two or three years' training and then may go into trances whenever consulted by private clients.

This longer training of Gã mediums is a severe discipline: 'Strict chastity, frugal fare, a hard floor to sleep on, insufficient covering during chilly nights.'[4] At first the medium may suffer from dumbness, and only learn to produce articulate sounds while possessed towards the end of the time of training. 'The great majority of woyo's fits, even when produced to order, are, I believe, perfectly genuine. But even so, a genuine fit, when repeated often, is capable of undergoing a certain amount of modification in character, and this modification can be and is brought about by the instructor's training.' Under possession such a medium may speak in a language of which she normally appears to have little knowledge (like the biblical speaking in tongues), but it may be found that she lived in a different area from the present one in her youth, and many West Africans can speak more than one language.

At the feasts of the gods, these mediums become possessed during the course of the drumming. They begin to rock and

[4] M. J. Field, *Religion and Medicine of the Gã People*, pp. 8, 100ff.

tremble, when their assistants rush them aside and prepare them for the dance, undoing their hair, and painting and decking their body with cloths, paint, beads, and bells. Then they may imitate and impersonate gods and spirits, changing personalities, giving messages, and performing feats which would be impossible in their normal state.

These women 'are the passive instruments of the gods and carry no authority whatever except when they are possessed. The priest himself is never possessed. He would be ineligible for the priesthood if he were. He receives the messages, and any instructions to the people based on these messages are issued by him. Each god has at least one *wǫyo*, her appointment is an official one, and she lives at the expense of the worshippers as does the priest himself.'

COMMUNAL TRAINING OF DEVOTEES

In most of the Yoruba and Ibo country of Nigeria the training of priests and mediums is private. Sometimes there appears to be little to it, beyond being officially appointed by the family that controls the shrine. At other times the novice goes to live with an older man for some time, on payment of a fee and performance of work for him. He undergoes ceremonial washings, the shaving of his head, and vigils. He learns the laws and taboos of his god.

Many of the Dahomean Yoruba and the Togo Ewe have come to adopt the system of training of acolytes and mediums, which finds its fullest development in the communal training of the Fǫn. The Fǫn system of training is social and carefully planned, and is undertaken in what are popularly translated as 'convents', a not inappropriate word, or cult-houses (*hũn-kpame*, 'spirit's enclosure' in Fǫn; *ile-orisha*, 'house of the god' in Yoruba).

The aim of the whole training in the convent is the complete change of personality of the neophyte, and we shall find this theme constantly recurring in the descriptions given in this and the following chapters. At the beginning the novice is possessed by the god, but when he emerges from the seclusion of the convent he is not simply a changed being, but a new and different personality. He does not recognize his own parents or former companions, he speaks another language as if he were a stranger from a foreign country, and he bears a new name. Henceforth it is absolutely forbidden to call him by his old name, and he will re-learn his old language slowly when he re-emerges from the convent to live among his family again.[5]

The period spent in a convent is now usually three years for a girl, but nine months for a boy. The new social and political conditions, military service and public labour, have reduced the longer period formerly spent by young men in the convents. Probably because of this the great majority, perhaps three-quarters, of Dahomean devotees are now female. Normally the novices are young people from ten to sixteen years of age, but occasionally the gods demand married people.

We shall first of all describe the recruiting ceremonies, and deal with life in the convent in the next chapter. The recruiting of neophytes takes place chiefly at the great annual festivals of the gods (not to be confused with the 'customs' of the ancestors). These are held in May or June, the beginning of the rainy season, the West African spring. The celebrations are marked by the parade of the gods, the sacred packages described in Chapter 7 are carried round the town on the heads or shoulders of priests.

The annual ceremonies last five to eight days. During this time old devotees who have left the convent and are leading a normal life in the outside world return to the cult-house, put on their robes, and revive their knowledge of the special dialect of the god. Between the dances they go round the streets, singing and asking alms.

Recruiting for the convent is done in various ways. It may be quite spontaneous. A spectator of the dances becomes infected with possession from the example of the other dancers, and he is rushed into the convent for training. More deliberately and publicly, during the festival the chief priest asks the heads of the principal families of the village if they have a child for divine service. There may have been a child vowed to the gods from its birth, as an answer to prayer. The next step is to consult the Ifa oracle, who declares the will of the gods. There is the desire to gain divine sanction for the choice of the pupil, since relatives of

---

[5] cf. C. K. Meek, *Tribal Studies in Northern Nigeria*, I.494, on the Teme, 'the boy remains silent, for he is a new being, who knows not his former mother'.

another branch of the family may be jealous if they have not been asked. Also if a neophyte were to die during the course of training, it would reflect discredit on the priest and the family. Hence the consultation of Ifa seeks to put the responsibility for the choice on the oracle, and also to find out if the pupil will stand the training.

The novice may be taken by night into the convent, particularly if he shows signs of unwillingness. More generally he will come forward during the daily dancing. But sometimes he is chosen secretly beforehand. The high priest and elder devotees choose privately the person whom they think will make a good pupil. The selected one is summoned to appear in secret before the priest. At the interview the priest puts a magical nut (*afoshe*) into his mouth, which is held to have the power of preventing the person interviewed from refusing to accept. The priest says to the candidate: 'The god has told me that he wishes to call you today. Do you agree?' The choice of refusal or acceptance is only apparent, for while the candidate reflects for some minutes, when he opens his mouth it is to say 'Yes'. He is then told to come and join in the dancing that day.

In the cults of the thunder and earth gods (So-Shãngo, Sapata-Shọpọna), in addition to public possession, there are remarkable ceremonies of imitated death and resurrection through which the neophytes regularly pass. These are not done in all cults, but only in the greater ones of Dahomey.

The dance is held on the open space in front of the convent. The door of the convent is covered with a mat, red, white, and black. In front are the stools of the priests. A goat is sacrificed early in the morning, and the blood is sprinkled on the principal shrines. Libations are also made at any other shrines in the neighbourhood. When the drums begin to sound a crowd quickly gathers, and the devotees come out of the convent and begin to dance, some wildly as though possessed.

The secretly chosen candidate soon cries out, and works his way through the excited crowd into the midst of the dancers, where he begins to twirl round quickly. He dances ever more furiously until he falls stark on the ground, as in an epileptic fit. The dancers, after circling round the 'corpse', wrap it in a shroud, and singing dirges they carry it into the convent.

The lay people believe that the neophyte has actually died, and there is probably a good deal of self-hypnotism on the part of the dancer, so that the role is realistically acted. It is said that occasionally the 'dead' one does not come to life again, and if this is so it may be due to over-excitement.

Once in the convent, the shroud is undone and drink is given. The novice is instructed in his future role and told how to act. Every night for seven nights he sleeps in his shroud. A goat is killed and its blood and skin are reserved for future use. On the evening of the seventh day the wrapped body is carried into the temple, and the body smeared with 'medicine'. Songs are sung round the 'corpse' and the parents may be allowed to attend this ceremony.

On the eighth day the ritual of 'resurrection' is performed. The neophyte is believed by outsiders to have been dead since the week before and is now to be raised up by the power of the god. So there is great excitement and anticipation. The usual acts of sacrifice precede dancing in the public place.

The supposed corpse is then carried out of the convent by assistants. It is wrapped in reed mats, as for a funeral, and smells abominably because wrapped in with it is the putrefying skin of the goat or fowl which was killed the week before. Women kneel by the corpse, sprinkle it with water and fan away the flies.

The priest then comes forward and, kneeling by the 'corpse', he calls upon the god for help to restore the dead one to life. Seven times he calls upon the 'deceased' by name, and it is not until the seventh time, when the relatives have got very anxious, that the body gives a grunt. The others then press round and unfasten the grave clothes. They lift up the neophyte, whose body is daubed red and white. With their help he staggers seven times round the drums and is then led into the convent to begin his training and become a new being, to the thunderous applause of the crowd.

The same rites are gone through for each neophyte in the great cults. The novice is now called a 'prisoner of war', since the god has captured him from his family. The duty of the family is now to bring presents of food to the convent. Except on the morrow they will not see their relative any more until the end of his monastic seclusion, but they must provide for his material needs.

I believe that these ceremonies are unique in West Africa, or at least developed to a point unknown elsewhere. There is some parallel in the adolescent initiation ceremonies which are performed in some parts of West Africa. Of the Mende Poro rites in Sierra Leone, K. Little says, 'The initiation rite and the whole time spent in the bush which follow it symbolize a change of status. The young initiate is supposed to be "swallowed" by the [Poro] spirit when he enters and separation from his parents and kinsfolk signifies his death. The marks on his back are evidence of the spirit's teeth. At the end of his time, he is "delivered" by the spirit and "reborn".'[6]

The Dahomean training of devotees is an extension and development of this, in order to fit selected young people for the service of the gods. Whether there is any connexion with ancient and classical rites and myths of dying and rising again, as I suggested in my first edition, I do not now know. The chief festivals are held in the springtime before the heaviest rains. The simulated death and resurrection may, possibly, have a connexion with the dying and rising of the seed, and with the new birth of those who are to be allowed to penetrate into the divine mysteries. The whole training stresses the change of personality, and begins with a triumph over death by the power of the gods, when mourning is changed into rejoicing.

But it should be noted that not all Dahomean cults have this rite of death and resurrection of the novices. Nevertheless, the training inside the convent, now to be described, is common in its main outlines to all the cults which have the conventual system of communal training of devotees and mediums.

[6] *The Mende People of Sierra Leone* (1951), p. 120.

CHAPTER NINE

Training in a Convent

THE SYSTEM of training the servants of the gods, priests, devotees, or assistants at the cults, and mediums, as practised in Dahomey is a subject of which little is known. The life and activities of those who enter the convents are kept secret, and normally no lay or uninitiated person is allowed to pass beyond its walls.

The following outline I was fortunate to secure from an ex-initiate, and it has been checked and supplemented by a priest and several other well-informed people. I believe such an account has not been published elsewhere.

In the cults that practise the imitation death and resurrection, the first act of the following day is usually for all the neophytes to go to a stream before dawn for a ceremony of purification. Only relatives and initiates may follow them; all other people must remain indoors. As they go they sing to warn all human beings not to look at them, even an animal met on the path may be killed.

After washing with new sponges, from new pots, goats and fowls are sacrificed. Blood, hair and feathers are put under the big toenail of each neophyte. The sacrifices are eaten on the spot, after being cooked. On return to the convent crowds now greet them as they enter in with joyful songs.

This is the last public appearance and the novices are seen no more for at least seven months. Their relatives bring food every day and put it in a common pot at the entrance to the convent. If a novice dies during the course of training, the parents may get no other indication beyond an empty calabash with a piece broken off. But initiated relatives may enter the convent and attend the burial.

Once in the convent the novice has all hair shaved off. This is kept in a secret place by the priest in charge. In some cults the first shaving of hair is put in a pot, and a fowl is sacrificed and placed on top of the hair. Fire is then applied to the hair, and though the fowl is only slightly singed it must now be eaten by the novice and his companions.

The hair is shaved off three times during the nine months' course. The second time the priest again keeps it. But on the third occasion, which is the day of finally leaving the convent, the priest makes a hole in the ground, arranges the hair round the edge of the hole and burns it; he keeps the ashes. The initiate is warned that if he is unfaithful to the god that hole will be his grave; it is then closed up again. The accumulated hair and ashes make charms to keep the novice faithful.

In some convents the novices wear only a loin-cloth and the torso is always bare. In others the rules are not so strict and more clothing is allowed, especially to the girls. But the clothes must never be washed and must be handed over to the priest before leaving. The dirt and sweat may also be used in making charms, as they are part of the personality. In most convents the body is rubbed regularly with oil, to beautify and strengthen it, so that it may be said that the god looks after his 'wives' well. The outsider will observe that most devotees coming out of the convent look in good health and well fed.

The novice is given an earthen pot from which he must always drink. A cock is sacrificed on this and blood and feathers daubed round it. If the family bring maize broth this must be drunk from the same consecrated pot, cold, for the pot must never be put on the fire. No other drink may be taken before this is finished, and then the pot is washed out and water put in again.

All novices of the same sex eat from a common dish, with the left hand which belongs to the god. All food that is brought must be put in the common dish, so that all partake of it together.

Girls eat apart from boys but in common with their own sex. They must not touch or take any object from the youths. No sexual relations of any kind are allowed between male and female novices, or of the priest with his pupils. Punishment for offences against this rule are severe; in olden days it was usually death or slavery; today beatings, heavy fines and dismissal are the penalties.

If a novice commits a serious fault he is judged by the priest and an assembly of older initiates. To give himself special powers the priest uses the *afoshe* nut, which is believed to guarantee the efficacy of his words. When the accused is brought in, the devotees state the case and give their opinion. The priest is silent till the end when he gives the final and irrevocable judgement. He says: 'The sacred things that our fathers handed down to us, you have spoilt. From today you will become mad (or fall into the fire and be burnt).' This curse is effective, as it is held to be the god himself who speaks through the mouth of the priest. The novice may die of fear, become insane or do himself a mortal injury.

Immediately after pronouncing judgement the priest quickly washes his mouth and chin, to remove all traces of the *afoshe*. He drinks palm oil, smearing it round his mouth. The reason is that his word may still be fatal, and if he happened to speak to his wife or child while still bearing the charm, some terrible evil would come upon them. It is a dangerous weapon, whence the saying: 'The *afoshe* can destroy the priest's house.'

The principal aim of training novices being to create new personalities, various methods are used to bring this about. One of the chief ways is by learning a new language and this is found in most convents. These languages have sometimes been called jargon; but, however imperfectly the devotees come to speak them, they are more than jargon. Perhaps in origin the purpose of using a special language was partly an attempt at imitating the ecstatic and unintelligible words uttered by mediums during spontaneous possession. But with the system of training mediums, and inducing possession with the object of obtaining messages that shall be at least intelligible to an interpreter, the language has become more fixed. In fact, today most of the languages used in possession are dialects from different parts of the country, and usually those of the original district from whence the cult of the god came.

Thus the dialects make a ritual or classical language of the cult in Dahomey. In the convents of the python Dăngbe, wherever it is found, it is the language of Ouidah that is spoken, and the devotees are called *Hwedanu* (-*nu* suffix shows the inhabitant of a specified town or region, e.g. *Dăhomenu*, inhabitant of Dahomey). The Sapata (earth-smallpox) devotees speak the variety of Yoruba that here is called Nago and are termed *Anagonu*. The thunder devotees are called *Popo*, from the Popo or Gẽ country along the coast from Cotonou. Followers of the ancestral cult are called *Mahinu*, from Mahi country in central Dahomey.

Some writers have noticed that in other tribes the cult songs may be in an ancient dialect, which shows the place of origin of the cult. But in Dahomey the initiates learn to speak these dialects as definite, and in a sense secret, languages. Morning and evening in the convent there are repetitions in the new tongue. The novice must forget his native language and adapt himself to the new one. When eventually he emerges from the convent, he acts as if he no longer understands his own language, as if he were a traveller from a distant country, which indeed he is supposed to be. He must greet other devotees in the god's language, and only learn his own tongue again slowly.

As nine months now hardly suffice for learning this new language, formerly it was longer, the devotees return to the convent at intervals during the year following their exit. Also before the annual festival, they go back to the convent for some days to brush up their dialect.

To affirm the new personality further each novice receives a new name, by which he must always be called henceforth for the rest of his life. When he is back in the outside world again, if anybody calls him by his old name he will fall down as if dead, or call out the person's name;[1] for his own self died on his entry to the convent. A heavy fine is imposed on the offender, sacrifice is offered to the god, and all or part of the training of the novice may have to be undertaken afresh.

The new language, new name, secluded life, new occupations, common meals, and common dress, all tend to bring the novice to an entirely new life and to help on the change of his personality.

The convent is generally a compound, composed of huts with grass of leaf-thatched roofs, joined together by walls between the huts, or surrounded by a single wall. There may be half a dozen to a dozen huts, and any number of neophytes, sometimes small, sometimes large.

The chief priest has his own hut, and another is used by an old initiate who prepares food for the novices. At least one hut is a

[1] See p. 91 below.

temple for the god. This is marked out from the rest by a bamboo flagstaff, some ten to twelve feet high, to which is attached a small white piece of cloth. To outsiders this is the distinguishing mark of a convent.

Common devotional exercises are held every fifth day, according to the day which is sacred to the god. The priest prays outside the hut, or kneeling just inside if it is small, with the novices gathered behind him. Only the priest may enter the temple, for he is the guardian of its contents. There he casts kola nuts on behalf of each member.

During the first days an old devotee instructs the novices in their conduct, telling them the rules for eating, drinking, and clothing. Every morning and evening, in addition to language classes, the neophytes learn the songs of the god, and prayers and blessings to be used when asking for alms after they have left the convent. Dances are learnt on moonlit evenings. Exercises and strenuous efforts are made to produce the state of possession. This possession by the god is carefully controlled by the priest, and is not allowed to get out of hand.

Novices are taught the minor duties of sweeping and cleaning in turn. In particular, they learn to make various articles of religious and secular use in raffia straw or palm fibre. They weave the raffia skirts and robes (the old style) which are worn by devotees and priests on leaving the convent and on special occasions; as well as raffia bonnets, necklaces, and armlets. Old devotees send into the convent for repairs and new robes to be woven for festival days and funeral rites, for at death every devotee is dressed in full regalia. Raffia objects are also made for sale to the laity: mats, fans, baskets, and switches. The girls who have to spend years in the convents thus earn themselves money.

After the third month the initiates receive the ritual tattoos of the god. These are a number of small cuts made by an old devotee with a small knife. They are chiefly on the face, neck, and shoulders of a novice. All women in olden days, and many today, whether convent initiates or not, have these tattoos made at puberty, mainly on chest, back, and thighs.

The scars and patterns of each god are different, but there are usually marks on the cheeks, neck, and shoulders. Probably over a hundred small scars are made on each shoulder, each one is about a quarter of an inch long and wide, in the shape of a diamond. There is also a double band made round the neck, where the cords of the sacred packages are tied on the festival days when the gods are paraded. It is said that if you are unfaithful to the god he will strangle you by means of these neck scars.

The marks on the face are distinctive. They are different from the tribal and clan tattoos by which various tribes, and especially the Yoruba, have been traditionally distinguished. There may be two or three deep and wide cuts, perhaps an inch long, on the cheeks. The scar is made dark and permanent by rubbing in a quantity of wood ash.

If the novice wishes other ornamental tattoos to be made on his chest and back they must be done now, for it is forbidden to have any more made once he has left the convent.

Sometimes the novices are allowed to go out of the convent for a little while every day after the seventh month, following a short ceremony. Usually they wait till the nine months' training is finished. They may be allowed out at night, and for this they must be dressed normally and cover their heads with their blankets. If they meet strangers they must not salute them, and the layman will not say that he has met men but spirits.

The night before leaving the convent, the novice receives final instructions from the priest about the ceremonies on the morrow, and about his future actions. He is now told of the god's taboos. The plants, fruits, and animals that are taboo differ with each god. He learns the laws of conduct: Not to kill, not to steal, not to deceive, not to be proud, to obey parents and elders, to be discreet.

'A devotee has no ears.' This proverb means that if anyone speaks evil of the god, or calls the devotee by his old name, he will at first pretend not to hear. On a third repetition he asks: 'Are you speaking to me?' If there is no reply now he takes no further notice, so as to avoid a quarrel at all costs. But if the persecutor insists the devotee will scream out and fall down as if dead, or he may leap on his opponent and pull his ears, letting out a piercing shriek at the same time till other devotees come to his rescue. The offender's name will be called out all round the village; he may be severely beaten and a heavy fine is imposed on him.

In addition to this calling by old names nobody must put his hand on a devotee's head, or insult him with certain words, 'dog' or 'fool'.

On the day of the final exit, or in some cases a few months later, a devotee is now authorized by the priest to have intercourse with his wife, and he must not do so without this authorization. Unmarried ones may now seek their fiancées. A small ceremony marks this permission symbolically. A girl is sought who is not yet nubile, and one by one each male novice sits on the same mat with her (which would normally be taboo), smokes a pipe with her, and then embraces her. For women, an uncircumcised boy is fetched and the same play is gone through. This makes the needed authorization. If a boy has never had any sexual intercourse he may now sit on his special drinking-jar, to vaunt his virginity. If he did so having formerly had intercourse, he would be severely punished.

When the training is completed a great ceremony is held for the coming out of the new devotees from the convent. Friends and relatives come in crowds to witness this ceremony, to give money and cloths, and to receive blessings. It is a costly affair, and the expenses are paid by the families of the devotees.

Each family gathers in the square outside the convent, with a basket containing cloths and gifts. After libations to the spirits of the locality the drumming begins. The devotees emerge from the convent in full dress. Each is dressed in a raffia skirt, two chains of cowrie shells across chest and shoulders, and bands of cowries round the head, arms, and ankles. Necklaces of coloured beads are worn, differing according to the god (blue, red, and white for the thunder gods, with red coral bracelets). Coloured ribbons, 'god's cords', are round their heads, decorated with sacred red parrot feathers.

The devotees dance for some time, showing off their newly learnt paces. In the thunder cult there is an interesting rite which is meant to prove the presence of the god. A pot is placed on cones of earth, or turfs, in the centre of the square where a fire is lit and oil put in the pot. The devotees then dance excitedly round the pot, till the oil is heated, when the fumes inside catch fire of themselves and the miracle of flame without fuel occurs. This is taken as a sign that the thunder god himself is present in power, and the devotees leap successively over the pot, amid the great cheers of the crowd at this omen of future success and blessing.[2]

This is the climax. The crowd shouts for joy, and friends and relatives cover the footprints of the devotees with pieces of money and cloth. The priest rises and gives out the new name of each devotee. After a short rest during the heat of the day, songs and dances continue till late at night.

A week later the initiates are redeemed by their relatives. Gathered in groups in front of the priest, he tells the families that these are prisoners that have been captured, which will they choose? Each family makes a pretence of looking out a good captive, but finally selects its own relative. A small present is given to the devotee, and he embraces his family and gives them one cowrie in return. He then goes home to live with his family, but he pretends still to be a prisoner from a far country, who has been exchanged for the true son of the family who is in exile.

For some days the devotees go round the streets, singing and asking alms, dressed in the raffia skirts and cowrie ornaments. With thumb and first finger of the left hand before their lips, right hands behind their backs, they move along slowly, humming a tune on the five-note scale. If the procession meets an old initiate they chant in the secret dialect which he understands: 'We are hungry and have nothing to eat.' On receipt of a small gift they invoke blessings on the donor. If they meet a non-initiate they sing in the same way, and though he does not understand their words he knows what is meant, and on receiving their benediction he says 'Thanks'.

After three months the devotees return to the priest who tells them to discard the raffia dress now, and wear a white cloth for three months, and finally a black cloth for three more months.

The post-novitiate period is then over. The devotee lives, dresses and works like a layman, except for the distinguishing mark of a cowrie bracelet, sometimes with a second row of black

[2] M. Herskovits, *Dahomey*, II.165, records a ceremony of symbolically 'mounting the goat'.

beads (like those worn by Gã mediums). Others wear a small fine wire ear-ring.

The keener devotees may undergo further training and are valuable and intimate helpers of the priests. Most of them only return for memory refreshing before the annual ceremonies. The more advanced carry the sacred packages of the gods on their heads or necks; these are called 'god-bearers'. The others do the dancing and accompaniments. They stay on in the convent for a few days after the ceremonies. On returning to their families they say that they have come back from a far country across the sea. This is a further trace of the resurrection idea, for all the dead are believed to go on a long journey, and to cross water before rebirth on earth.

Thus, not only during training, but every year in springtime, the devotees retire from the world, are believed to go on long journeys, and to return again to the world as from the dead. The emphasis on renewal of personality is recurrent and constant.[3]

---

[3] Some comparisons have been made with certain Ibo customs in building *mbari* houses. The male and female workers are called by the priest as sons and daughters of the spirit; during the building they live communally, eat special food, wear distinctive dress, are said to undergo ritual 'marriages', and sing special songs. But this lasts only for the short time of building and is not continued or renewed.

CHAPTER TEN

Personal Religious Rites

To INTRODUCE the third class of spiritual beings, the ancestors, we begin with the more personal side of religion. Most of the religious acts so far described are concerned with the community and great occasions of public life, whether in the regular cult of the gods or at times during the agricultural yearly cycle.

In the lives of individuals and families there are important events which have religious associations. These are what the Dutch writer Van Gennep called 'rites of passage', or transitional rites. They involve transition or crossing from one place or stage of life to another. Important among these are the stages of life: birth, the passage through puberty, the new state of marriage, the ceremonies of burial; these are the sacraments of personal and family life. Some of these rites have more religious importance than others, and we shall concentrate on the religious side. Religion permeates the whole of life, and if we try to separate sacred from secular it is simply for the sake of convenience.

BIRTH

A newborn child is often thought to be the reincarnation of some ancestor who is seeking to return to this life, or at least part of his spiritual influence returns. Childlessness is regarded as a great trouble because it prevents the rebirth of the family elders.

A baby is carefully scrutinized to see what marks of resemblance it bears to past parents; one of its names may indicate this, 'father has returned', 'mother returned' (Yoruba, *babatunde*, *yetunde*). Yet although the ancestor, or part of his spiritual complex, returns the child is known to be the result of the action of its human father and mother. A number of peoples think that every person previously belonged to a sky family before being born, and sickness and suffering may be attributed to the displeasure of the sky parents.

95

An Ashanti woman receives a present of a white cloth and some gold ornaments from her husband in the sixth month of pregnancy, the woman's child is said to wear the ornaments and cloth. In exchange she gives him a fowl and some eggs which he offers in the corner of his room to his patrilineal spirit (*ntoro*). A prayer is made at the three-pronged altar of the Sky God and the fowl is eaten by the married couple. The woman is restricted in her movements, wears protective amulets, and observes her own and her husband's taboos. When labour begins, in her mother's house, the women call upon 'Nyame, the family gods, and the woman's own god if she is an initiate. The child is hailed by its day-name as soon as it is born, the umbilical cord is cut with a wooden knife (old style) and the 'ghost hair' cut off. The baby is not coddled for a week in case it is a deceptive ghost and dies. On the eighth day the father gives it clothes and the grandmother takes it out for a sunbath at dawn, puts three white spots on its brow, and it receives a personal name. It may be shown to the grave of its dead grandfather, may be dedicated to a special god if delicate, and there are special rites for twins, and the third, sixth, and ninth children.

As soon as a Fọn woman is known to be pregnant the old women of the family offer kola nuts and pepper to the family gods; they promise further gifts if health and delivery are normal. In the third month the Ifa oracle is consulted, to discover what food and places are taboo to the expectant mother. She gives fowls and red and white maize paste to the diviner, in exchange for a charm to ensure a good birth. At delivery prayer is made to Mawu and the ancestors. The umbilical cord is cut with a wooden knife and buried at a special palm tree. Should a woman die in pregnancy or childbirth it is thought essential to remove the foetus, and it is 'red taboo' to leave it. In most regions the priests bury the mother and child in the forest and the family must not follow the usual burial customs. This is held to be an accursed death and the unfortunate mother is looked upon as the murderess of the dead baby. The priest who removes the foetus steels himself for this grisly operation with much strong drink.

A Fọn child is named on the eighth day, when its head is shaved, a fowl sacrificed, its blood poured out and the flesh eaten. Usually the mother does not go out of her house till the new moon, when the village 'moon-glorifier' comes with a little brush which he puts on the roof after brushing the yard, sounds a little horn, and calls on the mother to suckle her child when the moon appears. Only next morning may the woman leave the compound to take the baby's washing water to the kitchen midden, where stillborn children and placenta are buried. The Gũ women of Porto Novo may go out earlier, but there is a similar ceremony at the third new moon after birth. An aunt turns the child towards the moon, throws it gently into the air (nine times for boys, seven times for girls), and cries: 'Look at the moon, little one; we bless you at the coming of the new moon. When you see the moon, you see riches, prosperity, and long life.'[1] Both the Gũ and the Peda of Ouidah forbid their women to eat salt for nine days after the birth of a son, seven days for a girl.

A Yoruba woman at pregnancy sacrifices to her own and her husband's gods, and consults the Ifa oracle to find what food and taboos to observe; similarly at birth the taboos and special divinity of the child are prescribed by the diviner. A child is 'born with a name', according to the circumstances of birth and its place in the family. There are names for a child born with the cord round its neck, born face down, or feet first, wrapped in a caul, with extra fingers or toes, at the new year or on a holy day, when its father is away, or if the mother dies at birth. Twins have special names (Taiwo, Kehinde) and so has the one born after twins (Idowu). The child is usually named on the eighth day, though some say that boys are named on the ninth and girls on the seventh day. The child is first taken out of the room, water from a shrine is thrown on the roof and allowed to drip on the baby, who is then named by the family elders, a libation of spirit is made to the earth and the child's feet are touched with Ifa nuts.

When an Ibo woman conceives she wears a special cloth as a mark of union with Ala, the earth deity, and to drive away evil spirits. A fowl is offered by her husband at the shrine of Ala, and a dog sacrificed a month later and then waved round the woman's

---

[1] G. Kiti, 'Quelques Coutumes de Goun (Dahomey)', in Anthropos, 75ff. Some Northern Nigerian tribes hold a baby up to the rising sun, three times for a boy, four for a girl; see C. K. Meek, Tribal Studies in Northern Nigeria.

head to protect her by its influence. The woman wears protective anklets, and in some places smears her body with chalk. In labour both Ala and Chuku the supreme being are called upon, and yam is offered to the ancestors. The child must be born outside the house and should not fall on the ground, the head is shaved and the navel cord buried and the mother enters the hut backwards. Naming is often deferred till the twenty-fourth day, when the head of the family lifts the child into the air four times saying 'grow strong', and then asks the father to name the child. A diviner may declare that the child should bear the name of a departed relative as reincarnating his influence, and he is taken to the grave where a goat is sacrificed and waved round his head. Special names are given according to unusual circumstances of birth and sometimes of the day of birth.

There is often fear of supernatural trouble in the early days of a baby's life when it is still a visitor from the spirit world. An Ashanti child that dies before the eighth day is whipped and mutilated, the parents dress and eat as for a feast and then pretend to lie together, which is normally taboo for two or three years after birth. All this is done with the object of insulting the 'ghost child', and thus deterring its 'ghost mother' from sending it to be born again. The parents are not considered to be its real father and mother if the baby dies before the eighth day.

Such children are called 'born to die' (*abiku*) by the Yoruba and Fọn. They are greatly feared, and are sometimes said to be forest spirits incarnate which are always seeking to return to their own home. Protective bracelets and anklets and bells are put on children who are born after *abiku* babies. Such a surviving child may be given insulting names: slave, pig, fear, unloved, to deter evil spirits from carrying off such a worthless thing. Many circumstantial stories are told of the same children being born again and again and having the same deformity which proved their identity. Parents are often afraid to say how many children they have. They say they do not know, or give a number greater than the real number, or point to a post as the last born, so as to deceive any spirit of disease that may be hovering around to take away their youngest.

Various attitudes are adopted towards twins. In any case they are abnormal, and perhaps are thought to be like animals which are born several at a time, and so likely to bring disaster on the community. That this similarity to animals has been considered is seen in the suffix *-hãn* in some Fǫn personal names, meaning 'pig' and so a member of a litter. Sometimes twins are thought to be the children of fairies or of spirit paramours and so all the more dangerous. Many twins are born, and this is more noticeable in African society, where families are large, than in Europe where families are restricted to one or two children nowadays and twins are seen less often. It is interesting that the firstborn twin is often called the younger (as in the myth of the god Tano) and messenger of the second, as in the Jacob-Esau story.

The Ibo generally and some of the Yoruba formerly allowed twins to die. Twin babies were put into a large pot and exposed alive in the bush. The mother herself was driven out of the village for several weeks till the danger of her impurity was past. These practices have been forbidden since the beginning of this century, but may appear at times in out-of-the-way places.[2] In Ashanti twins born into the royal family used to be killed, as 'hateful to the Golden Stool', the national emblem. But twins in other families were taken into the royal or chief's household as servants or wives. They are always dressed alike and must receive identical presents.

By a reversion of the taboo attempts are made to placate the spirits of twins by offering them worship. A strong cult of twins is found among the Fǫn and many Yoruba. Twins are represented by wooden images (*ibeji*), which are decked in cowrie shells and honoured with gifts. They may be placed in a family shrine, or carried about by women. A child that has lost its twin brother or sister may be seen wearing a carved wooden doll image, tucked in the front or back of his cloth, a woman who has lost twins wears two images in her belt. Some northern tribes make such twins images shaped like phalli, with strings of cowrie shells attached.

A Fǫn mother of twins calls together other mothers of twins and gives them two little earthenware pots which are joined together by an arm; this joined twin-pot is very common. With the twin-pot, two cloths, four fowls and some kolas and cowries, and the women go into the bush calling on the spirits of dead twins.

---

[2] See F. M. Hensley, *Niger Down*, pp. 45-6.

Dead twins are said to live in the forest in the form of red monkeys, hence the Fɔ̃n call twins monkeys. At a chosen spot two mounds are made and sacrifice is offered. On returning to the village a hole is dug outside the mother's hut; in this leaves are buried, a mound is raised, and on it is placed the double pot. Offerings of fowls and libations of palm oil are made in these double pots, or in two pots or dishes placed side by side in many parts of West Africa. Even up in the Sudan similar twin cults are to be found among the half-Muslim population and twin pots or dishes are put in the house. Sometimes the first twin is said to come from the Sky God and the second from the Earth.

The Gã suppose twins to have the same spirit as the wild cow, and all the other twins rush about like wild cows when one of their number dies. When Gã twins are a week old they, like the Ewe, have a little clay pot put on a small platform outside the hut, in which offerings and libations are placed.[3]

Mention should also be made of an important cult made by the Fɔ̃n and some Yoruba to abnormal children. Everywhere idiots are regarded with awe, as beings that are perhaps in touch with the supernatural and therefore should be treated kindly. These are called in Fɔ̃n 'chiefs of the water' (tohosu), where in ancient times they were thrown. They are the chiefs of the 'spirits of the water' (to-vodũ). Every time a man and woman have connexion it is thought that a being is conceived who becomes a spirit of the water. The tohosu may range from monstrous deformations, simply to those children whose top teeth have appeared first. Care is taken to begin their worship early, as neglect is thought to bring sickness, misfortune, and sterility.

I witnessed the following tohosu rite. The women went first to a stream to fetch water, and returned singing and lifting up a dish of water and a white cock. They were led by two initiates of the thunder cult, buxom lasses in purple cloths, carrying the ceremonial thunder 'axe'. Outside the mother's hut sat several priests and diviners with cowtail switches and iron staves of office; in front of them was a calabash with cowries and shells for divining. On arrival the women went into a new hut, and then the devotees came out to fetch a small green herb each. Two of the priests

[3] M. J. Field, *Religion and Medicine of the Gã People*, p. 180.

went into a low temple near by and came out with the cult pot, wrapped in a cloth. The cock was sacrificed over this pot in the house. The *tohosu* child was washed with water and plants over the pot. The mother then came out and sat by her own hut opposite, carrying her abnormal child, an unusually large-headed child of about five years old. The priests having replaced the pot in the shrine and returned to their seat, a devotee plucked a handful of straw, touching the ground and then her brow as she passed the priests, and wiped all water from the floor of the hut.

Later a goat was killed, its blood put in a small earthen pot with a many-knobbed lid, and the flesh then cooked and eaten, together with other food, by the assistants and relatives. Henceforth the mother would make libations of palm oil in this pot for the child, and would hope to conceive again normally. She would always wear a bracelet of single shells as a protection against further abnormal children.

PUBERTY

Puberty is the passage from childhood to adult life, the real beginning of life as a full member of society. In some parts of Africa this is celebrated with considerable ritual, involving the separation of the youths from the rest of society for a time, but in many parts of West Africa such ceremonies are absent, or where they once existed they have ceased to function in modern times.

Rattray described at length the ceremony undergone by Ashanti girls after the first menstruation. Prayers are interspersed with social rites. Almost at once, on being informed by the girl of her condition, the mother pours some wine on the ground and invokes 'Nyame, Asase Yaa and the ancestors, and beseeches the mother of the ghost land not to take the girl away. The girl is spoken of as an infant, newborn to the adult stage. After five days' feasting she is now termed a mother and should become betrothed and soon marry.[4]

Rattray found no comparable rites for boys, but among other Akan groups in the Ivory Coast I have met with important ceremonies that used to be held every few years for the age-groups of

[4] *Religion and Art in Ashanti*, Chapter 7.

adolescents. The whole tribe is divided into seven age-groups, each of ten years' duration, and each group has four sub-groups. The names are always the same and men over seventy will be in the same name-group as newborn boys. The ceremonies are marked by trials of endurance. The young men live together for several weeks, wear only raffia shorts and daub their faces with red ochre and kola juice. At the end of the seclusion they run a gauntlet of beating with whips as they enter the village. Those who endure bravely are henceforth considered as selected soldiers. A second ceremony gives the right to take part in the weekly village council as adults with full votes.

Some Gã boys have a short ceremony, which is generally neglected now. The boy makes a small hut on the beach and is chased by elders who hit him unmercifully as he bends to get into the hut. He sleeps there for three nights, and then old women treat him as a corpse and prepare him as for the grave, as a sign that he is dead to childhood. After this he is dressed magnificently and given a big feast and many presents and can sit with the men. Girls may be enclosed in houses for periods varying from six weeks to six months. They are barred from exercise and are taught by old women. At the end of this time they are bathed with herbs, and transfer any bad luck to a scapegoat. Then they are dressed up in fine clothing and heavy necklaces and shown off for betrothal. The enforced seclusion has fattened them and this is considered an aid to beauty.

Fǫn girls receive presents at the first menses, and the diviner is called to find out what sacrifices should be made to the gods and ancestors; evil may be transferred to a scapegoat if it is foretold. Any marking with decorative tattoos is done now and after the third menstruation the girl is regarded as a woman and fit for marriage. Fǫn boys have little ceremony, but teeth may be filed and facial tattoos made.

Circumcision is not practised everywhere in West Africa. The Fǫn do not normally circumcise, but they say that a hunter should be circumcised, perhaps with the idea of a special purification or an ancient clan relationship peculiar to hunters.

Circumcision is the principal adolescent rite of Yoruba boys, though some are done in childhood and perhaps increasingly today with the growth in the number of modern doctors. Some people would say that this custom is most widespread among the Yoruba because many of them have become Muslims, but while conversion to Islam may encourage the spread and retention of circumcision yet it seems to be much older here than the comparatively recent introduction of Islam into Yoruba country. Some boys are circumcised at twenty years of age, others earlier. The youth must lie stiff like a corpse and utter no sound; the operation usually takes place early in the year during the time of the Harmattan cold wind, when healing is quicker. In northern regions the boys must wear no clothes and enter no house till they are healed, but they are well fed and sit with their friends round a fire in the market.

Girls may undergo what is popularly called 'female circumcision', or cutting of the erotic areas (clitoridectomy and cutting off the labia minora), and tattooing of shoulders, back, trunk, and thighs. Formerly marriage was impossible till these things had been done. Such female circumcision is found in scattered parts of West Africa, as well as other parts of the continent. Some of the Bini and Ibo practise it, as well as Yoruba. Dr Rattray found it here and there in northern Ghana, and gave his considered opinion that this was one of the few instances where the Government should intervene and forbid this cruel practice. There seems no hygienic reason for female circumcision, as there may be occasionally among males, and the practice scars women considerably, prevents rather than helps sexual pleasure, and causes much suffering and septic wounds from the unsterilized knives used.

Both Yoruba and Ibo have special rites for adolescent boys who enter the secret societies, and in olden days that might be all the youths of a village. The Ibo Mmọ societies were entered by youths who learnt there the secrets of life, and underwent an imitated death to their former self and rebirth to a high life. More will be said about these societies later. Ibo girls receive presents at the onset of puberty, a goat and yams from the father, and the mother plants a yam for the girl near her fiancé's home. The fiancé would send the girl's mother traditionally forty brass rods, four yards of cloth and some meat, and similar presents to her father. Some Ibo girls would be confined to the so-called 'fatting houses' for weeks or months before marriage, where they would be daily anointed, and with that and the restricted movement, should become plump and beautiful; the emergence was celebrated with a public feast and betrothal. Any circumcision, tattooing and teeth-filing should be done at this time.

MARRIAGE

Marriage is a secular contract, between two persons and families, and in many countries the religious element is not great and enters as a final blessing to the contract. At the basis of many West African marriage rites is an exchange of wine, which seems to have a religious significance. Dowry or 'bride-wealth' may be considerable, but there may be less dowry where the woman remains part of her own clan and the children will belong to her family, as among the Akan in a matrilineal society.

Both monogamy and polygamy are legal throughout West African customary law. One of the main causes of polygamy, or change of partner, is sterility. 'Be fruitful and multiply' is one of the most honoured commandments, which was no doubt necessary in the past days of high infant mortality. The first wife is usually called the 'house mother' and is senior to later arrivals.

The Akan have few new practices at the time of marriage because it is regarded as the logical outcome of puberty. The girl may have been betrothed from childhood and her parents have received presents and servants from her fiancé for years. Small gifts of rum are made on first inquiry and on agreement to the marriage, and 'head wine' is poured out to the ancestors to seal the contract. Dowry is called 'buying a wife', but this is not purchasing her person but the right of intercourse. The only formalities are the parents' consent, making gifts, and offering wine to the ancestral stool. Dr Busia gives interesting comparative lists of the few items of traditional dowry and the lavish and crippling expenditure in marriage under modern Ordinance.[5]

The great dependence of the Fǫn on the Ifa oracle makes consultation essential before any union is entered into; if it is agreeable then the fiancé makes gifts to the girl's parents and a

[5] *Social Survey of Sekondi-Takoradi* (1950), pp. 143–5.

libation to the ancestors. A goat may also be offered to the girl's special tutelary god; a banana tree is planted, wrapped in red, white, and black cloths, and a fowl is sacrificed. Prayer is made at the shrine in the company of the girl's aunt. After payment of the dowry, drinks are offered all round and a feast concludes the ceremony. When she leaves her home the girl is blessed by an old woman in the name of the ancestors, and water is poured on the ground. At their new house both husband and wife sacrifice to their ancestors.

Only the Gã seem to have separate houses for men and women after marriage and the men and women are in distinct groups. Women are independent of their husbands for money and property. But the financial independence of women is widespread, and many women engage in trade, and some journey great distances from home and may become rich with a number of employees earning money for them.

The Yoruba also depend on the guidance of Ifa, since the oracle originated with them. The popular practice of splitting kola nuts makes a ritual of exchange and union between the contracting families to the marriage. The dowry fundamentally consists of kola nuts, wine, pepper, and a cloth and headtie, but these are supplemented by money and much other clothing, and the young man has probably rendered long service to his future father-in-law. Sacrifices are offered to Eshu, the girl's family god, and the ancestors. The bride is taken to her husband's house at night, at the door her feet are washed, and she is then carried over the threshold into the house. Hence marriage is called 'carrying the bride' (*igbeyawo*).

This practice of lifting the bride over the threshold is found in various other parts of West Africa. The Agni of the Ivory Coast have the custom, where a companion of the bride takes her on her back and places her in the bridegroom's compound. But the custom is found in many countries of the world, as far apart as England and China. The root idea may be to avoid any danger from the spirit or influence of the doorstep.

The Bini, with their great emphasis on the ancestors, take kola nuts to the girl's ancestors when she is betrothed. The dowry completes service and gifts that the suitor has made over the years.

After the bride has gone to her new home she cleans her husband's ancestral shrine and prayers are said there for her.

An Ibo boy may have given years of service to his future father-in-law. When the 'wife-wealth' is finally fixed cowrie shells are given as traditional and basic exchange or as a 'fee for uncovering the wine'. The fathers of the young couple go to a shrine and wave the cult emblem round each other's heads and bind themselves to fidelity. The earth goddess, Ala, and the ancestors are asked for their blessing and if there is any later dispute over the marriage they are asked to help in settlement.

The importance of the dowry, or bride-price, is that it stabilizes marriage. The great exaggerations of modern times have weakened rather than strengthened the union, and to restore its original purpose, not abolition but reduction to the simple basic elements is desirable; exchange of drink or kola nuts is enough. Refund of the dowry could dissolve the union, but the difficulty of doing this prevented too easy divorce. The ability to take another wife also made divorce less necessary in cases of gross incompatibility. The difficulties of the modern marriage ordinances have been that they were based upon European rather than African customary law, and did not meet the obstacle of childlessness. European custom is not necessarily the same as Christian principle, and modern times need to see the application of Christian principle to African custom.[6]

BURIAL

Funeral and mourning ceremonies are long and intricate, frequently involving a first and second burial ritual, and we can only try here to stress the specifically religious side. Further references will be found in the next chapter.

When a person falls ill, all kinds of remedies are tried and the diviner may be called in. Although there is a firm belief in a spirit world, and indeed belief in a life after death is one of mankind's oldest and most universal religious beliefs, yet that life is not regarded in Africa as preferable to this one on earth. The world beyond is a place of shades and cold, although its organization may be on much the same pattern as earthly life, but this sunlit warm world is the better. Death is rarely regarded as natural, and

[6] See my *Bible and Polygamy*.

'carrying the corpse' may be practised to find out who is responsible for the death. If the deceased's wife is accused she will be allowed to undergo an ordeal by drinking the water in which the corpse has been washed; or a small kola nut is put in the dead man's mouth and then given to the woman with some of his saliva. If she is unharmed by these, she is accounted innocent.[7]

There are usually five phases to a funeral: the preparation for burial, the mourning before interment and wake-keeping, the interment itself, mourning after burial, and later mourning at varying periods. Considerable time and money are spent on a funeral and no pains are spared to see that it is properly performed, but for social and superstitious reasons.

As an Ashanti man is dying, a little water is poured down his throat, to help him climb the hill of death and his last gasps show what efforts he is making; old men keep a child near them to perform this duty and its omission is considered grievous. Then when he is dead rum is poured down the throat of the corpse, and on the ground for his spirit. The body is thoroughly washed, dressed in its finest clothes, the hair done, and money tied to the wrists for the journey to the next world and across the river of death. The body is then laid in state and public mourning begins, with wailing and wake-keeping. Dirges are sung, conventional or extemporary, and unaccompanied or to the sound of drums. Money is placed on the coffin by clan members, and prayer is made to the dead person for health, long life, and children. Sometimes a sheep is killed and food is offered. When the body is removed for burial a hole is made in the house wall, for it is unlucky to take death through the door; this is a widespread belief. At the cemetery the ground is knocked twice and a libation is made to the Earth Spirit to ask permission to dig. (This custom of knocking or setting down the coffin twice on the way to the grave has been retained by descendants of the Akan in Jamaica.) The Ashanti bury outside the village, in the 'thicket of ghosts'. Some think the body should be turned to face away from the village, others bury it facing the village because they think that when the mourners depart 'the corpse turns round'. Some northern tribes bury men facing east, and women facing west.

[7] See below, Chapter 14.

People return from the funeral quietly, but mourning continues for some days, and dirges are sung of which J. H. Nketia has given many notable examples:

> Farewell, thou priest. . . .
> Fare thee well, mother of the king. . . .
> O mother, do not leave me behind. . . .
> Father, come and take me away. . . .
> I call him, but in vain. . . .
> This death has taken me by surprise. . . .
> Send me something for you and I exchange gifts.[8]

On the sixth day further offerings are taken to the cemetery. A rough hut is made in which cooking materials are placed. A sheep may be killed and wine poured out in front of the hut. The deceased is invoked, requesting him to drink and be gone peacefully. The hair of blood relations is shaved and put in a special pot, and at sunset this pot, with some of the cooked meat and utensils, is taken to the graveside where the dead is told that ritual is finished. The path back home from the cemetery is closed by laying a creeper across it, to stop any spirits following the mourners. On return to the house, all sitting there move their stools slightly forward three times, showing that death has gone back and life forward.[9]

The second funeral ceremony of Akan people takes place at a chosen time when people are ready, from forty days to a year later. Three days after the death of an Agni of the Ivory Coast, the men meet together for 'hand washing' in wine, to fix the date of the final rites. Gin is poured out on the cemetery road, a sheep may be killed, and a small portion cooked and put on the grave. Eating and dancing continue several days, ending before Sunday when accounts are made up.

When these ceremonies are for a chief there are great processions, dancing, drumming, blowing of horns, drinking, and gunfiring. All visitors bring presents to the bereaved family. All stool property is displayed on the final day. Every chief has a blackened stool after death, which is believed to enshrine his soul; this is

---

[8] *Funeral Dirges of the Akan People*, pp. 44ff.
[9] R. S. Rattray, *Religion and Art in Ashanti*, pp. 160ff.

guarded in a hut, wrapped in a cloth, till the final day. Then a libation is poured out on it, and it is carried on the neck of a stool carrier, under a state umbrella, to be placed eventually in the clan stool house.

When a Fõn dies, the body is washed by the wife and best friends, the hair and nails cut off and buried in a bundle beside the corpse. Till this is done no tear must be shed. The corpse is dressed in its best, with a bottle of drink, a cowrie shell, tobacco, and a pipe. In the olden days mats or plain cloths were used to wrap the corpse; nowadays coffins are the rule. Food and money are put in the coffin for the spirit to use on its journey to the underworld, lest on arrival he is hungry and on asking his seniors there they refuse to give him to eat, whereafter he would become a wandering ghost. At the burial the sexton makes a libation to the earth to get permission to dig. Various methods are used, here as in many other parts of Africa, to prevent earth falling directly on the body. Generally the system is followed of making a side shelf (niche burial) into which the corpse is slid, or branches may be laid over the body. In the olden days most peoples, and still today many of them, buried the dead in the houses in which they had lived. This practice is undoubtedly unsanitary, but it is very ancient and probably was done with the thought that the dead man's spirit would remain in his own house. In towns where this is now forbidden by modern laws, the nails, hair, and washing-sponge are buried in the house as symbolizing the corpse which lies in the public cemetery.

Fine clothes may be left in the grave or may be removed. Formerly gold rings were buried, but today usually only silver rings are left. Those who have assisted in the rites have special purifications to be done before returning to their homes. In some Fõn villages the old woman who had watched by the corpse during the mourning goes naked to the market on the burial night, nobody being allowed to look at her; she washes there and on returning cries: 'Day has come.'

A final burial ceremony is held seven or ten days after death, when all the family have had time to assemble. Gifts of cloth are brought from the different branches of the family, one third of which should be put in the grave, one third given to the sexton, and one third to the family of the deceased. The Ifa horoscope and the Eshu (Lɛgba) of the dead person are destroyed. The diviner breaks their power by offering their taboos to these divinities; the taboos of dead people are often spoken or offered after their death to annul their power. The Eshu is smashed, and the Ifa nuts and calabash thrown into a stream or at a cross-roads, together with the amulets and charms of the deceased.

Devotees of a god are buried by initiates. Chaplets and bracelets are removed and kept by the children as heirlooms. The hair is shaved off, and part of the original ceremony of initiation into the convent may be repeated, perhaps with the intention of trying to resurrect the corpse. An Ashanti priest does not wear mourning or sprinkle himself with red ochre at a funeral, as other mourners do, but dresses in white as if death does not touch him. When he dies his body is clothed in white and white clay is sprinkled on it.

Wives have a long mourning period. They must let their hair grow and not wash with soap. Should they dress gaily it is taken as a sign that they had some interest in their husband's death. Unchastity during the mourning period is often taken more seriously than infidelity during the husband's lifetime. Some wives guard their husband's graves and specially notable are the royal queens at Abomey who still watch over the tombs of the kings; here when one dedicated woman dies another is appointed as 'queen' to carry on the succession of guardianship of the royal tombs.

When a Yoruba man dies the Ifa oracle is consulted to see if the death was due to witchcraft. The corpse should not be touched till this consultation is over, then it is washed and the hair shaved off. Then it may be tied in black and white cloths, or dressed in fine clothing with gold rings. Burial is from one to three days after death, and before it takes place the corpse may be publicly paraded and photographed. The grave is dug by the sons of the deceased; when the coffin is lowered into it a kid is slaughtered and its blood let run into the grave. The sons stand with their backs to the grave and throw food of maize pap on to the coffin and pray to their dead father for blessing: 'May you rest in peace, may this house know coolness, may I have children to throw pap on me.'[10] The grave is filled in, still with the backs turned to it. After the burial there is wake-keeping, with drumming, dancing, and funeral dirges.

The Yoruba rites differ from the Ewe principally on the religious side, by the activity of the Egúngún and Oro secret societies in the final ceremonies.[11] The widows are led out of the town on the seventh or ninth day by a masked Egúngún, to a place where there are mounds of earth, according to the number of women. Each mound, except one that represents the dead husband, has a yam on it. Each woman takes her yam as the last gift she can expect from the deceased. A week or so later one of the Egúngún comes at night to the house. All lights are extinguished and he calls on the dead man. Thereupon another who is hidden replies in the tones of the deceased and emerges into the house. An offering is made to him and he blesses the wives and children of the dead man as if he were the person himself. Eventually he leaves, giving blessings as he goes and is supposed to return to heaven. Many adults nowadays are sceptical of the identity of the masquerader but he used to be taken as the deceased by everybody.

When a woman dies the relatives are told to prepare a miniature hearth in a calabash. The mourners take it into the bush, the woman's name is called out three times and a reply comes from the grove. An Egúngún comes forward and receives the hearth, blesses the givers and returns. The hearth is later thrown into a river.[12] Some of the Ewe clans throw a woman's hearth into the sea. The hearth is the woman's special concern, and has respect shown to it during life, perhaps because of its connexion with fire and the centre of the home.

When an Ibo man dies his son should put four large yams on the roof of his hut, and a special person designated by the diviner then takes them and puts two at the foot of the corpse and one at each side, saying: 'When you return may your yams be as big as these.' This is called 'placing the yams in the hand'. Then a rite is held of 'making the face white'; a cock being held over the head and then sacrificed and eaten by the attendant women. The body

[10] E. G. Parrinder, *Religion in an African City*, pp. 43-4.
[11] See also Chapter 14 below.
[12] S. Johnson, *The History of the Yorubas*, pp. 138-9.

is washed, laid on plantain leaves, and smeared with indigo or dressed in fine clothes. There may also be a sacrifice of a dog, and blood put on the corpse's eyes. The corpse was formerly wrapped in a mat and buried in the house or compound, nowadays it is usually placed in a coffin and buried in a cemetery. As the earth is thrown into the grave the soul is thought to leave the corpse, and so the man filling it in shouts, 'Avoid the earth', meaning 'Be gone before the earth touches you'. Prayer is made for the rest of the soul of the deceased, to discover who has killed him, and for blessing on his relatives. In olden days slaves were buried with important men, one at the head and one at the feet. At Owerri a goat might be further sacrificed, its blood sprinkled in the vacant hut, and the wife and children given the meat to eat.[13] The Ibo cemeteries are remarkable today for the number and brilliance of coloured images on the graves, comparable to the profusion of artistic effort that used to be more widely expended on the *mbari* houses.

Among the Bini also there is an interval of some hours, as with the Yoruba, between death and the mourning and preparation for burial; it is thought that the soul may still be somewhere about and may return. Eventually the body is washed, the hair and nails cut off and preserved, and a goat sacrificed and the body anointed with the blood. Burial today is in the public cemeteries and few may be buried at home. When the body is put in the grave prayers are made that in the next birth on earth the man may not know the troubles that have come to him in this life. The blood of a hen is used to cleanse the feet of the mourners from impurities of the grave and the flesh is eaten by the grave-diggers. Later the nails and hair which had been cut off the corpse are tied in a white cloth, with chalk, salt, and cowries, and a white feather stuck in it; a goat is killed over this bundle which represents the corpse and it is buried to the accompaniment of dirges. For seven days goats and fowls are sacrificed and dirges sung night and morning. Finally a carved post is stuck upright at a shrine dedicated to the dead man in his house, sacrifices are made and the deceased is called on to come and eat with his children.[14]

[13] C. K. Meek, *Law and Authority in a Nigerian Tribe*, pp. 303–4.
[14] R. E. Bradbury, *The Benin Kingdom*, pp. 5off.

THE SOUL

Only a brief reference can be made here to ideas of the soul. This is a very complex subject, on which sufficient knowledge is not yet available from many West African peoples. The interested reader is referred to my *West African Psychology*,[15] where a first comparative study has been attempted of some West African thought about soul and spirit, personality and genius, ghosts and dreams, rebirth and possession.

For the Ashanti the *sunsum* is the personality expressed in the appearance and individual characteristics of man—the worldly and outward man. This personality-soul may wander about in sleep and be captured by witches. Then there is the *'kra*, a pre-existent spirit, which comes from heaven, like a conscience or genius, and which cannot be contaminated by evil. Each day has its spirit and the *'kra* is 'washed' or worshipped according to the day-name; nobody washes his *sunsum*. Then there is the *ntoro*, which is a tutelary or totemic force that comes to a child from its father.

Although the Gã claim not to belong to the Akan group, and some of their religious ideas differ considerably, yet they are neighbours of the Akan and on this subject use similar terms. Thus the *susuma* is the personality, the influence which marks a man by his speech. This wanders about in sleep and if it does not return the man dies; prolonged absence of the *susuma* causes illness, and it is believed that evil magicians can stick thorns or nails into an image and harm this soul, or call it up into a bowl of water and do evil to it. The spirit is *kla*, and it is sometimes said that all children born on the same day have the same spirit; people who live a long time are believed to have fed on other spirits and so strengthened their own.

For the Fǫn the personality-soul is *yɛ*, which is often compared with the voice, since it has a personal note of its own which distinguishes it from others. As the voice leaves the body at death, so does the soul; but it is also associated with the blood and power in men, and also with the shadow, though not identical with it.

[15] Lutterworth Press (1951). Unfortunately this book went out of print in 1960 and a reprint seems unlikely.

This soul comes from God (Mawu) and returns to him at death where it is judged for its deeds on earth. The spirit is *sε*, and is like a divine genius or conscience for it is often called Mawusε, the Mawu who lives in everyone's body.

The Yoruba word for soul or personality is the same as that for the physical heart (*ǫkan*), and it is closely connected with the blood. But it is a man's own power and mind; if a man is absorbed in thought it is said that 'his soul is gone'. It wanders about at night and may be attacked by witches. The spirit is *ęmi*, connected with the breath but not identical with it. At death it leaves the body and returns to God. It is closely related to divine spirits, the Spirit of God is called *εmi*, and God is Owner of Spirits (Εlεmi).

In Ibo again the life or personality (*obi*) is closely connected with the heart, and it is this soul which is believed to quit the dead body when the earth is thrown into the grave. A conception that is very close to this is the *mmuǫ*, of which the shadow is a manifestation, which can be harmed by an evil magician, and can be reborn on earth. But there is a further belief in a spirit *chi*, closely connected with the supreme God Chuku. Talbot calls this the Over-soul or genius. It acts as guardian to the human ward, brings him good luck, and is a spiritual god-parent or protector.

These souls are all believed to have the ability of detaching themselves from the body. There is never any doubt in West Africa of belief in a spiritual part of man's nature, on the contrary the difficulty is to sort out the complex strands of this spiritual belief. The belief in a wandering or separable soul is essential to the theory of witchcraft, to which reference will be made in Chapter 14.

CHAPTER ELEVEN

Ancestral Cults

BELIEF in the continued existence and influence of the departed fathers of the family and tribe is very strong in all West Africa. Not only are the ancestors revered as past heroes, but they are felt to be still present, watching over the household, directly concerned in all the affairs of the family and property, giving abundant harvests and fertility. They are the guardians of the tribal traditions and history; hence the secrecy, professed ignorance, or obvious falsification of tradition which often confront the inquirer into local history. People wonder if the fathers will be angered if traditional affairs are revealed.

The importance of the ancestors in chiefly, moral, and property concerns is stressed by Dr K. A. Busia. 'In every Ashanti village stories are always circulating about the ancestors. . . . The ancestors are believed to be the custodians of the laws and customs of the tribe. They punish with sickness or misfortune those who infringe them. . . . Constantly before the Ashanti, and serving to regulate his conduct, is the thought that his ancestors are watching him, and that one day, when he rejoins them in the world of spirits, they will ask him to give an account of his conduct, especially of his conduct towards his kinsmen. This thought is a very potent sanction of morality.'[1] The very land belongs to the ancestors, for they owned it and worked on it. So when it is said, the land belongs to the stool, or the land belongs to the chief, what is really meant is that the land belongs to the ancestors.

For many people, especially older ones who will soon join the ancestors, the invisible is almost as real as the visible, and they cherish many memories of the dead. People say that they have seen or held communication with the departed. The sick and dying have visions of those who have gone before them, and these 'phantasms of the dying' are very common. The dead are thought

[1] *The Position of the Chief in the Modern Political System of Ashanti*, pp. 24–5.

to be constantly near, even when they are not seen. Pious West African pagans before drinking will pour out a little wine from their gourds on to the ground for the fathers. Others put a mouthful of food on the floor before eating, and at evening meals pots are not entirely emptied, nor washed till morning, in case the dead come and find nothing to eat. Particularly in the evening, the ancestors are believed to draw nearer, and so after nightfall people will not sweep the house, or throw water out into the yard, without first calling out a warning.

One of the most important duties, therefore, is to see that the burial and later mourning ceremonies for the dead are duly carried out, and often great expense is incurred and debts are accumulated by this expression of filial feeling. Sickness and misfortune are often believed to be due to some neglect in fulfilling the last rites with due care. Bad dreams are put down to the anger of a restless ghost. Family life therefore is strengthened by emphasis on performing full duties to the dead. Old men and women and parents are honoured, and it is a great disgrace to be cut off from the family.

It has been said that ancestral cults are less developed where there is a strong pantheon of gods. One completes, though it does not oust, the other. The Yoruba, who are said to have 201 or 401 gods, have less important ancestral rites than the Bini. The Ewe have highly developed religious cults, but while they have annual ancestral rites there is nothing to compare with the Ashanti ceremonies for the ancestors held twice every six weeks. Benin and Ashanti were great warrior kingdoms, and so the soldier heroes were no doubt deified; yet Abomey and Oyo also were great powers in their day, but the gods were of supreme importance.

The most important ancestral customs of Ashanti are the Adae, a word meaning 'a place of rest or lying down', work being forbidden on that day. Rattray has recorded extensively the ritual and the frequency of the Adae ceremonies, which are tribal festivals.[2]

Throughout Ashanti country the Adae rite is held twice in forty-three days, once on a Sunday (Kwesidae) and the other on a Wednesday (Wukudae). On the day before the Adae, stocks of water, wood, and food are got in, as nobody must work on the

[2] *Ashanti*, pp. 92ff.

sacred day. Utensils are cleaned, stools scrubbed, and money counted out for the festival.

On the Wukudae described by Rattray, all assembled in the courtyard of the chief's palace. Led by the head stool-carrier, the chief and officials entered a small dark room in which were the ancestral stools on a low platform of poles and cross bars. When their cloth covering was removed they were seen to be blackened and crumbling, caked with clotted blood and fat. Water, which had been drawn early by an old woman, was poured out and the ancestors asked to wash their hands.

The chief, stripped to the waist in respect, then took a spoonful of mashed plantain and put the contents on the oldest stool, saying: 'My spirit grandfathers, today is the Wednesday Adae, come and receive this mashed plantain and eat; let this town prosper; and permit the bearers of children to bear children; and may all the people who are in this town get riches. The same was done at the other stools, but the names of those ancestors were not mentioned. The remainder of the plantain was scattered on the ground outside for the spirits of the stool-carriers of the dead chiefs.

A live sheep was then brought in and offered with similar words. The chief stabbed its throat, some blood fell on the floor, and it was taken outside and killed. The blood was caught and taken in to be smeared on the seat and edge of each stool, by the carriers, without speaking. The fat of the intestines was put on the centre support of the stools. Choice pieces of meat were put on skewers, roasted near by, then brought to the chief who put one on each stool, saying: 'Here is meat, receive and eat.'

A bottle of whisky was opened, the herald drank some first from a brass cup, then the head stool-carrier poured some out on each stool, addressing them at greater length than before. His speech, as previously, was punctuated by words of approval from those present. The rest of the whisky was drunk by the assistants. The meat remained on the stools till evening; one skewerful must be eaten by the chief and the rest by the stool-carriers.

The Sunday Adae differed little from the above. It was preceded by a 'wave offering'. A pot of water was waved by an old woman above her head, outside the palace, then quickly turned upside down on the ground; the idea being to stop any disagreement among those assisting at the rites. Yams were put on the blackened stools by the chief, a sheep offered as before, the meat placed on the stools and rum poured on them.

It will be noticed that there is no reference to the gods in these rites. Both gods and ancestors, however, were invoked in Brong Adae ceremonies which Rattray attended. The Brong are northern neighbours of the Ashanti, of the same Akan stock. They have no Sunday Adae, and their Wednesday Adae falls every forty-two days; they call it Muruwukuo.

In this ceremony the chief poured palm wine into a calabash in front of each blackened stool, calling on each ancestor by name to come and drink. At the last stool, wine was poured a second time into the calabash and the gods were called upon: 'Ta Kora (Tano) this is yours. Ta Mensa this is yours. Obo Kyerewa this is yours. Ati Akosua this is yours.'[3]

A procession was then made to the temple of the god Ta Mensa. The altar was draped in white and the brass basin shrine of the god was wrapped in a coloured handkerchief. Shrines of other gods were in the room and some blackened stools of dead priests. The chief and his spokesman (linguist) in turn gave wine to the priest, who sprayed a mouthful upon the wall, and poured the rest into a hole in front of the altar, asking the god for life and strength.

Among the Agni of the Ivory Coast sacrifice was offered to the royal stool every Saturday: palm oil, cooked plantain, and wine. A sheep was sacrificed less often and portions placed on the stool.

The stools are symbols of the dead. White stools are owned by almost every Akan and the soul (*sunsum*) is connected with it, and sometimes bound to it by symbolical chains. At death the stool is blackened with soot and egg yolk and is set in the lineage stool-house, or 'chapel of stools', which is part of the chief's dwelling. When not in use the stools lie on their sides so that no unwanted spirit may sit on them. Little dishes stand in front of each stool, for the 'soul food'. The Golden Stool of Ashanti was held to enshrine the soul of the whole people, and was used as a national emblem from about 1700.[4]

[3] Ibid. p. 117.   [4] See E. W. Smith, *The Golden Stool*.

The royal ancestral cult of the Fǫn of Abomey is called *nesuhwe* (*nesu*, the male organ, and *hwe*, a house). The ancestors of commoners were said to be the 'water-spirits' (*to-vodũ*), for they were supposed to live in rivers with other water sprites and lesser human and divine beings, and the spirits that are formed every time a man and woman have connexion. Today the *nesuhwe* cult has spread to all large and rich families.

The leading divinized spirits of the *nesuhwe* cult are the abnormal children (*tohosu*), the cult to which reference was made in Chapter 10. According to tradition King Abaka of Abomey (1680–1718) had one of these abnormal children, in whose honour the cult was founded, and each succeeding king is said to have had at least one such child. Each of these abnormal children is leader of the ancestral cults in one of the wards of Abomey. The cult is characterized by long huts in front of the royal palaces; no one else may build a hut for their cult as long as that of the leader. Round huts, with long roofs, contain altars for sacrifice to dead monarchs.

The cult of the dead is established by special priests and initiates ('wives of the water-spirits'), who are less trained than devotees of the great gods. These go to the stream carrying the typical earthen pots with many knobs on the lids, and red, white, and black mats. The priest calls the spirits to come from the water into the temple which is ready for them. The initiates who hold the pots shake violently when the spirits are believed to enter into them, and on returning to the village in procession each one is held by an assistant lest the spirit force him to return to the water. The pots are put in the long house and a cult is offered there by the dedicated servants. After the *tohosu*, the abnormal ones, the other dead of the family are installed with individual metal rods or 'standards' (*asɛn*, *ǫsãnyĩn*); these are like little iron umbrellas and figure prominently in all Dahomean religion at the altars of gods and ancestors.

The ancestral rites occur annually in May and June. The ancestors are 'fed' and their help is sought for sowing and harvest. The ceremonies last many days and consist of sacrifices, prayers, and dances by members of families and cult groups. The stools of the most important ancestors are exhibited under their decorated umbrellas on the great days, when the living chiefs are present with their stools, umbrellas, and attendants. Thus living and dead meet and mingle freely.

In the principal prayers the head of the family group addresses the ancestors outside the hut; thanking them for life and protection, asking them to accept the offerings now made, and to give fertility and prosperity to all the family. The priests of the ancestral cult kneel inside the huts, and the oldest one repeats the chief's words to the dead, represented by the metal standards. Afterwards he tells the crowd that the prayers are accepted and great rejoicings follow. The sacrificial animals are slain, and part of each is put on each iron standard so that the ancestors may eat.

In many parts of West Africa, there are important rites at the beginning of the yam season when ancestors and gods are invoked. This falls in September or October. Nobody may eat of the new crop till these sacrifices have been made. The Fǫn take goats and fowls to the shrines and the priests put slices of new yams there. The flesh of the victims is cooked and portions put on the standards of ancestors; I have counted over fifty at a small shrine. After the priest has tasted the food himself the people begin to eat and rejoice. The yam custom (*odwira*) of Ashanti is an annual purification and renewal. Fresh yams are offered at the shrines of the gods, in royal burial places, and to the ancestral spirits.

Some of the Ewe group, notably the Peda and Gũ of the coastline, practise the custom of removing the skull of dead people, in order to establish their cult. This is also done by some tribes of northern and eastern Nigeria; with some the head is removed and cleaned only a fortnight or so after burial, with others it is left till the dry season. Some tribes remove only the skulls of chiefs and royalty; others remove all heads.[4] It is said that the Fǫn of Abomey formerly practised skull removal, but the practice was suppressed by King Hwegbaja in the seventeenth century. Dahomeans still sing at the annual customs: 'The king has bought our heads on our necks.'

At Porto Novo and other Gũ villages the skull is dug up nine months after burial, seven months for a woman, when decomposition of the flesh is practically complete. The grave is opened and

[4] See C. K. Meek, *Tribal Studies in Northern Nigeria.*

the skull taken off; it is washed with soap and a sponge, a cock is killed and some spirits are poured with its blood on to the skull and prayer is made. The skull is then put in a sack and hung on the house wall, or placed in a pot.[5]

Eventually the village elders fix a day for all those who have skulls of relatives, to bring them together and give them to eat. The relatives assemble in the evening and the widow of the dead man may wash his skull if she has been chaste since his death; if she has not been faithful, but still performs the operation, she is said to be sure to die soon after. Any missing teeth from the skull are replaced by grains of maize, and it is then put in a pot and covered over. The pots are placed in a common room, each on a white cushion resting on a box. At night, the women come to sprinkle the pots with the blood of a cock and a hen.

Next day everybody comes to admire the pots, which are now covered with fine cloths and a hat each, two swords for each male, and pearls and ornaments for the females. Sacrifices, feasting, and dancing follow. In the afternoon, two young men are chosen to prepare a canoe, to take the skulls to the 'ocean-pit' and bury them. This is a metaphorical expression; the pit is dug in the family house, and the pots are all placed in it and covered over.

Up to a year later follows the Ago ceremony. On the evening of a chosen day the elders go to the sea, halting some way before arriving at the beach, to make a small mound. On this they pour a mixture of maize flour and water, and make a little tent over it with a bamboo mat. The oldest man calls on the dead by their names, one by one, to come and eat in the tent. He invites them all, and asks to be reminded if he has forgotten the names of any. After firing of guns, drumming and singing, all go home.

Next afternoon, the elders meet at the hut where the metal standards are, planted in the ground, one for each ancestor. The oldest woman pours alcohol and water on the standards, then makes some passes with red and white kolas; these are split to discover whether the dead are pleased. A man then seizes a sow that has been brought and the old woman pricks its throat with a sacred knife, so that the blood falls on the standard. After cooking, small portions of the sow's intestines are put on each metal standard,

[5] G. Kiti, in *Anthropos*, XXXII.419ff.

and the assistants eat the rest. A further ceremony is held a few days later, to give the dead to drink. After sacrifice of another sow some maize beer is poured out in front of the standards, a traditional drink that the ancestors used in olden days.

There is an annual ceremony (*gozen*) which is performed for the royal ancestors of Porto Novo. Long-necked pots of earthenware, brass, or silver are filled with water from the lagoons, one for each dead king. They are carried into the royal house of the dead in the compound of the 'King of the Day', by women stripped to the waist but otherwise finely dressed. Officials sweep the ground before them, and another carrying a whip calls out: 'Give way, the King of Sado is coming.' Sado or Tado in Togo was the traditional home of Gũ and Fǫn and some other Ewe groups. At this cry all passers-by crouch down, uncovering head and shoulders, till the procession arrives at the palace, where the pots of water are given to the ancestors to drink.

The Yoruba ancestral cults have their own special characteristics. However, the dead can be invoked at any ordinary times, here as among other peoples. Apart from the public rites, Yoruba may offer food or kill a cock for the 'great fathers' (*babanla*). This is done particularly in time of plenty, but if food is short the offerings may be neglected. A half buried pot or bottle, in the open or in a hut, may stand over the tomb, and here offerings are made. The dead are talked about in a familiar way, and a man will not speak of consulting the dead, or speaking to their spirits, but says: 'I am going to speak to my father.'

The chief Yoruba ancestral cults are connected with the Egũngũn and Oro cults. Egũngũn has already been spoken of in the previous chapter about funeral ceremonies, and both will be mentioned again in the next chapter on secret societies. Here we shall speak about the Egũngũn activities rather than organization.

Egũngũn, often contracted to Egũn, is said to mean 'bone' or 'skeleton', though some dispute this. But it is certainly a representation of the dead, in the form of figures masked and clothed from head to foot, which appear at funerals and on other occasions during the year. Egũngũn may appear at any time, singly or in companies. They join in town festivals and other public holidays, and in these days beg for money, often speaking in English.

They may be dressed in plain cloth, with webbing over their faces, or in sackcloth, and the more important have masks or horns on their heads. They may walk, run or jump about, and chase people with sticks or whips in their hands, or be led by assistants who beat back the crowds with whips. But they are always held to be spirits of the dead and speak in guttural or thin piping voices like the dead, whose voices are supposed to be nasal or broken.

The great annual appearances of the Egũngũn are the chief communal ancestral rites of the Yoruba. In early June, the time of farming, when the help of the ancestors is most needed, their visible representatives appear. Their appearance is preceded by a vigil all night in the Egũngũn grove, a clump of trees outside the town; this is called 'kneeling'. The blessing and help of the dead are requested, and sacrifices of fowls and goats are offered to feast them. When the robed figures appear in the town, often twenty or thirty of them at a time, they walk through the excited crowds, preceded by their attendants and policemen. They go first to the chief's house, and then perform plays there and at other places in the town. The June festivals usually last a week. They have been called 'All Souls' festivals', when the dead are remembered and their continued existence in the world beyond is affirmed. Finally the Egũngũn gather in the chief's compound and he prays for blessing on them and upon the crops. The harvest must not be gathered in until this festival, and produce is brought and put on the Egũngũn shrines and in the temples of the gods.

The Ibo also have ancestral ceremonies associated with secret societies, notably the Mmọ society, a word which means spirits of the dead. These masqueraders appear in public at the end of funeral rites, at festivals of the seasons, and on some other occasions. The Mmọ masqueraders are saluted as 'Our father', 'Owner of the village', 'Owner of the soil'.[6] In the dry season, from January to March, the Mmọ society appears in some places singing and dancing, and twirling the piece of wood on a cord known as the 'bull-roarer'. They go from house to house at night, while the women are strictly confined indoors, and demand gifts from the

---

[6] C. K. Meek, *Law and Authority in a Nigerian Tribe*, pp. 69–70.

householders and then disperse to eat a communal meal. At the beginning of the harvest this and other societies (Odo and Omabe) parade in the towns and receive sacrifices and gifts of new yams.

In addition to the societies, the ancestors receive regular attention. Under the presidency of Ala, the earth spirit, the ancestors are guardians of morality and owners of the soil. Sacrifice is offered to them periodically, or especially when a diviner says that it is necessary. Sacrifice is performed by the oldest man, or the head of the family; they are the family-priests and do not need an outside priest as in the case of the gods.

Ibo ancestors are called Ndichie or Ndi-Oke, and they are represented by pillars or staffs placed inside the hut, but facing outwards so as to keep watch. Food is put at these pillars and wine poured on them, traditionally whenever eating. But there is a portable stick (ofo) which is the most important symbol of the ancestors. This is used by the head of the family as the principal symbol of authority; it receives periodical libations and at communal sacrifices each man lays his ofo with others and receives part of the sacrifice. In some places this stick is thought to receive the soul of a dying man. There are also family stools (okposi) which are regarded as ancestral shrines.

The Bini are particularly devoted to the ancestral cults and it is said that the collective dead are the most important force in Bini society. The senior son establishes the cult of a dead father in the first room of the house, and here a carved staff is his symbol, in which there is a bell to call up the spirit of the father. Dual priests of the cult are the senior son and the senior surviving brother. In addition to regular offerings made to the dead there is a special Ebo ceremony held in October. All relatives meet at the shrine: sons, daughters, wives, brothers, and sisters. The two priests sit on either side of the altar, prayers are made and kola nuts are presented; all the attendants go to the altar to kneel down and pray, and their prayers are passed on by the priests. Then the priests offer a goat and sprinkle the people with its blood. At the end all the senior men lean over the altar and pray to the ancestors and to the king of Benin.

The royal cults have been of great importance in Benin. There is a myth that temples were founded as the body of a dead Oba (king) was carried home, and wherever liquid fell from his body a temple was built. In the past each Oba had a large temple built for him, with a semi-circular altar and staff. Today only one is left in Benin, with altars for past Obas in it. Here are to be seen the famous bronze royal heads for which Benin is renowned. There is an annual State ceremony (Igwe) in December that lasts a week, when sacrifices are offered to past kings and the Oba's own head. In annual sacrifices to the ancestors the Oba must sacrifice first, and others after him. For two or three months every year the Oba sacrifices every five days to the previous kings, and also frequently to his own head. Offering to the head among the Bini is paralleled among the Yoruba, where the Ori, 'head', is related to the destiny and receives offerings of kolas, wine, or animals. A man offers gifts also to his father's Ori, symbolized by the big toe.

In all these varieties of ancestral observance the question arises whether it is worship. This has been much debated, and it is of considerable importance in the spread of Christianity and Islam. If the dead are worshipped like gods, then this worship is incompatible with the adoration of one God. On the other hand if the dead are like saints, then certain forms of Christianity and Islam have found room for veneration of saints in their systems. In any case, both believe in a life after death, in the continued existence of the departed, and in their interest in men on earth as a 'cloud of witnesses'.

Some writers roundly declare that Africans no more worship the dead than they do elders and chiefs here on earth. They prostrate to chiefs, or kneel before elders and seniors, and bring to them gifts and requests. On the other hand, it must be said that the prayers and attitudes men adopt to the ancestors differ very little from those taken up towards the gods. Both are senior and potent forces, and need every reverence. Some would say that the gods were all once ancestors who have been deified, or they may be natural forces personified like men. Some gods, like Shāngo, clearly combine both human and natural attributes, the storm and the king. In the ancestral cults the elders of the family are priests, whereas in the temple of the gods there are specially separated priests, but this makes little practical difference to the types of worship offered to each spiritual power. It can hardly be denied that prayers are made *to* the ancestors, and the only possible way in which such cults could be reconciled to a monotheistic faith would be by permitting prayers to be made *for* the dead *to* the supreme God.

NOTE ON HUMAN SACRIFICES

Many of the human sacrifices of olden times took place in connexion with funeral and memorial ceremonies, and much more rarely in the cults of the gods. It was at the 'customs', the funeral and commemoration ceremonies, that the rulers of Abomey, Kumasi and Benin (the 'cities of blood') got their reputation of being blood-thirsty despots. The Abomey kings were particularly despotic at times, but a careful contemporary observer who visited Abomey remarked: 'When the system is examined, these prostrations are merely keeping-up of ancient customs. And although no man's head in Dahomey can be considered warranted for twenty-four hours, still the great chief himself would find his throne tottering if one of these customs was omitted.' And again: 'Gezo, we are assured, has no delight in human sacrifice, and continues these awful scenes solely out of deference to ancient national customs.'[7]

Similar things were said in explanation of the large sacrifices at Kumasi and Benin. Many other towns had smaller sacrifices, Oyo, Ife, and so on, and many funerals were accompanied by two or three human victims. The motive of the funeral sacrifices was the conviction that important persons who died must be accompanied by servants fitting to their position. The same belief, with human sacrifice, was found in ancient Egypt and Mesopotamia, till about the thirteenth century B.C.

While the king of Ashanti's corpse was being washed, attendants were killed at each stage, to carry his bath-mat, sponge, soap, bath robe. At Porto Novo a principal official was the 'skin chief', and on the king's death this functionary was killed, skinned and the body of the king wrapped in the skin for burial. Another official announced the king's death from the roof of the royal residence, and was then shot down by an officer.

[7] F. E. Forbes, *Dahomey and the Dahomeans* (1851), II.17, 32.

Many of the victims were resigned to their fate and took poison as soon as the king's death was announced. Yoruba monarchs had special wives and ministers who were always known by the name which indicated that they would 'die with the king' (*abǫbaku*). Other previously chosen victims were called 'king's souls' during their lifetime. This custom also probably served the purpose of seeing that many people had an interest in keeping the king alive as long as possible, and so of preventing palace revolutions. Queens who were not mothers took poison to accompany the king of Dahomey. A sacred dwarf was buried alive in the tomb; he was given a lighted lamp to light the king's path to the city of the dead.

Today, these people who were formerly buried with the king or chief may still take their part in funeral processions, and have their hair and nails cut off and buried as symbols of their presence with their dead master.

Not only at the funerals of kings, but at annual or even more frequent occasions of remembrance of the dead kings, further victims would be dispatched. It was thought that they would go down to the land of the dead, and they were charged with messages to take to the departed monarchs. So there was a constant flow of blood, daily at times in Abomey, and visitors had to step over pools of fresh human blood.

It is true that there were other victims of sacrifice. Some were criminals who had been condemned to death, but whose merited punishment was held over till the ancestral ceremonies, and they were well fed in the meantime so as to be healthy messengers. The rest were prisoners of war, the least excusable category, though many warlike expeditions were undertaken to supply the slave trade.[8]

Those days have gone, and though we may explain, our explanations do not excuse the practice of human sacrifice, or alleviate the cruelty and suffering caused to many innocent people. Occasionally still there are rumours of people disappearing at the funeral of a great chief, and constant vigilance is needed to erase the last traces of this cruel custom.

[8] See pp. 71–2 above.

CHAPTER TWELVE

Secret Societies

SECRET SOCIETIES, closed associations, cult groups—various terms are used to describe the groups and clubs of restricted membership and mysterious activity.

Many of these so-called secret societies were of religious inspiration. Some were connected with initiatory and adolescent rites and served to strengthen male prestige. Some of the most important are concerned with the dead and, as we have seen, they are active at funeral and memorial ceremonies. Hence description of them may well follow on consideration of ancestral cults.

These societies seem to have been less common in some places where there was a strong central monarchy which suppressed rival organizations, especially Ashanti and Dahomey. There is little to report from these regions. In Togo there is a *yehwe* (spirit) organization, but this is a cult of one of the gods, and its followers are trained on the lines of the communal initiates of the gods in Dahomey. The principal secret societies are in Nigeria, west and east. There is however one society that is peculiar to Dahomey, that is the Zãngbeto of Porto Novo.

ZÃNGBETO

The Zãngbeto society is strongest in the region of Porto Novo, though it is also found along the coast into Nigeria at Badagry. It is said to have been introduced by the founder of the Porto Novo kingdom. Few writers have mentioned the society, and little research has been done into its origins and practices. I was fortunate to secure some information and songs from a member.

The name Zãngbeto means 'hunters of the night'. They are also called 'spirits of the sea', since they are said to come from beyond the lagoon, which is perhaps meant to indicate return from the country of the dead, across the water.

The outward symbols of the society are long robes of grass,

sometimes crowned with horns or a mask. These are commonly seen in the daytime hanging in the open or under a thatch shelter. Near by there may be the horns which the attendants blow. It is a grave offence to touch these grass robes, or to say that they are worn by men; formerly the punishment was death.

The *zãnsi*, 'wives of the night', go through the streets at night in their grass robes, with rattles and gongs, and with attendants blowing on hollow horns called 'night noses'. The *zãnsi* speak in a nasal falsetto, like the Yoruba Egũngũn; there is a wide-spread belief that the noses of the dead are broken and so their impersonators speak nasally.

In semi-public performances in the moonlight two masked figures may draw together, one wriggles out of his costume into the other's, while his own robe sinks to the ground. This is taken as a proof that the spirit is not a man. Sometimes a masked costume is put to float on the lagoon in the moonlight, and a *zãnsi* comes up into it by diving under the water, and so he is taken as a lagoon spirit.

The chief of the Zãngbeto is the Zãngãn. His attendants are called 'flies' that discover any danger to the society and spy out secrets. They meet in a grove in the bush, the path to which is marked by a large Eshu with horns; this shows the layman that the grove is private to the society. A small hut in the grove contains the belongings of the members.

The Zãngbeto society serves as an initiation society for young men, as well as representing the spirits of the dead. A candidate for initiation must pay gifts in cash or kind, and is then told when to appear in the grove. On the night chosen the *zãnsi* assemble in their robes, but their chief is in civilian dress. The Zãngãn is the only person who is generally known to be a member of the Zãng-beto, and the names of the others are kept secret. The candidate is questioned about his knowledge of Zãngbeto. Does he really know what it is? There is a ritual interrogation, to which the devotees chant in chorus. 'If you wish to know anyone you may do so, but the layman ("not-wife") does not know Zãngbeto. This one here? Chorus: He is Zãngbeto. That one there? Chorus: He is Zãngbeto. And I myself? Chorus: He is Zãngbeto. And you yourself? Chorus: He is Zãngbeto.' Thus the candidate understands that Zãngbeto is inexplicable, even material objects are Zãngbeto for they remain still during the day, but at night they may move about and take other forms and places. This is followed by trials of beating with sticks, to prove the courage and endurance of the candidate. If he is strong and successful, then he is admitted as a 'wife of the night'. (It should be noted that this is a purely male organization.) There is a feast following the admittance, the cost of which is paid by the neophyte. The Zãngbeto society still continues today, but chiefly as night guardians in towns and villages. Women and non-initiates must remain indoors when they hear the horns which tell that the society is out. In towns all people going home late are stopped and questioned by these guards. A kindred society in Porto Novo got out of hand and was closed by the Government.

EGŪNGŪN AND ORO

We have already twice mentioned the Egũngũn society, in its associations with funerals and ancestral rites among the Yoruba. Farrow quotes a proverb to show that different Yoruba societies prevail in different areas: 'Oyo has the Egun cult; Egbo has the Oro cult; Ijebu has the Agemo cult.' Egũngũn is said to have come from Oyo, but it spread widely no doubt during the time of the extensive rule of Oyo.

The Egũngũn masqueraders appear in the daytime, robed from head to foot in a variety of dresses. The commonest, 'children of Egũngũn', can appear at any time and dance to please people and win their alms. The 'elder Egũngũn' sometimes wear wooden masks and are feared for their magical powers. Others play tricks and represent animals into whose form they pretend to change. Others again are specifically concerned with representing people who have recently died, and also performing at the annual ceremony for the dead.[1]

Admission to the society is on the advice of the Ifa oracle; kola nuts are cast at the Egũngũn grove shrine, beer and gin are offered, the blood of a fowl sprinkled, and its flesh cooked and eaten. In some areas (e.g. Ilaro) it is said that girls may join the society, but normally it is reserved for males. The society is

[1] See the Ethnographic Survey, *Yoruba-speaking Peoples*, pp. 18ff.

spreading among the Gũ and Fɔ̃n of Dahomey; they call it *kufito*, or the French word *revenants*.

The Oro society also represents the ancestors (at least this is the general opinion; Bascom denied it, but Idowu affirms it). It is the collective male ancestors, protectors of towns and villages. Formerly Oro was the executive arm of the secret secular council, the Ogboni (see below). Evildoers condemned by the Ogboni were taken away by the Oro society and executed in Oro's grove; their skulls were afterwards nailed to a tree in the market-place and part of their clothing hung from the branches. Oro still rounds up undesirable people and keeps witches on the move.

Oro is a purely male organization and ensures masculine domination. When Oro comes out all women must stay indoors, huts must be closed, and lights put out. Usually the society is out at night, but occasionally in the daytime. There used to be an annual festival in the spring which lasted a week, and during the whole of this period women had to stay indoors, day and night, except for a short interval during the day when they were allowed out to fetch water and food. This is impossible to enforce in modern towns and in many villages, with the ease of communications and the spread of Christianity and Islam. Some of the younger members were said to go about naked during this period, confident that they would meet no women, to show off their manhood; and stories tell of indiscreet women who came out or looked out and were killed by the society.

The chief public sign of Oro is the 'bull-roarer' or rhomb, which is known in other parts of the world. When this piece of wood is whirled in the air on its cord it makes an uneven roaring sound, which is called the voice of Oro. Several sizes of these may be used to produce different notes. Any male may join the society on payment of a sheep or fowls and may attend the meetings, but office is restricted to certain families. The grove of Oro is in the bush, guarded by a palm-frond and sentries who stand on the path during meetings and exact passwords from all comers.

In Ijebu country the Eluku society acts like Oro, as a nocturnal society, taboo to women, whose presence is announced by piercing shrieks. It is also called Agemo, the chameleon, which is represented by a masked and robed figure, and is prominent in funeral rites.

In Lagos and neighbourhood there has been the Adamu-orisha society. Its members dress rather like the Egũngũn, in gowns covering the face and all the body, and with the addition of broad-brimmed hats. They carry hollow sticks filled with seeds, which make a weird noise. The chief public display of the society is a play given at funerals of important people. The object of the play is said to be to lay the spirit of the dead, so that it no longer wanders about. The play lasts for a day and is followed by a feast.

Among some Yoruba in Dahomey and parts of Western Nigeria there is the Gɛlɛdɛ society which is represented by a dancer wearing a wooden mask, often elaborately carved, sometimes as an animal like an alligator, or with female characteristics. Outside villages are clearings where Gɛlɛdɛ dances are taught at night; drums coloured blue and red, with designs of snakes and birds, are set aside for Gɛlɛdɛ.

Mention was made of the Yoruba society, Ogboni. Some would call this the third major 'secret society', but it is principally a political organization with its lodges in all parts of Yoruba country. The Ogboni served political ends and curbed the powers of the chiefs in olden days, though as a secret society there were tendencies to abuse of power. But religious actions formed part of its work and it is said that formerly human sacrifices were made at the initiation of new members. The society is said to worship the earth, and the symbols of the society are metal images of human figures known as Edan; these Edan were formerly kept secret but today can often be seen. The Ogboni society has lost much of its earlier power and new forms of local and central government have confined most of its activities to funeral rites. A Reformed Ogboni Fraternity was founded in 1914 for Christians who admired the society, and it has been the subject of much debate. Members say that there is no ritual inconsistent with Christian teaching, but since it is secret nobody outside can confirm this. Muslims usually forbid their members to belong to it.

NDAKO GBOYA

A famous society is the Ndako Gboya of the Nupe, often called Igunnu by other people. This has been prohibited in modern times, was revived, and then forbidden again in Bida emirate, but it is to be seen in other parts of Nupe country and among the Yoruba. The title means 'Ancestor Gboya', and it is confused by strangers with a *gunnu* ritual and dance which is one of the principal features of Nupe religion. The origin of Ndako Gboya is obscure, and as an organization it seems to be comparatively recent; as a cult society training initiates it is about a century old.

The chief activities of Ndako Gboya are masquerades, during the course of which ordeals used to be administered and people tried for witchcraft. A woman accused by the maskers would be forced to dig the ground with her bare fingers and if blood appeared under her nails she would be proved a witch; it must have been very hard to prevent this. The bull-roarer was sometimes used, and dances were performed during which witches were accused by the maskers apparently at random.

The masks of the Ndako Gboya are different from any others used in Nigeria, as they completely hide the person inside, have no resemblance to a human body, and so are the more strange and spirit-like. They consist of high bamboo frames, about twelve feet high, covered with cloths of one or various colours from top to bottom, and often with ribbons of cloth hanging from rings round the central cylinder. These look like great rolls of cloth as they stalk through the streets, and it must not be said that there is a man inside, but a spirit. The masker is saluted as friend and chief, and in a shrieking voice he gives greetings and blessings to those he visits.[2]

MMỌ AND EKPO

The principal Ibo society, which impersonates the dead by means of maskers who appear in public at funerals and seasonal festivals, is the Mmọ society. Initiation into the society is begun when boys are about ten years old. They undergo an ordeal of beating by a masker and then parade round the village; this enables them to follow the maskers in procession and not hide away as before; they are then 'children of Mmọ'. The full initiation follows several years later and is a ritual of death and rebirth. The dead are called up from the underworld, in the form of a masker, and the naked

[2] S. F. Nadel, *Nupe Religion*, pp. 188ff; and picture in *Religion in an African City*, Plate 10.

novice is made to undergo ordeals symbolizing a visit to the spirit world and proving his powers of endurance; this includes eating charcoal and bones while the members of the society feed on wine and yams. In the morning the novice emerges exhausted and dirty from his adventures as if he had come from the underworld, and is then told the secret of the masks and their occupants and sworn to secrecy.[3]

There are various grades of Mmọ; some parade the village at feasts, or chase witches away, others appear at funeral rites and pour fowl's blood on to the eyes of the corpse. Women are kept in their place by oaths sworn in the name of Mmọ and are not allowed to use such oaths themselves.

The Odo society is also an Ibo company of maskers who appear in December and impersonate the dead; they speak in croaky voices like the dead and receive gifts from houses that they visit. Any who refused such gifts would be beaten by Odo's attendants. New yams are also offered to Odo and he appears again at this season to receive sacrifices. Boys are initiated into the cult, and while they learn that the masks are occupied by men they believe that Odo is associated with the costume and that those who impersonate him are possessed of his spirit.

The Ibibio ancestors are represented by the Ekpo society, which appears at the yam harvest. The members wear wooden masks which are often highly carved and decorated and have become famous for their intricate and often fearsome appearance. Every village had its Ekpo lodge, and non-members and women might be roughly handled and injured during Ekpo appearances. Membership of Ekpo and office holding conferred high social status. A comparable society was Idiong, connected principally with funerals and dramatic performances with figures and masks.

A fairly recent 'leopard society', Ekpe Owo, has appeared, but not much is known about it. It was suspected of murders where the bodies of victims were found marked as if they had been mauled by leopards. Similar societies have been known in the Ivory Coast and Liberia. These leopard societies were often dangerous, anti-social, and much feared by ordinary people. They were sometimes cannibalistic. The members of the societies in the Ivory Coast

[3] C. K. Meek, *Law and Authority in a Nigerian Tribe*, p. 66ff.

met in the heart of the forest in secret clearings. A peculiar drum note called the members, and as soon as this was heard all non-members shut themselves up in their houses. Candidates for admission were made to drink narcotics, to reduce them to a highly suggestible state. The chief principle of the initiatory rite seems to have been the acted birth of the neophyte from a leopard mother. He was put under a leopard skin, with iron claws in his hands and dragged from under the tail, as in a birth. At the meetings human victims were killed, and sometimes eaten, and the new member was charged with the duty of providing a victim for the next meeting. He would generally choose a member of his own family, ostensibly so as to avoid vengeance from another clan. But it may be noted that witches are often said to have no power of killing those to whom they are not related and only eat members of their own clan. Whether the whole conception of witchcraft, eating of souls, and meetings at night, which now seem to be only imaginary, derives from ancient leopard societies, is a question that deserves investigation. We shall refer to this in a later chapter.

It is clear that the leopard societies are very different from the other secret societies that we have examined; the latter are mainly concerned with initiation and ancestral customs. Still, any secret society can be dangerous, if it gets out of hand. Meek, the anthropologist, says that the secret societies were often used for committing brutal judicial murders, they bullied and exploited women, and the Churches should continue to take a strong stand against them.[4]

BLOOD PACTS

A private secret association used to be made by means of blood pacts, of which the basis was the exchange of blood which thus provided an unbreakable link of blood relationship. This was an extension of the practice of having a 'best friend' who acted for a man in special rites, notably at funerals, shared his secrets, and helped him in trouble.

A story told in Dahomey says that the blood pact originated between a hunter and a forest spirit. The hunter is variously said

[4] Ibid. p. 79.

to have delivered the spirit, disguised as a deer, from death; or the spirit appeared suddenly to the hunter, exchanged blood with him, and then revealed to him forest secrets and the knowledge of herbs, whereby the hunter was able to make great medicines and become a famous doctor.

Several varieties of blood pact are related by Paul Hazoumé in his book on the subject.[5] The most common form, the main outline of which was followed in different regions, took place at night in the heart of the forest. The friends, men or women, knelt in a circle, completely naked, without even bracelets or rings. A ring was cut in the ground behind them, by passing a knife to each, from hand to hand behind the back, to the left. A hole was made in the middle of the circle and a human skull put beside it. Water, a snake's head, and various crushed leaves were put in the skull. The knife was passed round again and each person made a small cut on the back of the left hand, just above the thumb. The wound was dried with a piece of cotton which was thrown into the skull. After all had done this, the skull was passed round and everybody had a drink from the mixture. An oath of mutual fidelity was then sworn and disaster promised to the unfaithful, and the gods invoked as witnesses. A plentiful meal followed at which all revealed their plans.

Many notable persons entered into pacts with their allies, to ensure their fidelity. King Gezo of Dahomey made a pact with a Brazilian trader, Francisco da Souza, whom he rescued from a pot of indigo in which the trader was being soaked during the preceding reign. His successor, King Glele, made many pacts with his spies in enemy towns, to make sure that they could be trusted. On these occasions the king himself would rarely be present, but would be represented by a high official and symbolized by a royal staff placed between the contracting parties.

[5] *Le Pacte du Sang au Dahomey* (1937).

CHAPTER THIRTEEN

Diviners and Oracles

THE DIVINER seeks to interpret the mysteries of life, to convey the messages of the gods, to give guidance in daily affairs, and settle disputes, to uncover the past and to look into the future. He is not necessarily a priest, serving the shrine of a god, though he often is one. He is generally an expert in medicines and herbs, in addition to his work as a seer. The Yoruba say that their oracle god is the elder brother of Osanyin, the doctor's god, being thousands of years older and so the diviner knows all the herbalist's remedies.

Diviners accumulate a vast store of secret knowledge, and have a deep acquaintance with human nature. The diviner is the wise man of the village, and although his practices are open to abuse, in general his profession is honourable and highly respected. To him people go in all the crises of life, betrothals, marriages, before and at the birth of children, at the appointment of a chief or king, before a journey, in time of sickness, in time of loss or theft, and at any time for guidance and comfort.

The secrets of diviners are closely guarded, and it is difficult to tell the extent and manner of their knowledge. They maintain, and some serious writers believe them, that they have esoteric secrets of which modern science is ignorant. It is certain that they sometimes seem to gain knowledge of people's deeds, or the whereabouts of their lost or stolen goods, by methods which are not easily explicable. Some would say that they have secret agents to listen to village gossip and watch suspected people; others claim that they practise telepathy and have powers of prevision.

THE IFA GEOMANTIC SYSTEM

In West Africa divining is most highly developed among the Yoruba with their divining system called Ifa. This was adopted by the Dahomeans, perhaps in the last century under the name of

Fa, and has become as popular with them as with the Yoruba.[1] The Bini and some of the Ibo also use this system or some variation of it, and one of the two major systems of Nupe divination, Eba, also resembles part of the Yoruba system.

The Ifa system is connected with a god called Orunmila, 'Heaven knows salvation', who is said to have been a child of the supreme God and to be his deputy and oracle on earth. Ifa is sometimes called the system and Orunmila the divinity. But there are also records of myths which represent Ifa as a historical figure, a man of great wisdom and skilled in medicine, who founded the sacred city of Ile-Ife. In the olden days, it is said, the gods were often hungry and sacrifices were few, and it was the demoniac Eshu who showed Ifa the system of divining by which he could both benefit men through foretelling the future for them and also help the gods through the thank-offerings that men would make to them in return. There is a great body of stories connected with Ifa in which nearly all the gods occur, and which is a fund of information on Yoruba religion that is still only partially recorded. This shows the importance of Ifa as intermediary between men and the gods, and therefore he is connected with all of them.

Nearly all family houses in time past have had shrines of Ifa or Orunmila. These would be usually on a shelf in a corner of the room, and would consist of a bowl or covered dish holding at least sixteen palm nuts used in the process of divination, some cowrie shells, and some carved sticks. A grove in the bush would be used for special consultations of the oracle and receiving initiates. Still today the hold of Ifa is very great, few pagans dispense with this attractive means of discovering the unknown, and many Christians and Muslims find it hard to relinquish the practice.

The diviner is called a 'father of mysteries' (baba'lawo in Yoruba; bokonõ in Fǫn) and so he is very properly called a seer. The diviners hold a full consultation of Ifa every fifth day, the 'day of mysteries'. They generally dress in white or light blue robes and shave their hair.

There are two principal methods of Ifa consultation, according to the importance of the occasion. Both are based upon the same

[1] See the long and detailed study of Fa by B. Maupoil, La Géomancie à l'ancienne Côte des Esclaves.

principle of calculation. Basically the system of divination is a series of 256 figures or permutations, each with its own name, and these are worked out either by using sixteen palm nuts or by casting a string or chain of eight half nuts or shells.

The full or greater consultation is done on a small board or planchette. This may be rectangular or round, and the edges are often decorated with carvings of faces, snakes, tortoises, crocodiles, and divining cords. The Babalawo often makes a preliminary sacrifice to Eshu, then he puts the divining board on a cloth or mat and sprinkles it with powder or sand in which he will make the marks of divination. Two finely carved bell-sticks (*iṛọkefa*) made of ivory or wood may be laid beside the board and lifted up in invocation or tinkled to show that the consultation is beginning. China basins or calabashes containing palm nuts are put beside the board. There must be at least sixteen nuts, and usually there are several more.

The diviner sits in front of the board, perhaps bare to the waist, and sets aside two of the nuts to which sacrifices may be made invoking a successful consultation. Then he takes the remaining sixteen in both hands, puts them against his breast and makes a further invocation. Then with all sixteen nuts in his right hand he 'beats' or passes them rapidly to his left hand. If two nuts are left in the right hand, he marks one stroke on the powdered board. If one is left, he marks two strokes. If none are left, or more than two, then the turn must be begun again. He continues passing the nuts from one hand to the other, and making marks according to the remainder, until on his board there is a figure of eight single or double strokes, arranged in two columns of four each.

The figures are usually marked with the middle finger of the right hand for one stroke; with the middle and forefingers for two strokes. They are written on, or pushed on to, the board from the bottom upwards, and the right column may be written before the left, and the second stroke above the first. Only when the four figures are complete is the second column begun, to the left of the first, and again written from the bottom upwards. This is a kind of writing, or mathematics; but as the diviner is usually illiterate the way in which he marks the strokes may or may not be significant.

A diagram will show the simplest figure, where all eight swoops have left two nuts, marked in two columns of one stroke for each turn:

I   I

I   I

I   I

I   I

This is called a double figure (*meji*), as both sides are the same. The name for a figure of four single strokes is *ogbe*, hence the double figure given above is *ogbe meji*.

As there are in each column four strokes, any of which may be single or double, it is clear that sixteen combinations are possible on one side (4 × 4). A little calculation will show that there are 256 possible permutations for the two sides taken together (16 × 16).

In describing the patterns of the Ifa system it is customary in most books to write identical pairs of columns, calling them 'two' (*meji*). All sets of double marks would be *oyeku meji* (see diagram facing). But this is rather confusing for it tends to give the impression that the throws of nuts always give two identical columns, whereas in reality this is quite rare, and almost always the two columns are made up of different sets of marks. If the two sides are different, the names are combined, as *ogbe-oyeku*.

Because of this we shall only give here each of the sixteen possible varieties of marks which can occur in one column. But it must be understood that there are always two sides, the final pattern must always be a double figure, of two columns, each usually different from the other. To write the full set of 256 possible combinations would be too long, and unnecessary, as the following diagram gives the basic signs.

The order in which the figures are given varies from place to place, except that the first two and the last two are usually the same. The names of the figures are Yoruba, and in Fǫn and other Ewe systems they come from the same roots, though some of the consonants and vowels may change (Fǫn changes r to l). Other lists may be seen in the writings of Herskovits, Spieth, Dennett, and Lucas. The names now written were given to me by the chief Babalawo of Ibadan.[2]

[2] *Religion in an African City*, pp. 34–5, and later revised.

1. I ogbe	2. II oyeku	3. II iwori	4. I odi
I	II	I	II
I	II	I	II
I	II	II	I

5. I iroshu	6. II ǫwara	7. I bara	8. II ǫkarã
I	II	II	II
II	I	II	II
II	I	II	I

9. I ogunda	10. II ǫsa	11. II ika	12. II oturupǫ̃n
I	I	I	II
I	I	II	I
II	I	II	II

13. I oture	14. I irete	15. I ǫsɛ	16. II ofũ
II	I	II	I
I	II	I	II
I	I	II	I

When the set of eight marks, two columns, of figures has been obtained by casting the nuts and marking on the board, the great point is the interpretation of the scheme. It is here that the skill and memory of the diviner are displayed.

Each figure represents a chief (*odu*) or section. There are 256 Odu, according to the basic number of combinations, and some diviners claim that there are 4096 sentences and stories connected with them (256 × 16). Each Odu is characterized by a short sentence or proverb, which is often quite obscure to the inquirer and so light is shed upon it by a story which is traditionally attached to it. Finally the application is made by the diviner to the needs or requests of the inquirer.

The conjunction of two Odu is regarded as favourable or sinister according to the traditional proverb or legend which the diviner has by heart. This gives an oracular reply, and undoubtedly impresses the inquirer by its mysterious nature, and then its application to his needs. Since many of the Odu contain myths of the gods, the practical application may be to make a sacrifice to the god named and so avert a threatened danger or obtain his protection for a project in hand.

The lesser form of consultation is called Ọpẹlẹ (in Yoruba; *ogumaga* in Fọ̃n). The Babalawo does this every day and on all minor occasions.

Here the diviner uses a cord or chain which has four half-nuts, often mango nuts split in two, at each end of the cord, making eight in all on the cord which is two or three feet long. Each half nut is rounded on one side and flat or hollow on the other, convex and concave. As the cord is held in the middle, with four nuts on either side, a figure can easily be made similar to that marked on the divining board after casting the palm nuts in the longer Ifa system. A concave surface of each nut equals one stroke, and a convex surface two strokes. Thus with one throw of the cord a figure of eight signs is produced, equal to that made in the longer method with greater elaboration.

The consultant gives a penny, or franc, and puts it on the ground. The diviner takes a cowrie shell, places it beside the penny, and then adds a nut to them. The inquirer takes these three into his hands and whispers over them what he wants to obtain. The diviner puts the Ọpẹlẹ cord on the three objects, covers them with a little cloth bag, then takes up his wooden or iron divining bell and invokes the spirit of the oracle, saying: 'In the morning, or in the evening, hear what he has said.' Or he may call up various spirits: 'Spirits of the east, spirits of the west, spirits of the sea, spirits of the north, agree with all I say.'

The diviner takes up the Ọpẹlẹ cord by the middle, four nuts hanging on either side; he twangs it, holding both ends, or swings it round and may say: 'You come from Ile-Ife, as you do there so do here; if in truth you come from the house of Ife, tell the secrets of this man's heart.' He then throws the cord on the ground, or on a mat or cloth, and according to the way the eight nuts lie so he has his Odu and proceeds to interpret it as before.

Further manipulations may be done. The diviner takes up the penny, and the consultant puts the cowrie in one hand and the palm nut in the other. The diviner then says that Ifa will decide whether the cowrie or the nut are in question. He casts the cord again; if a majority of concave sides are on his left, the left hand of the consultant must be opened, if not, the right. If the left hand holds the cowrie it may be taken as a sign of misfortune or danger, to avert which the inquirer must bring articles of sacrifice to the diviner, and the former receives some leaves and sand from the divining board with which to wash. The diviner may even make a small rough Eshu of clay and put it in a calabash; a goat's blood is poured on it and it is given to the consultant to throw into the bush to get rid of the bad luck, or he may put it at a cross-roads, to prevent any evil coming that way; such objects are often seen at cross-roads.

The Ifa system of divination is used at all the important occasions of life. At the birth of a child the oracle is consulted. The Fǫn go into considerable detail at birth and adolescence, to find out what god the child is to worship and later to work out his horoscope.

Before the arrival of the diviner at the child's home, the head of the family brings out a big calabash which contains the palm nuts of the Ifa of each member of the family, each in separate calabashes or basins. The diviner puts his divining board (opǫn Ifa) on a mat or cloth on the ground. From a sack he brings out various stones and bones, which represent the gods and spirits of the dead. A young child of the same sex as the baby sits by the diviner. He divides the bones into two groups and takes one in each hand while the officiant turns his back. The Babalawo then casts the Ifa nuts and tells the youth to open one hand, according to the figure obtained. That one is set aside. Then the same operation is repeated, until all the bones have been gone through and there is only one left. That one represents the god whom the child must serve. The baby is given two palm nuts to wear round his neck.

In adolescence, at ten or twelve years of age, a Fǫn child is given eighteen palm nuts in a sack, in exchange for the two that he wears round his neck. Fowls and drinks are given to the diviner, who prays for the boy and offers one of the fowls to Eshu.

At about twenty or twenty-two years of age an adult Fǫn should obtain his life horoscope, though this is often delayed for years. Considerable offerings are needed for this, as fees and for sacrifice to Eshu and Ifa; at least one goat and sixteen fowls. At dusk the man goes into the bush with his eyes blindfolded, guided by the diviner and elders. A mat is spread out and the board, bells and bowls of Ifa are displayed. Often the consultant himself is shown how to change the nuts from one hand to the other, under the guidance of the diviner, and thus he works out his own life horoscope. The figure which is obtained on the board is engraved on to a small triangular piece of calabash, about two inches by three, and it is put with the divining nuts into a cloth bag, four or five inches square, and fastened by a string bearing several cowries. The consultant carefully guards this horoscope in a small covered calabash, which is a symbol of heaven and earth. If he has a big house a special room may be set aside for Ifa, or a corner of the living-room will be used for a shelf on which the calabash rests. If at any time he needs to be reminded of the interpretation of the horoscope, or to discover if what is happening to him is part of his fate, he may go to any diviner who will read the signs of Ifa according to the traditional Odu.

Women do not normally consult Ifa, unless they are childless and are advised to do so by the diviner. Instead of the male collection of eighteen nuts and a piece of calabash, women may have seven nuts given to them which are kept in a straw bundle and may be worn wrapped in the waistcloth.

The choice and training of diviners varies in different places. The office is often hereditary, but there are not usually special lineages exclusively associated with it, and any adult male who feels drawn and can undertake the training may become a diviner. We said in an earlier chapter that the training of a diviner, at least among the Fǫn, is not so carefully organized as that of priests and devotees of the gods. Yet both here and in Yoruba country the training of a diviner is usually three years, and sometimes up to seven. But it is private training with an older diviner.

The novice pays the diviner who is training him fowls, goats, and money, according to the length of service. During the whole of the apprenticeship he is considered as the diviner's son, 'son of the cult', or 'son of mystery'. He works in the fields, as well as learning the occult secrets. At the beginning of training the diviner takes two palm nuts, sacrifices a fowl on them, and gives them to the novice after rubbing them in palm oil, and he smears his body with the same oil. They represent his Ifa.

In the first year the novice learns the names of the Odu and their signs. In the second year he learns many of the proverbs and stories associated with them. In the third year he learns to practise divination and all the subsidiary rites of the cult.

At the end of the novitiation all the diviners of the district gather together. The novice has to provide a number of goats, fowls, and drinks. The party goes to a grove and there the novice learns the final secrets of Ifa. He draws up his own horoscope, which is said to show his future success as a diviner. He is told that Qrunmila is his god, yet he will worship other gods as well, for Ifa is the spokesman of them all. The initiation is said to be crowned with an ordeal of fire, in which the new Babalawo takes flames from a lamp into his hands, without his skin being burnt.

The fully-fledged diviner prays to Qrunmila every day, ringing his bell and calling upon the gods. Every day he throws the Qpẹlẹ, to learn whether the day will be favourable, and he performs rites and makes sacrifices if the omens are against him. Normally he prays alone, but on the evening of the first appearance of the new moon he calls his family together and prays for them all, and they respond.

The Ifa divining system, or some variation upon it, is used in west and east Nigeria, Dahomey, Togo, and parts of the seaboard of Ghana. The Akan generally do not use Ifa, though they have simpler ways of consulting oracles, some of which are mentioned below.

The complicated Ifa system, with its calculations of at least 256 figures, and mythical interpretations that are given of them, suggests derivation from eastern sources. Divination is, of course, worldwide, but there are many varieties of method and some may have no relationship to others. Some European astrologers, whose systems are now being introduced to Africa, have somewhat similar markings to Ifa, but they are usually arranged under the twelve signs of the zodiac, though occasionally sixteen houses are mentioned. The chief concern of European, and much Eastern, divination is the interpretation of the stars, mythical astrology, but there is no trace of this in the Ifa system.

Muslim diviners in Nigeria often use a pattern similar to Ifa, making marks on a board covered with sand but apparently at random and not using palm nuts to help in arriving at a pattern. The names given to the pattern are drawn from local and Islamic lore. Further north in the Sudan a popular and influential book, by Sheikh Mohammed Es Zenati, taught some of the main principles of notation and interpretation of sixteen signs, which are attached to persons of Islamic tradition.[3] In Senegal some diviners connect the signs with the planets; others have parchments with rough sketches of the human body, with sixteen figures placed in different parts of the body; and yet others use a square figure divided into four triangles, each containing four of the figures, and perhaps representing the elements of fire, earth, water, and air.

Whether the Yoruba, who have by far the most highly developed divining system in West Africa, received it from Muslim peoples to the north is not certain. The Yoruba have certainly been more influenced by Islam than any other peoples we have been dealing with, except the Nupe, but that influence is fairly recent, not going back much before the beginning of the nineteenth century. Yet according to Dahomean tradition the Ifa system was introduced to them from Yoruba country during the reign of King Agadja (1708–28). But even such apparently precise information may not be as exact as it seems; it is common to credit some achievement to a popular king, and there are signs that the system was known on the coast before then. A tradition at Oyo was that the Ifa system was introduced in the reign of the ninth Alafin, Onigbogi, some hundreds of years ago.[4] Another tradition says it came from the Nupe country, but the Nupe have nothing so complex today.

One of the most interesting traces in the history of this kind of divination appeared in the extreme west of Ghana in 1714. Father Loyer, an early missionary, described a diviner at his consultation: 'He then throws sawdust of boxwood colour on the little board that he puts down, after which he takes the nuts from out of his cup where he had put them, and moves them about again in his

---

[3] See *Bulletin du Comité d'Études historiques et scientifiques de l'A.O.F.*, XIV.27–136.

[4] Johnson, *The History of the Yorubas*, p. 32.

hand for a time and makes marks with his middle finger on the powder.'[5]

The Ifa type of divination has been practised in West Africa for centuries, and its hold is still deep. Whatever its origins, and these are virtually unknown, it has become thoroughly naturalized. No doubt in the course of its development it has become highly complex, especially among the Yoruba and Fǫn. The names of the Odu do not correspond, I believe, with any known Islamic tradition, though there is room for research into the meanings of the names of the Odu. They have become attached to the myth-ology of various gods, as well as including many more secular stories. Some Dahomean diviners connect each figure with one of the gods of their pantheon: Mawu, Sapata, Gu, and so on. They are thus brought into the tightly knit scheme of Dahomean theology and the naturalization is complete.

OTHER DIVINING METHODS

The Nupe have two methods of divination, both of which have points of resemblance to the Yoruba system and so deserve brief mention. The Eba system is older, now much forgotten and degenerate, and seems to date from the time before the Nupe kingdom became dominated by Islam. It resembles more the Ǫpẹlẹ divination method. The diviner uses eight cords, each of which has four half-shells. They are picked up two at a time from the ground, one in each hand, and then thrown down again. This is done four times, to use all the cords. The pattern then made on the ground by the cords is interpreted by a key of eight pieces of gourd, each of these has marks, called houses. The interpretation seems to depend on similarities between the pattern of the cords and the marks on the gourds, but this appears to be rather erratic and arbitrary. Incantations are made during the throws of cords which refer to proverbs and sayings, and are supposed to give a clue to the patterns of cords.

The second Nupe system is called Hati and is done in the sand, often by Muslim teachers. Sand is smoothed on to a mat or cloth and signs are marked on it with the tips of the fingers. In the middle

[5] Quoted in Labouret and Rivet, *Le Royaume d'Arda*, p. 28.

is the 'sign of the king', which resembles an Arabic figure, and a
key sign is made for the day of the week. Then the sand is wiped
clean again and the real divining begins. Small dots are marked in
the sand from the left bottom to the top right-hand corner,
apparently at random. Sixteen dotted arcs are made one under
another, in sets of four. There is some wiping out, and the final
figure has sixteen signs in four rows. These sixteen signs are again
called houses; the names given to them are in Arabic or a degenerate form of it. The interpretation varies, and sometimes the signs
are connected with the stars, or with the elements of fire, air,
water, and earth. There are written keys in Arabic which most
Muslim interpreters use, and they then apply the answers to the
needs of the client.[6]

Bini diviners use the full Ifa method of geomancy, or the shorter
cord which they call apɛlɛ. A variant on this which is very popular
is the use of four strings each holding four shells with a concave
and convex side to each. According to the way these fall the interpretation is given. Diviners also use small images of human beings,
animals, and objects, which they throw on to plates and give the
answer according to the pattern which is made.

The Ibo diviner (dibia) uses four cords to which fish bones are
attached, or two strings with four pieces of calabash attached to
each. The cords are held in each hand and thrown on the ground
in front of the diviner, and the interpretation depends on how the
pieces fall, whether face up or down. Each combination suggests a
recognized topic. If the right string leaves the top piece of calabash upwards and the other three face down, the topic is a woman.
If the bottom piece is upwards and the other three down then the
matter is urgent. Having determined the meaning of the first
string, the diviner then turns to the second and selects a meaning
which fits the first; perhaps the woman in the first pattern is unhappy in the second. This interpretation is one given by a diviner
of the Jukun people of the Benue region, northern neighbours of
the Ibo, and whose divination system is closely similar.[7]

Divination by means of a cord with objects attached to it, then,
is one of the commonest methods in West Africa. A variant of this

[6] Nadel, *Nupe Religion*, ch. 2.
[7] C. K. Meek, *A Sudanese Kingdom*, pp. 326–7.

is used in Ashanti, in the method called Nkontwima. This consists of seven strings of antelope hide, fastened with beads, cowries, teeth, and horns. In inquiries or ordeals people sit round the dealer in Nkontwima, who draws out the strings at random. The person before whom one particular string, called *tonto*, falls is the person sought or guilty.

Another Ashanti form of consultation is *nsuo ayaa*. A pot or bowl is filled with water, leaves, cowries, and marbles, and a sacrifice is offered. This is operated by a priestess who stirs the mixture and invokes *nsuo ayaa*. When the god responds to the invocation, she takes the spoon out of the mixture and the will of the god is determined by the nature of the object picked up by the spoon.

Such practices are widespread in West Africa. Water-gazing and the manipulation of nuts and shells in water are often met with. Mirror-gazing is frequently practised, to discover some unknown thing or person, or to pick out witches. Entrails of fowls are read by priests and their apprentices. An initiate is taught during his training how to read omens from sacrifices. The colour of the kidney is often thought to be particularly important, and if it is black that is a bad omen and the operation must be begun over again.

It would be as difficult to list or describe all methods of divination, as it would be to describe all European or Indian fortune-telling and horoscope manufacture. These latter charlatans send their advertisements and products, at high prices and with much deception, to flood the African market today. The difference between the traditional African diviner and the modern commercial African charlatan, or the European quack, is that the Babalawo is usually a wise man, with a deep knowledge of character and a concern for the individual and public good. The Babalawo is a respected counsellor, who settles palavers and gives advice in big undertakings. His counsels rarely have the superficial character of the modern Western quack, who works on a purely commercial basis, and usually sees and knows nothing of his consultant or correspondent, and cares even less for his hopes and fears.

The replies and predictions of the Babalawo and other traditional diviners may be borne out by events; miscalculations are easily forgotten and successes are acclaimed. Although the Ifa and some other systems appear somewhat rigid and mechanical, the possibility of uncanny combinations exercises a fascination upon diviner and inquirer alike.

SÉANCES

A much older and rival method to the Ifa divination is the spiritualistic séance. The attempt to get in touch with the dead and obtain a message from them is perhaps as old as intelligent man. A classic example is the 'medium' (not a witch) of Endor who professed to call up Samuel for Saul. So in West Africa it is believed that the soul of a dead person may be consulted anywhere from the hour of death, regardless of the place of death. The Fǫn hold that souls can be consulted with special success at Oyo in Nigeria and at the mouth of the river Adan in Ghana.

The simple offerings made at the graves of the dead imply belief in their continued existence and their willingness to help their relatives. In Porto Novo old women often act as intermediaries with the dead on behalf of their families. The supplicant stands or kneels outside the small hut which contains iron standards as altars, and the aunt or grandmother kneels inside; there is just room for her. The bamboo matting that serves as door to the hut is rolled up and the old lady bares herself to the waist in respect. She breaks kolas and puts them in front of the standards, pours water on the ground as a drink, and puts yellow maize flour and palm oil on the standards, which are blackened and clotted with previous offerings. She presents the special requests, to the dead in general, or to a named ancestor. They are asked for help and for 'fresh air'. To get a reply from the dead the same method is used as in offerings to the gods; cowrie shells and kola nuts are thrown on to the grave or in front of the symbols of the dead, an uneven number or a majority falling convex would be taken as a sign of disfavour.

More specific séances, to make the dead speak, may be held in a house, or behind a screen or in front of the shrine of a god. The 'medium', the person who is intermediary between man and the dead and who professes to speak in their name, may work openly or prefer to be covered by a mat or blanket. One that I observed in Yoruba Dahomey worked openly in a room. He took an ordinary cooking-pot and put it upside down with its mouth on the ground. Four or five sprays of leaf from a nearby tree were plucked by the medium, and held together with two stones. The stones being wrapped in the leaves, they were rubbed on the pot in a circular clockwise motion. This circular movement was continued throughout the operation, the leaves wearing through and scraping on the pot and making a rumbling noise. The medium soon began to speak in a low tone, calling up the spirit by name. A murmur was gradually distinguishable, apparently coming from the ground. The medium interpreted this mumbling in his own voice, though the mumbling sound seemed to come from his throat even when his lips were not moving. He explained to the inquirer what the spirit needed, and what warning or promise he gave. This was really all the ceremony did, though there may often be longer and more complex consultations.

Ventriloquism, making sounds that seem to come not from the lips but from the belly (*venter*), or throwing the voice so that it appears to come from other people or things, is a worldwide practice and is well known in West Africa. Yoruba followers of the god of medicine, Ọsãnyĭn, often practice ventriloquism and claim to get messages from inanimate things. I have observed several of these; sometimes they claim to have a spirit in a little bag which they carry and from which squeaking noises seem to come, or they may make answers appear to emerge from the altar of their cult before which they crouch. Their chief symbol is an iron bar with a bird on it, and this bird may be supposed to talk.[8]

Some diviners go into a trance, in which they become apparently unconscious. On return to their senses they report what they have seen in the spirit world. Others put an assistant into a hypnotic state by washing his face with various medicines. In this trance state the assistant tells what he sees in the occult regions, but on regaining consciousness he has no knowledge of what has passed. Unless the proper medicine is applied, it is said that he may not regain full use of his faculties. Many seers claim to be able to apply medicines to the eyes, by the use of which those long dead may be seen, as well as fairies and other spirits. Such mediums

[8] *Religion in an African City*, p. 36.

declare what the dead require and what sacrifices should be made to please them.

A common method of getting a message from one recently dead is by 'carrying the corpse'. This is done to find out from it whether death is due to natural processes or the evil deeds of an enemy. Some peoples have no conception of any natural death or accident; 'An enemy hath done this thing.' I have seen a procession of devotees of Nana Buku leaving the village to consult the dead outside. It was headed by a woman carrying a white fowl in the left hand and a brush in the right. Then came three female devotees carrying staves. A rolled mat containing the nails and hair of the deceased and wrapped in a blue cloth was carried on the shoulders of two women. This was the 'corpse'. Other devotees followed bearing the characteristic long brushes of Buku, of red-dyed raffia, the handles studded with cowries. With these they flicked the path as they went, singing a low dirge. Outside the village the mat was asked whether its owner had died well; if well, the bearers of the mat advance; if badly, they retreat. In the latter event, an inquest would be opened at once.

In many places corpses are carried round the village, or they used to be, though a mat may be substituted if the practice is kept up today. The bearers often say that they are moved against their will, and they may stop and point at some person as guilty, even when he is closely connected with themselves and it would be in their interest to protect him. It is said that there is an irresistible force in the corpse, by which the dead man impels the bearers and makes his will prevail.

ORACLES

The Ifa and other methods of divination, and the spiritualistic séance of consulting the dead, are oracles in that they believe that the god or departed spirit speaks to men by these means. There are other oracular methods and some famous oracles in West Africa.

An interesting oracular method is used by the priest or priestess of Nana Buku in Dahomey. A mixture is prepared from the bark of two trees, one male and the other female. These are always collected during the night, and there is a taboo of eating palm oil on the journey for the person who gathers them. The priest faces the shrine which is divested of its usual straw covering. A tiny metal standard is fixed in the ground in other cults or away from the shrine. The priest sits on a stool on a mat. An assistant brings the bark of the trees in a sack and two small grindstones, some water, sapodilla nuts, cowries, and cocks. After grinding down some bark into a red powder the priest touches the head of a cock, which is held by an acolyte, with a cowrie which is presented to the shrine and then thrown aside. The same is done with a nut, and with a small gourd in which the powder was mixed with water. The assistant holds the head of the cock back and its beak open, and the priest pours the mixture down its throat. If the bird vomits the mixture and takes no harm, the person concerned or accused is innocent. If the cock struggles and dies, guilt is held to be proved. It is said that a different paste may be substituted which mixes less easily, and even that the acolyte can dexterously break the bird's neck as the poison is being poured in.

A famous oracle which has come from Ghana in recent years is Nana Tongo, known elsewhere as Atinga. Rattray described a visit to the home of this oracle in the Tong Hills of the Northern Territories of Ghana in 1928.[9] Here was a shrine of the spirit of the earth, Tong, of the Talense people. For various reasons this spirit became very popular and people travelled from all over Ghana to tell their troubles to the spirit. The shrine was in a deep cave, and as people shouted their troubles into it an echo, or sometimes a long wail, emerged. Before long the powers of Tong were claimed as a cure for witchcraft and priests who bought its powers travelled far and wide claiming to cure witchcraft. The movement spread rapidly through Ghana, Togo, Dahomey, and Nigeria. It came to be known first as Nana Tongo and then by corruption as Atinga, and under this name came to Nigeria where it caused such a stir that it was finally forbidden by the Government in 1951. The priests of Nana Tongo used an ordeal, like that of the fowl at the shrine of Buku described above. The person accused of witchcraft would have to take a fowl, together with gifts of money and gin, to the witch-hunters. The fowl's head would be partly severed and then it was set free to run about till it died. If it died with its breast upwards, the accused was innocent;

[9] *The Tribes of the Ashanti Hinterland*, pp. 361ff.

it fell in any other position then he was guilty. As it is unlikely for a dying fowl to fall on its back, guilt would usually be assumed. But the accused could have another try, on payment of more money, gin, and a fowl. This ordeal-oracle became very popular, and many people were tried and convicted of witchcraft on this lack of evidence.

Some towns have famous oracles; such is Doumé in Dahomey where the main shrine of Buku is found, and Siari in Togo. At the town of Krachi in Togo there is a popular oracle called Dente. Here people come to consult the oracle who is said to live in a cave in the forest. A priest sits in the entrance to the cave, which is covered with cloths. All the consultants must sit with their backs to the cave and offerings are passed outside by the priest. There is an assistant within who gives the messages of the god.

Caves are favourite places for oracles, probably because of the echo. At Abeokuta the cave under the rock is said to produce a low singing sound in the heat of the evening. In Northern Nigeria there are caves with rock-gongs and wall paintings which are used, or were in the past, for religious ceremonies. But one of the most famous oracles was that of Aro Chuku, in the territory of the Aros, a section of the Ibo people in Eastern Nigeria. The Aro Chuku oracle became notorious in the last century because of its use in the slave-trade by the owners of the oracle, and its organization of other oracles for the same purpose. There were other oracles such as the Agballa, the Igwe, and Ogba in Ibo country which were subordinated to Aro Chuku. A writer of the time described some of these oracles and gave the conditions necessary for their success: a quiet place far from main roads; natural features to inspire a sense of dread, such as caves, valleys or groves; a system of spies or travellers to get to know local disputes and have them referred to the oracle, and a secret system for disposing of victims of the oracles. The victims would be said to have been 'eaten' by the oracle, but would have been smuggled away through the back of the cave to be sold into slavery.[10]

The oracle of Aro Chuku, called Ubinokpabe or 'Long Juju', received visits from pilgrims from all parts of Ibo country and

[10] S. R. Smith, quoted in K. O. Dike, *Trade and Politics in the Niger Delta*, p. 39. note.

beyond. At the height of the organization pilgrims would have to go through agents of the oracle in different villages, to learn the taboos of the oracle and pay fees. On arrival the disputants were taken to the mouth of the cave and the priest told the god the stories of the inquirers, or disputants to a quarrel, and the reply of the god came out in a muffled voice. There might be heavy damages to pay, or one of the litigants would be seized for the god. Visitors always took back water from the sacred stream at the cave and used it as medicine for themselves and sick friends. Sand from the river-bed might also be taken home and used in setting up a local shrine of Chuku. The organization of the oracle was destroyed by the Government in 1901, but visitors may still go to the cave and stream and pray to Chuku there.[11]

[11] C. K. Meek, *Law and Authority in a Nigerian Tribe*, pp. 44ff.

CHAPTER FOURTEEN

Charms and Magic

DOCTORS AND MEDICINE

PRIESTS AND diviners are generally also expert 'doctors' and administer 'medicine', a term that covers both natural healing agencies, leaves, roots, and the like, and also the invocation of magical or spiritual influences that are thought to be associated with them.

Although the word 'fetish' is now abandoned by serious writers in its indiscriminate application to all African religion, we have noted that some writers have suggested keeping it to describe the magically made objects which we now try to portray. For reasons given in the second chapter I think it best to drop this word 'fetish' altogether, and to use 'charm', or 'amulet', or 'medicine', words long familiar in English and which have not the disparaging connexions of 'fetish'. Certainly the use of magical medicines has been found in every country of the world and is not something peculiar to Africa. It is most important to get rid of the notion that African beliefs and practices are something queer and unusual.

There is no doubt that West African doctors have a wide knowledge of the properties of many roots, bark, leaves, and herbs. They are called 'observers of plants' in Fǫn and 'workers in roots' in Twi. They are certainly acquainted with some little-known poisons, and perhaps some that are still unknown to science. Some poisons may be given of which the effects are immediate, others produce no visible result for some time, and yet others imitate the symptoms of common diseases. These, of course, are used by evil doctors, and no honest man would think of giving them to his patients. A good doctor may treat a sick man for months or years. He may diagnose and prescribe medicines, and often lead to a complete cure.

Yet the 'medicines' given by a professional 'doctor' are often, perhaps principally, chosen for imagined or spiritual reasons.

Many medicines are selected because of some observed or fancied resemblance to the illness. A spotted leaf may be thought to be a good remedy for a spotted skin, and a sharp quill ought to act as protection against enemies of the soul. This is 'sympathetic magic' that acts on the principle of similarity, that 'like produces like', or sympathy, that there is a hidden affinity or relationship between the sick person and the remedy. Many such objects are part of the stock-in-trade of the medicine-man, and a glance round any market will show extraordinary collections of curious objects which are supposed to have curative or protective power: skulls, skins, bones, dried bats, dried lizards, porcupine quills, red parrots' feathers, twigs, leaves, horns, and so on.

The purely herbal use of ordinary leaves and plants as purges, sedatives, and plasters is often known to people outside the professional religious classes, and these may be of greater medicinal value in the physical sense. Christian converts distinguish between the legitimate use of herbal remedies, and the more magical or sympathetic use of the medicines applied by the medicine-man.

A young Agni woman when asked what leaves she used for treatment, said she did not know. But when she was in a trance she plunged into the forest and plucked unthinkingly those leaves that came to hand. When we asked her if all sickness of the same type did not require the same treatment, she replied that no two sicknesses were alike, but that they depended on the people who are sick.

With a profound belief in a spiritual universe, the doctor and the patient never look on the treatment as purely material. Power of thought and will in the doctor, faith in the patient—these are essential ingredients. In addition there is belief in the invisible efficacy of the remedy, provided the correct word is spoken over it or a true invocation made.

We may call this attitude 'magical', but the doctor's belief is not unreasoning, however strange to the scientific way of thinking. In fact he is a kind of scientist, in that he seeks to discover and use the laws of the universe, not only of inanimate nature but also spiritual forces. He believes that there are powers that are hidden, secrets that can be tapped; not necessarily that he can force these powers to a different purpose, but that there are laws which may be set in motion by the knowledgeable, as an electrician uses the forces of nature to light his house.

Much of the doctor's practice is 'sympathetic' magic, based on the belief that using part of a thing, or a copy of an object, may affect the whole. To wear the horn of an animal is thought to procure the protection of or against the whole beast. To destroy the nails or an image of an enemy will cause him to die. A violent pain must be cured by a painful remedy; hence painless and tasteless hospital medicines are often regarded with scepticism. From the scientific point of view this attitude may be misguided; it is not illogical.

The word for medicine and charm in Yoruba is *ogŭn*, and a good doctor is *onishegŭn*, who is the owner of medicine. In Ibo, medicine is *ọgwu* and the doctor or medicine-man is *dibia*. The Fọn call charms *gbo*, and the medicine-man or plant-observer is *amawato*. In Twi the charm is *sumãn*, and the doctor *sumãnkwafo* or *dunseni*.

THE POWER OF MEDICINE

One of the best studies of West African magical medicines is given by Dr Field.[1] She prefers to avoid the word 'magic', as it so often seems to mean miracle-working, and she prefers to speak of 'medicines', even when there is a spiritual rather than a material value attached to a remedy. Each medicine is believed to contain a power, or breath of life, and may be the abode of a spiritual being, a minor god or an impersonal force. Essential to the medicine is an outward form or apparatus through which it can work. In this it differs from a god who can act without any material form. The medicine will act for anyone, if he has observed the proper ceremonies in becoming the owner of the medicine, and observes its taboos carefully. So medicines can be bought and sold.

Medicines may be thought to have no power in themselves, or the power may be latent and only aroused through the action of a medicine-man. They are agents through which invisible beings or powers work.

Various kinds of uncleanness spoil the power of medicine.

---

[1] *Religion and Medicine of the Gã*, Part II, Chap. 3.

No medicine can keep its force if it is taken to a latrine; so a man may be murdered in a latrine, for his protective charms do not work there, and hence chiefs avoid public latrines. Another uncleanness is menstruation, and hence women are sent to a house outside the medicine-man's compound during their monthly period. It is blood that is powerful and can act for or against a medicine. The chief necessity for ensuring the working of good medicine is said to be upright character, and good medicines cannot be used for killing people.

To be efficient the medicine must not only be good in itself but it must please the patient's soul. One of the commonest causes of sickness is a troubled soul; anger, remorse, worry, witchcraft, all these can cause sickness. The soul may need food, and if it is very ill it may require another power to come and wrestle with it and so the medicine-man is called in. He may just say, 'your soul needs a fowl', which is then sacrificed. But more usually he gives some potent medicine for washing or drinking.

There are various ingredients which go into the preparation of an efficacious medicine. It is not just a simple herb, but must be prepared, mixed with other elements, and have a spell uttered over it. Herbs are essential ingredients to most medicines, and gods have particular herbs that they favour. Some animal content is also often needed, either a sacrifice or the blood, skin or fur is used. Alcohol is an important third ingredient, and rum is usually poured on to new medicine.

In the preparation of large or important magical medicines for protecting villages or chief's houses, a mixture of herbal, animal, and alcoholic elements is buried, and often the animal part will be buried alive. A doctor's compound usually has a mound of clay, stone, or cement, which is the burial-place of a potent protective medicine. A chief's house may have a cow buried outside it; in olden days it was a man.

Good descriptions of charms are found in a number of authors. It is difficult to clear a way through the great variety of such objects. I have tried to classify a number of them as private and public, protective, and offensive. Only general principles can be indicated.

PERSONAL PROTECTIONS

A most powerful protective charm, called by Rattray 'the greatest *sumãn* in Ashanti, the father and elder of all *sumãn*', can also be paralleled in Dahomey and Nigeria.[2] It is a small broom of palm fibres, of common type but with sacred objects attached to it. Clotted with blood and cowries, it may contain a piece of cloth from a menstruating woman, and has touched the tabooed objects avoided by its owner, and all manner of dirt. Its nature is vicarious, as it takes every evil upon itself. It has its own taboos, things that are 'hateful' to it. Fowls and sheep are sacrificed to it. Rattray gives the following prayer: 'Kunkuma, receive this fowl and partake; if any one poisons me [i.e. does something to make me break a taboo] let it have no power over me; if any one takes a gun and points it at me, do not let it have any power over me.'

The horns of wild or domestic animals are worn as protections, the strength being in the horn, like horse-shoes in Europe. Many people carry about such horns with them, or have them in their houses. The horn is stuffed with leaves and powders, and spells are uttered over it. Teeth of lions, crocodiles, snakes and other creatures, usually wrapped in leather, are often tied in pairs and worn round the neck or waist. Animal protections are thought to have the power of the animal in them.

Gun-shots wrapped up are worn against accidents or attacks. If the wearer is then killed by a gun-shot, his medicine-man will give out that the shot was not made of metal but of some other material, such as buffalo hide. This was said when King Gezo of Abomey was killed by a sniper on the way to Abeokuta. The new Okyenhene of Akim wore a cap, supposed to be able to avert all bullets aimed at him, at his father's funeral in 1944.

Blacksmiths' knives or shears are worn wrapped in leather or cloth, since being harder than other metals they should protect the owner against cuts and attacks with knives. Miniature knives that cannot be drawn out of their cases are worn to defend their owner against other weapons, and should prevent these from being drawn also. A bamboo whistle wrapped in goat's skin is a big

[2] *Religion and Art in Ashanti*, pp. 12–13.

charm; if the wearer is plotted against, he has only to whistle the name of the plotter and all is undone.

Very common are small objects, which are called amulets or talismans. A leather packet, often worn round the neck, may contain dried leaves, or texts from the Qur'ān. Muslim Hausa traders are great salesmen of these amulets. Girdles round the waist, or hidden out of sight, are protections against loose-living. Knots are often used, the knot having the virtue of tying or preventing a spell.

Another protective charm is a chewing-stick, decorated with red parrots' feathers. A cock is sacrificed over it by a diviner, and the stick is then chewed by its owner and the pieces spat out on the roof of his hut, every day for a week. This should prevent evil words and quarrels.

Iron bracelets or chains are used against sorcery. Similar objects may be used by a woman to help conception or prevent 'unpregnancy'. Weakly and malformed children, and especially those that are born after others have died (*abiku*), wear heavy and rattling bracelets and anklets to drive away evil spirits. Rings on the fingers and toes are meant to prevent bites of snakes and scorpions; small rings of twisted iron or copper imitate the snake. Practically everyone uses these.

The smaller charms are not worshipped, or sacrifices made to them generally. But they are prepared by and obtained from qualified men, and then sold in the market. They are not just any curious object that happens to strike the fancy. Even the rings have been heated in a pot of snake ashes, with the idea that a snake 'will not bite his own'.

PUBLIC PROTECTIONS

Most houses are protected by charms hanging above the doorway or stuck in the rafters. Quranic texts on strips of yellowed and dusty paper float above the heads of chiefs and notables who are far from being Muslims. Bundles of sticks or dripping bananas are fastened over Christian doorways. Half calabashes, or bowls wrapped in coloured cotton threads, hang over doorways; sometimes there is a large collection inherited from predecessors.

Many Yoruba and Ewe houses are protected by crudely carved

wooden figures with human features, that are fixed in the ground outside the door of the compound or tied by a chain. They have been put there on the advice of the Ifa oracle, and are house guards which should chain down any evil influence that arrives. Or there may be a simple chain cross the doorway, and of course the demonic Eshu is there. Other mounds are more modern and made of concrete with a chain embedded in them.

Nearly all fields are protected with charms; from a simple wisp of straw on a bamboo pole, to a complex packet of bones, skin, and leaves. Nobody would dare to steal from such a field, unless the thief had a stronger counter charm, in which case the owner prepares an even more deadly guardian. Similar packets of sticks, feathers, and bones protect houses, piles of stones, and other forms of property. The agricultural charms may represent the god who has been asked to bless the harvest.

Outside some Ewe and Yoruba villages may be seen a pole or branch which forbids entry by one path, or by half of the path, on alternate moons. The position of the pole is changed at each moon.[3]

Very common in West Africa is a protecting arch or small doorway, with a palm frond above it, on the path leading to a village or a sacred grove, or to the place where a religious ceremony is to be held. The arch is made of two poles, six feet or more in height, forked at the top where a cross-bar or palm-frond joins the two supports. The arch may be plain, but usually it has fastened to it bones, bamboo matting, a raffia basket, a dead or dying fowl. Elaborate bundles of this kind are placed to guard Ibo *mbari* houses and other sacred or important places.

OFFENSIVE CHARMS

The use of offensive charms is 'bad medicine' or 'black magic', and no reputable doctor will engage in it. Such practices are left for the evil magician or sorcerer, who works in secret and at night, and is much feared. He practises such things as 'tying up a man's shadow', 'pointing the finger', 'invocation shooting', and 'hot pot'.

One of the most feared Yoruba offensive medicines is Shigidi, which is personalized into a demon. The magician makes a rough

[3] E. G. Parrinder, *The Story of Ketu*, p. 77.

figure of clay and decorates it with cowrie shells and feathers. Then sacrifices and incantations are made to it, and the evil spirit is called up and sent out to do harm to the enemy. It may be offered its taboo food and told that the enemy has insulted it. Off it goes like the wind and chases the enemy back, running all the way and beating him unmercifully. So the story goes. But it is said that if the enemy has a more powerful charm, or offers Shigidi his favourite food, it will come racing back and take its revenge on its owner. It is said that human sacrifices were formerly offered to Shigidi.

A sorcerer will lay a trail of 'prepared' soil across the porch of an enemy's house or right round it. I have seen a man nearly die of fright on seeing what proved to be quite harmless soot. Salt and water is sprinkled on the charm to remove its ill effects. A similar trail of soil or sand is laid round a house and is believed to stop witches entering at night. A liana held down with pegs should catch hold of a witch and it is thought that even if she tears herself away she will leave a trail of blood.

Similarly, an amorous youth will put sand and a preparation of leaves across the doorway of an empty hut, then having sent to call the girl that he desires, she must be his if she crosses the threshold. Other love philtres are made of powdered bones, the name of the woman is uttered over them by the diviner and the woman will come, it is said. Some will rise up in the night as if forced by an invisible power. A jealous woman will seek a charm to make her rival impotent, and many witchcraft accusations are based on the belief that somebody has been using charms of this kind to prevent conception or kill babies.

Other charms are believed to make men invisible, so as to be able to enter huts unseen at night or even in broad daylight. Hunters are convinced that there are charms or spirits in the forest that can make them invisible. Other potions make people fall into a deep sleep, so that their houses may be burgled. In fact, every event has its excuse.

Nails, hair, spittle, sweat, urine, washing-sponges, and water, sleeping-mats, dirty clothes, are all intimately connected with the body, and so may be used in preparing offensive charms against the people to whom they belong. Therefore great care is taken in the disposal of these things, especially by chiefs, who always have an attendant by them with a spittoon, for magical not for hygienic reasons.

There is a great fear of evil magic, and direct poisoning is also common. Both suggestive means and the actual contamination of food and drink may be used. Estimates of the amount of poisoning are difficult to make; the idea of 'natural death' is strange, many people die without a doctor's post-mortem, and there are few registrations of deaths.

Good doctors make medicines to counteract the effects of harmful magic. The doctor who is called in to help a sick or frightened person may pretend to produce medicines that he claims have been buried about the house, or to remove worms or hidden charms from a baby's head or arms or belly. He may return the attack and prepare a medicine against the enemy, or content himself with a more powerful protective charm for his client. Sometimes attack is the best method of defence, though of course prevention is better than cure, and so most people provide themselves with charms against all possible ills.

MAGIC AND RELIGION

Priests and diviners are the principal makers of charms, for they have the necessary knowledge, which has been acquired from other doctors. There is always a reason why the object is thought to have magical power, and it must have been properly prepared by an expert.

Priests and seers are often hunters, and so they live in closer contact with nature than other men. They learn the ways of animals and the properties of trees and plants, their natural elements as well as all kinds of curious associations gathered round them. Many hunters are said to understand the languages of birds and animals and to be able to change into animal form. They are believed to be in contact with the spirits of the forest, the dryads or fairies. Some of these are believed to be experts in medicine and tell their secrets to hunters after making a pact with them.

Magic and religion are closely entwined in most countries and at many stages of religion. It is rare to find a priest such as the head of the temple of Tano who told Rattray: '*Sumãn* spoil the gods, but I cannot stop most priests using them.' Dr Edwin Smith, in an important lecture, maintained that the word 'magic' should no longer be used. He rejects the theory that magic came before religion, for there is no evidence of this, and also the theory that magic is elementary science. It may be experimenting with material forms, but the magician always believes that there is a spiritual power at work in his magic. Therefore magic is a form of religion, even if the lowest form.[4]

Dr Field draws a distinction between a medicine and a god by saying that 'the one is implored and the other commanded. I use this phrase reluctantly, as it is a well-known one and likely to be challenged as a cheap tag, but it does happen to fit the . . . situation as I have learnt to see it after many discussions with various priests and medicine-men.' A god is implored and has worship, a force is commanded and is medicine. The god has his own will, and his worshipper must pray 'thy will be done'; whereas medicine can be set to work if you know the secret. 'A priest can only pray; medicine-men can work wonders themselves.'[5]

These charms may be considered as in the lowest grade of religion, or as mere superstition, but they play a great part in the lives of millions of people. 'The labour and infinite pains, the prayers, the spells, the sacrifices, the abnegation, the heart-burnings, the disappointments, the hopes that are inseparably bound up in each one of these poor fetishes we can only imagine in part, but they should never be quite lost sight of when we are considering such objects, or judging the makers of them.'[6]

WITCHCRAFT

Witchcraft is believed in everywhere in West Africa, though with varying degrees of intensity. The belief has virtually disappeared from modern Europe, though it was widespread from the fifteenth to the seventeenth centuries under the stimulation of the Inquisition and professional witch-finders. With the growth of education in Europe, and the reduction of infant mortality to a

[4] *African Symbolism* (1952).
[5] M. J. Field, *Religion and Medicine of the Gã People*, pp. 80, 111.
[6] R. S. Rattray, *Religion and Art in Ashanti*, pp. 21-2.

very low level, the belief disappeared. For belief in witchcraft explained sudden death and misfortune to those who were ignorant of the causes of these things.

A special number of the journal *Africa* was devoted to a study of witchcraft in different parts of the continent (October 1935). At the outset Professor Evans-Pritchard, one of the greatest authorities on the subject, defined the sphere of study. 'There is much loose discussion about witchcraft. We must distinguish between bad magic (or sorcery) and witchcraft. Many African peoples distinguish clearly between the two and for ethnological purposes we must do the same. Witchcraft is an imaginary offence because it is impossible. A witch cannot do what he is supposed to do and has in fact no real existence. A sorcerer, on the other hand, may make magic to kill his neighbours.'

We have seen that 'black magic' is an offensive action, deliberately undertaken against the community and condemned as such. The bad magician is best called a sorcerer, he is usually male, and works in secret and alone, preparing evil poisons and charms. The witch is thought usually to be a woman, who has no poisons, and meets in company with other witches.

The most valuable studies of witchcraft in West Africa are those which Dr Field has done in various parts of Ghana for the last twenty-five years.[7] She says that 'its distinctive feature is that there is no palpable apparatus connected with it, no rites, ceremonies, incantations, or invocations that the witch has to perform. It is simply projected at will from the mind of the witch.' Again, although witches declare that they have eaten people, sharing different parts of the body, 'all this sounds rather like secret orgies of simple cannibalism. But it is not. It is only a manner of speaking. It is the victim's *kla* (soul) which is stolen and "eaten". The relatives of the victim agree that the physical body is never injured—except by the ravages of disease—and there is no evidence that it is ever disturbed after burial. . . . Not only is the eating at these feasts not a physical eating, but the gathering is not a physical gathering. The witch's *kla*—which maintains breathing a physical

---

[7] *Religion and Medicine of the Gã People* (1937) and *Search for Security* (1960). My own Penguin, *Witchcraft* (1958), deals with European and African witchcraft at length.

life—remains with her body on her bed and to ordinary eyes she is in normal sleep.'[8]

Evans-Pritchard says that 'a witch cannot do what he is supposed to do', that is eat somebody else's soul, and the medical point of view as Dr Field explains is that witches suffer from the 'obsession' that 'they have the power to harm others by thinking them harm'.

Very likely many people accused or confessing to witchcraft suffer from nervous complaints, they hide or imagine evil thoughts under a calm exterior. Dr Field's latest book is by far the best, and in fact practically the only, study of witches from the psychological point of view. There is a great deal of neurosis, hysteria, and psychic maladjustment, and all these contribute to the belief in witchcraft.

The confessions of witches are extraordinary and are often taken as proof that the accusations are true. Witches often confess to having 'killed' members of their own family, even their children, whom they would not normally hate. I heard an old woman admit, on accusation, to having killed eleven people. Yet she was a poor old thing, with little sign of ability to do much harm. But is a confession proof of action? Today we have learnt only too sadly, from Nazi and Communist forced confessions, that people will admit to the most unlikely things. 'Confession is good for the soul', and some people like doing it. It is said that for every reported murder the police receive confessions from a number of people who had nothing to do with it.

Dr Field records confessions from some of the five hundred stories she listened to. People admitted to killing their babies, and eating them. Others said they were still devouring a sick man. Yet the man could be seen, sick it is true but not eaten, lying on his bed. It was not the material body that was eaten, but 'the soul of the flesh'. In other words, any wasting disease, mysterious complaint, or unexplained malady such as polio is put down to witchcraft. And as for the babies, infant mortality is very high. If a child dies, the husband accuses the wife. She does not know what has happened, perhaps in her sleep her soul fed on the baby's soul. Or she is a second wife in a polygamous household, with no

[8] *Religion and Medicine of the Gã People*, pp. 135, 141ff.

children herself, or a mother-in-law past the age of bearing. A child of a co-wife dies, and the other wife or mother is accused. Under beating she confesses. Of what value is that? What is needed to cure witchcraft is increased child welfare and hospital treatment for expectant and nursing mothers, so that the infant mortality rate goes down to the lowest possible level.

Witches are called *ǫbayifǫ, aze, ajɛ, amozu,* in Twi, Fǫn, Yoruba, and Ibo. Some people use the term 'witch' for both men and women, but in most places women are believed to be in the majority. Dr Nadel, who also made a valuable study of witchcraft among the Nupe, says that some Nupe witches are men, but they are not so dangerous as the women, and the head of all Nupe witches is held to be a woman.[9] In the Atinga witch-hunts in Dahomey and Nigeria in 1950, in many villages only women were accused of witchcraft. Usually children are not accused of witchcraft, though a girl may be believed to inherit witchcraft from her mother and to have witchcraft latent within her.

Witches are said to be in league, and so witchcraft is a social affair. At night they are thought to leave their bodies asleep in their houses, while their souls fly off to a meeting. They may fly on the backs of birds or fireflies, or actually turn into owls, bats, or black cats. If the animal is killed it is thought that the real body of the witch will die at the same time. Witches fix spiders' webs across the doors of their houses so as not to be wakened while their souls are absent.

Witches are believed to meet in hollow or high trees, iroko, or baobab and the like. There they may sit naked or dance in a lewd fashion. As vampires they are thought to suck the blood or eat the soul of their victims. New members bring a victim, perhaps a child of their own family, and together they cook or eat the limbs raw. When they eat the heart or the liver the victim dies.

Do witches every really meet? In the Middle Ages in Europe there were many tales of witches going to their 'sabbath', to eat unbaptized babies, and investigation would prove that the witch was lying unconscious in a trance, or asleep, all the time. Yet when she came to her senses again, the witch would describe in detail the orgy which she believed she had attended. Learned judges

[9] *Nupe Religion,* Chapter 6.

decreed that the evidence of the confessions must be taken as valid, since in the nature of the case witchcraft was invisible, and so there could be no outside watcher of witches' meetings.

The importance of dreams in the interpretation of witchcraft is considerable. One of the commonest dreams is that of flying or leaping great distances. Psychologists today interpret this as due to a feeling of wellbeing and buoyancy. But people who take dreams literally will believe that they actually fly like birds. Also in dreams many hateful thoughts, which are repressed in conscious life, come to the surface, or adulterous and envious thoughts. On waking a man may well believe that he has been misbehaving, or quarrelling with other souls. A great deal of the belief in witchcraft is due to self-deception, suggestibility, and the power of thought. If everybody believes in witchcraft, then all evils will be blamed on it, and people will accept accusations of guilt.

WITCH-HUNTING

The witch-doctor is a respected figure in society. He is not a witch himself, though he may have special powers akin to witchcraft. But his task is to cure those who are bewitched and check the powers of the witches. At least this was so traditionally; modern laws usually forbid any accusations of witchcraft though they are not always effective.

Some people get haunted with the notion that they are bewitched. It is believed that when the body of a witch is asleep in her house her soul flies on to the roof of the hut of a person whose heart she covets. Despite the darkness and obstacles she can see into the hut, and draw out the victim's soul to eat or hide. When the victim awakes he is ill, of an inexplicable and sudden complaint, and he may die of fear unless properly tended. So a witch-doctor is called in, who is perhaps also a priest or a diviner. He will make a pretence of finding where the soul is hidden, accuse a suspected witch and oblige her to release the soul, or he will beat loud gongs in the sick person's ears, and this harsh treatment should drive the evil spirit away.

People become very distressed and ill by getting an obsession that they may become witches. A woman of my acquaintance said she had been invited to join another witch to hunt for souls.

On refusing she had been cursed and soon fell ill. She believed the witch was clinging to her invisibly and sucking her life away.

The regular witch-doctors may be called in for occasional help, and sometimes they are kept very busy, but they generally stay in one locality and have other work to do. Some of the secret societies, as described in Chapter 12, have a special function to chase witches away; Oro and Ndako Gboya in particular specialize in this.

Nowadays there appear from time to time groups of new witch-hunters, often young men who use a mixture of old and new methods to hunt out witches. Such a movement was the Bamucapi which swept across Nyasaland, the Rhodesias and into the Congo in 1934. It is beyond our scope to speak of them here, except to note that although many people surrendered articles and bones supposed to be used in witchcraft, Dr Richards who inspected hundreds of these saw no human bones and nothing beyond ordinary charms, mostly protective and a few offensive.[10]

The Nana Tongo or Atinga movement of witch-hunters spread from Ghana, across Togo, Dahomey, and Nigeria in the 1940's. Here again piles of objects that witches surrendered revealed nothing that could not be used for personal magical and usually protective purposes. They used the ordeal with a fowl, described in Chapter 13, and imposed fines and beatings on their victims. It is interesting to note that husbands very rarely defended their wives, for perhaps the wives came from other villages and had lost children in childbirth. But a number of young men could not believe that their mothers were witches and fought the Atinga successfully to get their mothers freed. A mother's best friend is her son, and human affection triumphed over superstition.

Other methods are used to chase away witchcraft and evil from towns. In Porto Novo and Abomey there is an *Avo* ceremony held annually or less often to drive out all evil spirits. The sacred packages of the gods are carried through the town, and devotees make a pretence of seeing evil lurking in corners and chase it out with brushes dipped in a pot of water; others fall to the ground and pretend to struggle with the evil spirit. Finally many small Eshu are made of mud and wood, representing the spirits that have been caught, and after a parade through the town they are

[10] E. G. Parrinder, *Witchcraft*, pp. 166–7.

thrown into the lagoon. Similarly in Ashanti there is an annual *Apo* ceremony, which consists in cleansing the town, driving away evil, parading the gods and sprinkling them with water.

It is sometimes said that the belief in witchcraft is useful, for it is an essential part of the social (or ideological) system and helps to relieve the tensions of family and social life. But Nadel says firmly: 'The relief offered by witch-hunting and witch-punishing is no more than temporary and their capacity to allay anxieties no more than illusory: for if witchcraft beliefs resolve certain fears and tensions, they also produce others.' In fact belief in witchcraft is more like a drug which poisons the system, or a false remedy which is itself very dangerous. 'We may liken witchcraft beliefs to a safety valve: but let us be clear that the engine which needs it has been badly constructed; nor is the safety valve itself safe.'[11]

It is sometimes said that belief in witchcraft is on the increase, in these days of modern towns and new ideas, and general insecurity. But in fact there is no evidence for the extent of the belief in any previous century, since there are no reliable records; and it is not really likely that modern times are as upsetting as the earlier centuries of the slave trade and tribal wars. Education will slowly dispel some superstitions. Medical and child care will remove many unexplained diseases. But nobler beliefs and a new religion would lift the load of false beliefs and prejudice. It took centuries for the superstition to disappear from Europe, and it will fade out in Africa in due course if the forces of enlightenment are maintained and increased.

[11] *Nupe Religion*, pp. 205–6.

CHAPTER FIFTEEN

Totems and Taboos

SACRED ANIMALS

THE WORD 'totem' was adopted from the American Indians, to indicate the use of images or emblems by groups and clans to represent some animal or plant after which the clan was named. Anthropologists have extended this use to refer to people in other parts of the world which are divided into groups named after animals, and sometimes use images of those animals.

'Taboo' (or tabu) is a word taken over from the peoples of the Polynesian and other Pacific islands to indicate a special or forbidden thing or person. It has been linked with totems, since totem animals are taboo to their followers. But there are many taboos and prohibitions which have nothing to do with totems. The whole question has been complicated by the powerful theory of the psychologist Freud who would derive all taboo, and even religion, from totemism. But, while recognizing many of his findings as valuable many people reject the principal theory of Freud.

In West Africa there are certain animals that can be called totems, of some clans, though they do not necessarily worship them. The python is often sacred, especially in river areas; the Fọ̃n and Ashanti dare not eat it, but the Yoruba may do so. Many chiefs rear leopards and regard them as sacred. Crocodiles are revered in the city of Ibadan, and elephants elsewhere.

The Ashanti and Fọ̃n both give funeral honours to a python that they find dead in the bush; white clay is sprinkled on the dead snake and it is buried by members of the clan to which it is taboo. The lizard is sacred to the Adjukru of the Ivory Coast; one that is found dead is buried in a white cloth. Other tribes bury leopards, crocodiles, and tortoises like human beings. The Fọ̃n, whose royal family is said to be descended from a leopard, bury a dead leopard with full ritual. The Gã also bury leopards, in a white cloth and with a rum libation. The special burial of these animals indicates a thought of blood relationship with them. But nowadays people may not remember this, and simply say that the flesh is taboo to them because it gives them a pain.

Occasionally a taboo animal is ritually killed, as by the Ashanti in the annual yam (Odwira) ceremony. There the king publicly struck an ox, the taboo of his totem (*ntoro*), with the golden State sword. The beast was then killed and eaten by the executioners. Next day at the shrine, the king prayed to the family god: 'You were sharp but I took that thing which you abhor and touched you [with it], but today I sprinkle you with water that your power may rise up again.'[1]

In some special religious ceremonies the skins of animals are worn, generally those of the totem animals. This is clearly so in the secret leopard-men societies. Ashanti and Fǫn priests sometimes wear leopard skins round their waists, daub themselves with white spots, and dance in imitation of the animal. The Oyo war chief, Kakanfo, wore an apron of leopard skin as part of his insignia of office. Often monkey skins are worn in dances, and as caps.

Animals are often taken as family symbols. The most popular are the elephant and the lion; these are royal animals and would seem to be adopted as much from admiration of the strength of the animals as from any idea of origin from them. Lions and leopards are modelled in clay outside the houses of kings and chiefs; the elephant is a frequent symbol in royal stools. Animal symbols are found in the regalia of the gods, they are woven into coloured cloths and painted on temples. The masks of secret societies are often carved in animal shapes.

Some of the most distinctive features of certain West African peoples are the facial tattoos. These are slowly being discontinued nowadays, but the Yoruba in particular are noted for their prominent face marks. The royal family of Oyo have not only three marks on each cheek, but long ribbon scars along arms and legs. A description and illustration of Yoruba marks is given in Johnson's history.[2] Similar long face and arm marks are to be seen in northern Dahomey and Ghana. That the Yoruba marks are

[1] R. S. Rattray, *Religion and Art in Ashanti*, pp. 136–7.
[2] *The History of the Yorubas*, pp. 104ff.

ancient is shown from their appearance on the stone figures, particularly in the large collection at Esie.

Some of these marks are related to totemistic myths. The royal family of Abomey claims descent from a leopard, and the king has five claw marks on each temple. Princes have five marks on one temple only, and the other side is tattooed for the king during the enthronement ceremonies. Lower classes have three, two, or one mark.

The Ibo either do not have such tattoos, or have only a small one at the side of the forehead. The Ashanti do not practise tattooing, but some of the Akan tribes on the Ivory Coast have a small mark in the middle of the forehead. The Gã of Ghana have small slanting cuts on both cheeks.

The members of a totem clan often believe that they are related to the totem animal by a common origin. A notable instance is the myth of the leopard, emblem of the royal Fǫn lineage. It is said that a certain Princess Aligbonu was seized by a male leopard, lying in wait at a spring. The attendants fled in horror, returning with warriors to kill the beast. They were amazed to find the leopard gone and the princess alive and well. In due time she gave birth to a son, a well-formed boy but hairy and long-nailed. He grew up to be a mighty chief, Agasu, and his descendants are called Agasuvi, 'sons of Agasu' the leopard, a name of the royal family today. In their migrations the Agasuvi took with them the skull and jawbone of their totem ancestor, which were buried finally at Allada, a sacred royal city of Dahomey.

Agasu and Aligbonu are both worshipped. Devotees of the leopard are called 'leopard-god-wives'. The Queen Mothers of Abomey were called 'leopard mothers' and the royal wives were 'leopard wives'. They were preceded everywhere by servants with bells on their necks crying: 'Make way for a true leopard wife.' All males had to bow and lower their eyes, and even ordinary queens had to avoid contact with them.

Members of the royal family of Porto Novo are also called leopards. When princes are buried they have their faces bound up in cloths, as it is said that one must not look a leopard in the face. The king of Porto Novo must never look at a leopard, nor at a gazelle, the latter being the name of the traditional founder of the town. The Alafin of Oyo, and other chiefs, is also called the leopard.

The Malabu, of north-eastern Nigeria, say that the human ancestress of their tribe gave birth first to a leopard and then to a human baby. The two children fed from the same breasts and grew up together. Their descendants were supposed each to have a human or a leopard counterpart.[3]

In northern Ghana the Nankanse have a leopard taboo because, they say, the first father of their tribe was blind but a leopard licked his eyes and he regained his sight and swore for ever to respect the leopard. It is said that when an old man of the leopard clan dies he 'rises up' a leopard. At adolescence a boy is told the clan secrets by his father; they are hidden from women who do not become leopards. He says: 'When you see a leopard, do not kill it. If you kill it, you have killed me. . . . When I die. . . . I will rise up a leopard.' After death he will return to the compound as a leopard, enter it to look round and see that all is in order, and then return to the long grass; the enlightened boy may watch this but must not harm the animal.[4]

On the other hand animals may be associated with myths that have no clear totemistic meaning. Such are the stories about creation. The Fǒn associate the python with the first man and woman; their eyes were sealed up and he opened them. This recalls the Genesis story, where the snake opened their eyes, gave them knowledge, and perhaps revealed the mystery of sex; the snake is an obvious phallic symbol. This is even clearer in the Ashanti story that the python taught the first men and women the secret of procreation. These ancestors are said first to have come up out of the depths of the earth, accompanied by a leopard and a dog. A popular Agni legend says that man came down from heaven on a chain, in a brass pot covered with the skin of a white sheep, and accompanied by a dog who had stolen fire. There are countless such myths; the chain motif recurs sometimes, as in Nupe, but the animals are very common: dog, chameleon, bat, sheep, tortoise, spider, hare, and so on. They play different parts in fables about creation, the arrival of death, disease, fire, and the like.

[3] C. K. Meek, *Tribal Studies in Northern Nigeria*, I.13.
[4] R. S. Rattray, *The Tribes of the Ashanti Hinterland*, I.233ff.

EXOGAMY

An important feature, often clearly connected with totemism, and much stressed in the writings of Sir James Frazer, is exogamy: the rule whereby a person could in no circumstances marry or have sexual relationships with another of the same totem. The question is complicated by different systems of inheritance, of totem and material goods, and the resulting diversity of attitudes towards marriage and children.

Here there is a distinct cleavage in our field. The Ibo, Yoruba, and Fǫn on the eastern side are patrilineal, the children belong to their father's lineage and inherit his goods and totem, if any. The same obtains of the Gã and some of the Ivory Coast tribes in the west.

The central Akan group in Ghana and the eastern Ivory Coast is strongly matrilineal, the children belong to the mother's lineage. In a number of tribes in northern Ghana it seems that they were formerly matrilineal, but later the father's lineage prevailed. The same has been suggested for some of the Nigerian peoples, because this would explain some inconsistencies and stories of different practices in the past, though this hardly amounts to historical evidence or proof.

The reason given for matrilineal inheritance among the Akan is the belief that the body comes from the woman's blood (*abusua*, in Ashanti and Agni), whilst the spirit (*ntoro*), like the semen, comes from the father. The clan persists through the female element, which alone can transmit the *abusua*, for this disappears in the males. So the cult of the ancestors is of those on the maternal side.

Rattray gives a thorough investigation of the matter, and the peculiar exogamic laws which it involves. 'Sociologically the *ntoro* plays a less important part than the *abusua*, which decides the whole succession to property and stools, but it is none the less important. . . . We come to the law that, while prohibiting a man's marriage with his father's brother's daughter (entailing no breaking of the rule as to the blood or clans), it actually enjoins a man's marriage with his father's sister's daughter. The explanation lies in the facts that (1) the *ntoro* descends through the males, and

(2) (like the *abusua*) is exogamous.' The above marriages, 'though they do not infringe the law of the *abusua*, do infringe that of the *ntoro*, while the marriages permitted, i.e. that of sons and daughters of parents who are brother and sister, infringe neither.'[5]

Inheritance of property goes to blood brothers in order of birth, then to sister's sons, uterine cousins, first cousins, sisters in order of birth, nieces and female cousins, the family head, the mother of the deceased, and children of slave wives in order of birth. The child inherits its totem (*ntoro*) from its father. There is a cult of the *ntoro*, 'washing the ntoro', which partly compensates for the lower prestige of the father. Rebirth of a clansman or clanswoman is only believed to be possible through the same *abusua* to which the dead ancestor belonged.

That this system weakened a father's authority is suggested from experiences of the related Adjukru of the Ivory Coast. A young Adjukru begins to work for his father but a day comes when his mother rebukes him for giving all his energy to his father's service, and reveals to him the secret: 'You are not his heir.' From then onwards the son slackens his work for his father and seeks to get married. The marriage arrangements are a father's last duties, and are soon completed as girls are married at puberty. From then on the young man works for his maternal uncle.

Yoruba, Ewe, and Ibo have the patrilineal rule of descent. Children are affiliated to their father's lineage, they inherit from him and the eldest surviving son succeeds to his title. If a man has daughters but no sons, then his grandson, one of his senior daughter's children, may be adopted as heir by arrangement with its father. But sometimes if there are no sons the title may pass to a brother or more remote relative.

There are always some rules of exogamy, and prohibitions of marriage within an affinity list, but these vary considerably. Marriage is almost always forbidden between close kin, and often within the village ward. Sometimes marriage is forbidden between any people descended from a common ancestor within seven generations, a descendant of 128 grandparents, but beyond this marriage to remote kin may be permitted.

Sometimes totems appear in the marriage rules, sometimes just

[5] *Ashanti*, pp. 37ff.

some remote human ancestor. One of the names given to a Yoruba boy is the *orilɛ* which indicates the totem or family origin, though this is often lost to mythology; these are sometimes names of animals: elephant, ram, bird. Marriage within the totem was formerly forbidden, though now this rule may be neglected; a woman could not adopt her husband's totem, though a man might marry into his mother's family.[6]

PERSONAL TABOOS

Morality is the behaviour of man in society, the distinction between right and wrong. It is governed by custom, which is usually ascribed to the positive command of an ancestor or a god. On its negative side it is expressed by taboos, prohibited actions and relationships. If a man breaks a taboo he expects the supernatural penalty to follow, and his friends may desert him or punish him still further, like Job's so-called 'comforters' who tried to discover what taboo he had broken.

Moral commands are like those in the Ten Commandments, with the exception of the first two. Parents are highly respected; the names of the gods are sacred and days are consecrated to them; murder, adultery, theft, covetousness, all have their prohibitions. These were more strongly insisted on in the ancient kingdoms than today. Sexual morality is nearer the Old than the New Testament pattern, as polygamy has been the rule, or at least freely permitted. But unchastity is greater today, with the rapid loosening of ancient sanctions, than it was formerly.

Taboo refers particularly to the sacred character of people and things, and the uncleanness that follows violation of the prohibitions with which they are surrounded. It is normal that kings and priests should be hedged about with strong taboos. The same obtains of members of particular crafts and occupations, smiths, hunters, weavers, and so on. But taboo enters into the life of the ordinary man, surrounds his words, clothes, eating, names, oaths, and sexual relationships.

We have referred to the great care that is taken in the disposal of all cuttings and excretions from the body. Hunters and priests in particular have taboos of cutting their hair, or do it in a special

[6] S. Johnson, *The History of the Yorubas*, pp. 85–6.

way, for hair has a virtue of its own (as in the story of Samson and the Nazirites). There are fables of giants the source of whose power lay in their hair; often 'medicine' was hidden there. Perhaps the many styles of female hair-dressing, now popular in West Africa, originally had special meaning, but today they are largely fanciful.

It was the custom of many West African men to eat separately from their wives and womenfolk. This is a sexual taboo found in many other parts of the world, and no doubt much of the Western intimacy of the sexes seems promiscuous, but the rising status of women makes for more equality and removes some disabilities.

Taboos shield many relationships of men and women. Menstruous women may be segregated, or forbidden to prepare food. Antagonism to and avoidance of the mother-in-law is very common. Obscene jokes and fables are delighted in, by a reversal of the taboo. A very common West African taboo forbids a man to have intercourse with his wife while she is still suckling a child, and this may last two or even three years. This is one of the great hindrances to monogamy, as the second wife may be taken about the time that the first wife bears her child. Thus a woman may bear a child only every three or four years, unless the previous one dies and she may resume intercourse with her husband earlier.

The taboo of men dressing in women's clothes is reversed at certain ceremonies, and occasionally priests put on female costume, the taboo increasing their awesome character. The priest of the Ibadan mountain dresses as a woman, with hair braided in female fashion, at the annual festival.

A curious custom existed at Abomey, which allowed certain women of noble family to take 'wives' for themselves. They were married to young girls by the normal contracts, and then lent out to men who had gained their owner's favour by services rendered. The children belonged to the female 'husband'. Some of these old matriarchs still exist, with their attendant wives.

Taboos of eating certain animals have been dealt with previously. There are taboos of the right and left hand. Some people will not take money from the left hand. They will not pass on the left side; bees passing on the left are said to bring bad luck. After enthronement, an Agni king might never cut anything with his right hand.

The 'minister of the right' was the most prominent official in Yoruba and Fǫn kingdoms.

Various crafts have special taboos, particularly hunters. Their wives must not eat meat, and must be chaste while the husband is away on an expedition. If a hunter sees animals having intercourse, that is taken as a sign that his wife is unfaithful and his own life will be in danger unless he returns home. Blacksmiths are often a separated profession, the members being endogamous, only marrying within their own ranks. There is a special clan of glass-makers in Nupe; apprentices to the craft have to marry into the glass-workers' kinship group, and so they form a matrilineal enclave in an otherwise patrilineal society.[7]

Weavers are sacred in Ashanti; their wives may not speak to them during their monthly periods and can never be weavers themselves. In Yoruba country, female weavers have special types of looms; some work a large loom against a wall and sit with their backs turned to the door. Others sit in holes in the ground, about two feet deep, in their houses, perhaps to cover their sex. Women also might not be stool-carvers in Ashanti. Pottery, however, is usually in the hands of women, except for the making of pots in human form.

We saw in Chapter 10 that twins are sacred persons. Other abnormal individuals may be so also, such as albinos. Dwarfs and hunchbacks are commonly chosen as heralds and jesters for chiefs, sounding their praises and memorizing national lore.

TABOO WORDS

Speech can be important and an idle word taken as a fatal insult. Hence the fearful nature of insults to one's father or mother, calling out their name may be taken as a spell against them.

Insults and threats can be based on the taboos of the person menaced, used either as a curse or else as a means of obtaining some desired object by threat. In Ashanti the expression now rendered by 'I swear an oath', means: 'I shall mention the hateful, or weighty, or forbidden word.' This is used instead of the actual word in a threat, or an appeal to an ordeal. In the north, the name of the totem animal is the taboo used in swearing an oath.

[7] S. F. Nadel, *A Black Byzantium*, p. 274.

Typical oaths on the Ivory Coast are sworn by the dead, by the river god, or by the three royal coffins of past kings. The last oath is taken on the enthronement of a chief.

Breaking an oath, especially one made in the name of a god or ancestor, is greatly feared. A Fɔn who even belches in illness is regarded as an oath-breaker. The remedy is for a relative to take water from a spring, with some sea water; in front of the shrine he swills his mouth with the water and spews it out, right, left, forwards and backwards.

A vicious gag was used in Dahomey, and in Ashanti a knife was thrust through the cheek, for condemned criminals and prisoners. This was to prevent them cursing the king or the nation on the way to execution, when the bitterness of death was passing. If any prisoner managed to work his gag free and uttered a curse, later misfortunes to the State would be ascribed to the irrevocable word.

The 'strong names' which African kings gave themselves were based on similar notions. Most kings had a number of these names and took new ones in moments of success or reverse. No name was a 'mere name', it was charged with magical power. Some of these names might not be used by ordinary people. In the same way, hunters' guns, bows, and arrows have strong names to ensure their efficiency.

The king's death was not announced directly, but by a euphemism. At Abomey only when the successor had mounted the throne, and eight days after death, was the decease of the previous monarch made public by the phrase, 'it is night' (literally, 'the night is dead'), a sentence which is used every day at dusk. After the final burial of the king it was said, 'He has gone to Allada', the town of the totem ancestor. At Porto Novo it was said: 'The house is broken.' In Ashanti they announced: 'A mighty tree has been uprooted' or 'He is absent elsewhere.' The Agni said: 'A branch of the tree has bent', or 'The king's head has struck the ground.' At Oyo they said of the dead king: 'He has entered the vault.' And at Dassa they cry, 'A leaf has fallen', when a prince dies, and 'A tree has fallen' or 'A mountain has fallen down' when a king dies. They say, 'An animal has taken another road' when the king is buried.

There are sacred numbers: Forty-one, 'forty of the god Lisa', in Dahomey. Forty less one is also used. Mungo Park noted a flogging of forty stripes less one, in the western Sudan. Three and its multiples, and seven, are generally sacred. At Porto Novo, during funeral rites, a male corpse is put nine times in the grave before final rest, a female seven times; for nine evenings following, a fire is kept up at the threshold of the funeral chamber, seven evenings for a woman. The same nine-seven theme is observed in infancy rites and in skull removal. The belief is current among Fǫn and Yoruba that men have nine pairs of ribs, and women seven, and so women are inferior.

Five is generally regarded as unlucky. In Ashanti the third, sixth, and ninth children are lucky, the fifth unlucky. If the first three children are boys, the third is extremely lucky and is greatly favoured. Three is the figure for a man and four for a woman, in many Akan tribes.

In the class of taboo words we may put those curious cursings and insults of chiefs and kings, and even gods, that so puzzled early observers. This is seen in the Apo ceremony of northern Ashanti, where Rattray found the true meaning of the custom to be an annual purification of the mind and thoughts, whereby men had freedom to speak out anything that was in their heads and tell their neighbours just what they thought of them. By this safety valve the soul was quietened and relieved.[8]

The annual festivals and saturnalia were also times of breaking taboos. The Gã have an annual 'hunger-hooting' ceremony, at the end of the old food and before the new is harvested. Young men carry about sexual symbols or dress up as women, and even chiefs and priests are taunted with their weaknesses or sins. So in the Yoruba festivals of the farm goddess, Orisha Oko, or annual hill festivals as at Ibadan, there was breaking of taboos; and reinforcing them on the following day. Yoruba kings also prescribed occasionally a period of liberty to mark the close of a successful reign. This was the Bebe festival which lasted three years, and liberty of speech and action were allowed to rich and poor, without action for sedition. 'No riot or fighting is to be heard anywhere, all provocations must be suppressed while the

[8] *Ashanti*, p. 153.

Bebe lasts, for no one is to be prosecuted during that period.'[9]

At Ketu and other Yoruba towns when the announcement was made of the election of a new king, there was an outburst of shouting and lampooning against him. Mud and stones were thrown at the door of his house, and insults shouted at him until people had cleared their minds. Thenceforward it was a capital offence to speak against the king.

ROYAL TABOOS

The person of a king or chief is hedged about with taboos. No doubt this is because, as Frazer pointed out, in early societies the king existed only for the well-being of his subjects. It was his duty to order the course of nature, to make the rain fall and the crops grow, and if he failed to do so he could be dismissed or even killed. His life was often a burden to him, because of the taboos that closed him in.

The king's palace and burial quarters were sacred, and in various regions it is reported that when they were repaired all the work had to be done in one day, before nightfall. It was taboo for women to leave their houses during the royal repairs.

Human sacrifice was offered at the foundation of a palace or of a town. The kingdom of Dahomey traditionally derives its name from a neighbouring chief Dã, who was killed to build the town 'on the belly of Dã'. The name may also be connected with the snake Dã. But there is little doubt that a foundation sacrifice was made. A hunchbacked weaver is said to have been sacrificed at the foundation of the Yoruba town of Ketu, and to have given it his name. At Oyo, when the king entered the inner precincts of the palace for the first time at his enthronement, a special entrance was made for him and closed up again at his death. A man and a woman were sacrificed there, among other animal victims.

Sometimes the king is forbidden to appear after sunset. At Dassa the 'mountain king', who is not the town chief but perhaps represents the original owners of the soil, must not remain in the village below after sunset but must regain his hill palace. At Porto Novo the reigning monarch may not go out after sunset,

[9] S. Johnson, *The History of the Yorubas*, p. 163; E. G. Parrinder, *The Story of Ketu*, p. 71.

for that is the time when the 'king of the night' (literally 'owner of the forest') is supreme, and it was formerly taboo for the two rulers to meet. The King of the Night controls the gods and the secret societies. He is not the owner of the soil however; another official fills this office and at the close of the coronation ritual he says to the new king: 'Today it is finished, I have appointed you, you are king.' He then goes home without looking behind him. He must never again see the king, enter the town, or leave his house in the daytime. These taboos are still observed.

In most parts of West Africa the king should not be killed. If he was unworthy he might be told, 'We reject you', as at Oyo. At Abomey he was sent a packet of parrots' eggs; or the royal sandals might be whipped off by the first minister, as happened to King Adandozan who was then interned for life. A king of Ketu was induced to go out on a prohibited day and met the tabooed eunuch, ruler of the market; the king returned to the palace and quietly took poison.

The king of Porto Novo had a taboo of seeing the sea, though this has been broken nowadays, with payment of sacrifice. Some of the other Ewe tribes forbade their rulers to look at rivers. The original reason for this may have been because the sea, or river, represents the water which must be crossed at death. Thus the kings of Abomey were said after death to embark for the under-world at the 'lagoon of death' (ku-to-nu, the modern port of Cotonou). The Fante believe that the dead go up the river Volta, to build villages there till their rebirth. The Gã give the dead presents 'to cross the river', and to pay for a cure for the mortal sickness in the underworld.

Formerly many kings alone had the right of wearing sandals, and even today the heir-apparent in some places leaves off his shoes lest he be thought to usurp the king's place or be plotting against his life. In many places the king alone might sit on a stool or a hide mat. Nobles would leave their shoes and sit on the ground in the royal presence.

It was thought that the king should not come into contact with the bare earth, or even toil the soil with his hands, lest the crops be ruined by this contact of two potent forces. At great cere-monies in Ashanti the king could not walk unaided. His feet were lifted one after another by an attendant, for if he were to stumble when acting for the nation a great famine might follow.

At Nupe nobody could be killed in the presence of the king. An organization known as the 'king's hangmen' ensured that criminals were killed in places far away from the capital.

In council Yoruba kings were masked with a veil of coloured beads, and in olden times they never appeared in public with uncovered face though they do today. The kings of Abomey once practised this, but King Tegbesu (1728) abolished the veil in council. The king in council spoke little, or quietly behind a cow-tail switch, to be interpreted by a minister. The 'linguist', so named in early West African literature, was not an interpreter but a spokesman, a necessary intermediary between the divine speech of the king and the commoners or visitors. The lightest utterances of the monarch were charged with power.

The king was indeed a demi-god, and it is understandable that worship of gods and ancestors came to mix easily. At Oyo the Alafin was supposed to have no natural father or mother. If they were alive at his accession, they were asked to 'go to sleep' quietly. At Porto Novo the Migǎn, minister of the right hand, was taken as the king's father, and the Aplogǎn, supervisor of cults, as his mother. At the coronation ceremonies the Aplogǎn took the new king on his back, bound with a cloth like a child to its mother, and lifted him over the threshold into the palace.

The king must be well built. A left-handed or hammer-toed king was disqualified. On the other hand a prince born shod, that is with the feet wrapped in the foetal membrane, was regarded as predestined to royalty.

Strong taboos surrounded the eating and drinking of the king for, as a god, he had no need of food like mortals. Kings ate alone, being served by an attendant who turned away his head while the monarch ate; the latter gave a cough when he had finished. His food was cooked either by his first wife or by a woman past the menopause. When the king of Abomey ate, a queen called out 'the day is going out', and all queens and servants would bow and close their eyes. If he had to eat in public, the eunuchs and wives held cloths round him to veil him from the common gaze.

At Oyo there was a ritual eating that was magical rather than cannibalistic. The king-elect partook of a dish prepared from the heart of a previous king; hence the phrase to become a king was 'to eat a king' (*jɛ ọba*). But kings were not killed, and the kingship did not descend from father to son but went in turn through seven families [10]

At Dassa the corpses of all princes are carried up the mountain to be inspected by the 'Mountain King', to find out the cause of death since a prince was not supposed to die naturally. On the day of the king's death no hammering is allowed in the town, no pounding of meal, and no wood may be chopped. At Dassa a drum was covered with a human skin and beaten with the arm bones. This is done at night so that not even the drummers, but only the new king and that once only, may look at the drum which is then hidden under the mountain till the next king dies. Before burial the corpse of the king of Dassa is hung from a rafter and dried over a slow fire; cuts are made in the soles of the feet so that all liquid drains away and the body becomes dry and taut and better preserved. The king of Porto Novo was wrapped in the skin of an official. This process of preserving the body of the king may be compared with the custom of some north-eastern Nigerian tribes who peel the skin off the bodies of dead kings and nobles.[11]

At Abomey, for three days after the king's death no fire must be lit, no water drawn, no personal washing done; nobody must sit on a stool and no market may be held. Grindstones are taken down. All the population has to shave the head, and cover the head and chest with clay.

The bones of dead kings of Ashanti were preserved in a mausoleum, where the reigning kings officiated in ancestral cults. At Abomey the royal tombs are still maintained; they are large huts in the compound next to the old palace which is now a museum, and are cared for by a succession of royal wives appointed for this purpose.

[10] S. Johnson, *The History of the Yorubas*, p. 43, note.
[11] C. K. Meek, *Tribal Studies in Northern Nigeria*, I. 196–7.

CHAPTER SIXTEEN

Religious Change

NO SOCIETIES and no religions are static, though they may appear to change little for long periods. In modern times all societies are undergoing rapid change and religions with them. The slave trade and the tribal wars which it provoked, then the coming of colonial rule, and finally the establishment of independent States, brought a succession of political changes. Social changes were even more profound: the cessation of wars, the new ease of communications, the growth of trade and wealth, the great spread of education, all these and many more factors have produced a social revolution. Along with these have come not only the new outlook introduced with Western education, but the new missionary religions, Christianity and Islam. We cannot speak of West African religion as if it were untouched by all this. Much of the old faith of centuries has crumbled and disappeared. But much remains under the surface and continues to influence men's thinking. It is a mistake either to look at the religion as if nothing had happened, or to treat it as vanished without a trace. Neither the isolationist nor the archaeological attitudes are adequate to modern times. A process of culture-change, or acculturation as the Americans call it, must be recognized. The mixed religion of today is as real as the paganism of yesterday, and both must be studied.[1]

In the last chapter we spoke of kings or chiefs and the customs surrounding them, and often we had to speak in the past tense. The position of the chief is as indicative as anything of the great social and religious changes of our times, as Dr Busia has so well shown in his valuable study. At the basis of Ashanti religion and society, he says, was the ancestral cult. 'The whole legal and political system of Ashanti is bound up with ancestor-worship,

---

[1] For a valuable recent study of social and religious change in Africa see M. Wilson's *Communal Rituals of the Nyakyusa*, and especially the last chapters.

which provides an organic unity between political and religious authority. . . . Ancestor-worship is the basis of the chief's authority as well as the sanction of morality in the community. The chief is the one "who sits on the stool of the ancestors".'[2]

The position of the chief was weakened by colonial rule, dividing the chief from the people, and by the rise of modern politicians who mostly came from the new coastal towns. New riches in the hands of other people, new education, more social and political power, all these have weakened African chiefs. But direct religious challenge also assailed the chief. Christians refused obedience to the chief on several grounds: objection to swearing oaths in the traditional way, to providing sheep for sacrifice in legal cases, to carrying stools or swords on ceremonial occasions, even to doing communal labour on the roads. The objections crystallized in the refusal of Christians to observe Thursday as a day of rest sacred to the spirit of the earth; this would have been tantamount to recognizing the existence of a pagan god. ·

Dr Busia puts the problem fairly from both sides. 'The cleavage centres round two questions. Belief, and the liberty of the Christian. They are both political as well as religious questions. . . . To recognize the existence of Christians in the community, the chief must surrender to the Church his traditional authority as a religious head. This is the problem which Christianity presents.'[3] There is no easy solution, in fact there has not been one. When the Ashanti Confederacy Council of Chiefs ruled that Thursday must be observed, the Churches Christian Council appealed to the Asantehene and the Chief Commissioner. The matter was shelved. It was hoped that time would solve the problems.

In greater or less degree the problem of old and new has arisen everywhere in West Africa. But there have been concessions as well as objections on both sides. In Ashanti as elsewhere men have been elected as chiefs who were both educated and Christian, and they have usually felt obliged to perform some of the traditional ritual acts of their office. 'They were enstooled in the stoolhouse, where they poured libations to the ancestors whom they had succeeded.'[4] Like the Oni of Ife they might not go to the

[2] *The Position of the Chief in the Modern Political System in Ashanti*, pp. 136–7.
[3] Ibid.   [4] Ibid. p. 38.

shrines themselves, but a deputy would be sent. Only rarely, as in Ibadan with Chief Akinyele, were all pagan associations expunged, the symbolical staff of office changed for one which had no images on it, and the annual festival (Oke'badãn) confined to a simple holiday with licentious songs and dances banned.

Dahomey has remained the country where the old religion has persisted most strongly organized still, followed perhaps by Ashanti. But even in Dahomey the chiefs have often had Christian education, and the politicians are often Christian. In the first parliament of independent Togoland thirty-six of the forty-seven deputies were Christian. In Eastern Nigeria the success of Christianity has been most sweeping, and here Islam has hardly penetrated at all. Nearly thirty years ago Meek could write: 'The people of Onitsha have adopted Christianity in no uncertain manner, and the Obi himself has become a Roman Catholic. All that remains to him of his old prestige is the presidency of a society which functions feebly, and a certain sentimental regard by the people, which can only be galvanized into a genuine loyalty by an Obi of very exceptional personality.'[5]

There is also the great invasion of the Muslim religion from the north which is a major factor of modern times. This has only happened since the beginning of the last century, and is a result both of the Muslim revival under the Fulani and the opening up of modern communications and establishment of peace, which enabled Muslims to penetrate right down to the coast. The effect of Islam has been greatest so far on the Yoruba, little on the Ibo or Fọn and not a great deal in Ashanti. But all the coastal towns have their Muslim communities, and being spread by African laymen, and those in close touch with the people, this religion has many advantages. As a monotheistic and anti-idolatrous religion Islam, like Christianity, brings great challenges and changes to African life.

The process of religious change brought by Islam has been acutely analysed by J. S. Trimingham, in books that no student of African religion can safely ignore.[6] In an important diagram he shows the impact of religious forces that work out in at least six

[5] *Law and Authority in a Nigerian Tribe*, p. 195.
[6] Especially *Islam in West Africa*, pp. 21ff.

ways. There is the effect of Islam upon paganism: the process and psychology of conversion to Islam, the pagan reaction to Islamic influence, and the way in which pagan myth and ritual may be affected by Islamic myth and ritual. Then in reverse there are the ways in which paganism affects Islam: local custom may hold its own against Islamic law, there are reversions from Islam to paganism, and particularly there are pagan elements which remain to condition Islam—belief in spirits, ancestral cults, magical practices, ceremonies of birth, marriage, and death.

In similar fashion paganism and Christianity interact. Christian and Western customs in politics and economics, and also religious teaching, affect traditional beliefs. Examples may be seen in the Western-type school, application of Western ideas in law cases, nationalist and political movements, and the degradation of the dowry system by a money economy. In religious conversion the growth of great Churches with their organization is of great importance; and so also is the sectarianism of the so-called African Churches. Paganism also influences Christianity, once again through the separatist Churches which retain more magical practices than do the orthodox. In the days of European rule the very separation of the races produced a colonial ruler-attitude which attentuated Christianity, and this may be continued under independent rule, with a minority claiming undue privileges. Customs such as dowry, polygamy, and ancestral cults brought varying measures of compromise and adaptation into the Christian community.

But the two new religions also influence each other, and this again is a part of the modern African scene that must not be neglected. There has been little direct conversion on either side, and there is a good deal more tolerance between Christians and Muslims in West Africa than has been seen in other countries and at other periods in the history of these two religions. But the West brought economic and social revolution to the Muslims of Africa, abolishing slavery and warfare, and introducing Western economy and education. That the northern Muslim areas have taken to education less quickly has also meant that politically they have been less advanced in Western style. Western law has also slowly affected traditional Islamic law, as it has done much more rapidly in Egypt

and Turkey. In reverse Christianity has been affected by the
official governmental recognition of Islam, a religious neutrality
policy which often meant freedom for Islam and restriction for
Christianity, as well as the maintenance of feudal systems and the
application of Islamic law to everyone.

In the study of West African religion today there is room for a
good deal of research to be done into the ways in which the new
religions have affected and are still affecting the old. How far has
belief in a supreme God been affected? In Nupe, for example,
whose rulers are Muslims but most of whose people are pagan,
the supreme God Soko may be approached direct only by the
Muslims, it is thought, whereas other people must approach him
through traditional rituals. Yet belief in a supreme God may be
strengthened by the fact that the new religions are both monotheistic. In the old days, priests have said, nobody built a temple
for Qlọrŭn or Chukwu, but today he has many temples.

How far do the nature gods survive? It seems that these are the
first to go under the impact of a new religion. In the Atinga witch-
hunting many temples of gods were pillaged for their images, and
some were burnt down, but the ancestral shrines were left severely
alone. It may be that some of the old gods will survive as fairies in
fables, or turn into local saints of wells and hills, as happened both
in Christianity and Islam, but there is little sign of this as yet.[7]
The ancestors, too, may turn into saints and have prayers made
for, or even *to*, them, but this is in the future, and the nearest to
it at the moment is the popularity of All Souls' festivals and the
way in which even Protestant funeral cards bear the words
'pray for him', and the insistence on memorial services.

The magical side of religion, its lowest and yet persistent
aspect, continues to be attractive. If pagan charms in the form of
special leaves may not be worn, then verses from the Qur'ān and
Psalms are worn as potent protections and curses, and crosses and
scapulas replace magical beads. The magical so-called books of
Moses and Solomon, vast frauds invented by European charlatans,
sell at exorbitant prices and vie with the Ifa magical system
in popular esteem. And all kinds of European and Indian
magic, magical pens, magic words, charms to procure success in

[7] See J. S. Trimingham, *Islam in the Sudan*, Chapter 5.

examinations, promotion in business, fertility, and prosperity, all these rival the old herbal and magical remedies. On the medical side there are as many quack medicines as there are ones that have some valuable healing value.

The festivals of all religions are adapted to one another. The Christian Sunday and the Western calendar provide holidays for all and are a great convenience. There is no reason why a Muslim should not observe Christmas, since he believes in Jesus the Messiah, and an Egyptian Muslim has written one of the most moving studies of Good Friday.[8] On the other hand Muslims press for observance of the birthday of the Prophet and their two great Ids. But pagan festivals can easily be adapted, especially as so many of them are connected with agriculture: planting, first-fruits, and harvest. It is here that the new religions can become naturalized and no longer appear as foreign systems.

Festivals of family life witness to the mixture of religion that is symptomatic of our day. The eight-day naming ceremony often mingles Christian hymns with libations to the earth. Dowry in some form remains, and polygamy is widely practised. Adolescent initiation ceremonies have tended to die out, and there has not been the experimentation that has been done in East Africa with Christian schools of initiation.

A notable effort at reforming and retaining an old religious society has been the Reformed Ogboni Fraternity, which some of its followers have claimed to be an African Christian Gnosticism. But its spiritual and intellectual claims have been too slight to support this claim, and the strong stand taken against it both by Islam and by the Roman Catholic Church outweighs the indecision of the other Churches.[9]

On the other hand there have been some efforts at a reaction against Christianity and a complete return to paganism. Both in Ghana and Dahomey public political ceremonies have been marked by libations to the ancestral gods, while Christians and Muslims have either been excluded or pushed very much into the background. And organized pagan reactions have appeared in the small Ethiopian and Orunmilaist Churches. Qrunmila, we have

[8] K. Hussein, *City of Wrong*.
[9] See E. B. Idowu, *Olodumare, God in Yoruba Belief*, Chapter 15.

seen, is the patron god of the oracle, but is only one of the Yoruba gods, and the claim that Qrunmila was to the Yorubas as Christ was to the Jews or Muhammad to the Arabs has no basis in history. This cult is only one of the old pagan cults, and cannot speak as the whole of Yoruba religion. Similarly the Ethiopian Churches which claim to be truly African have only adopted the name of Ethiopia for their purposes and have not the true link with the Ethiopian or Eastern Orthodox Churches that the African Greek Orthodox Church has in Uganda.[10] And the National Church of Eastern Nigeria, with its God of Africa, seems to have died out since its political purposes have been served.[11] The *Eglise des Oracles* at Porto Novo was the French Dahomean version of the Qrunmila cult.

These various cults show degrees in which new beliefs have been mingled with old, and different ways of reaction to modern times. There is a great deal of mixture, and this is evidence of vitality and interest in religious thought. Old cults revive occasionally, or take new forms as in the Atinga witch hunters, then they decline again. Their place is taken by churches, mosques, or the new separatist or prophetic churches. Some of these latter are of particular interest in that they centre round a leader, build a community, and are often highly successful and noted for their efficiency and honesty. Such are some of the religious communities in Nigeria and Ghana.[12]

The censuses that are taken from time to time in West Africa reveal ever larger numbers of people who claim allegiance to Islam or Christianity, and it seems certain that the religious future of the countries must be divided between the two great historical and scriptural religions. At the moment however it is difficult to say how many of those who claim the name Christian or Muslim ever really accept the obligations of faith and worship; it is often the 'done thing' to take the name of a higher religion.

At the same time there are still millions who hold to the old paganism, either fully or partially. These are becoming fewer in the four main groups with which we have been dealing, but they

[10] See F. B. Welbourn, *East African Rebels*, Chapter 5.
[11] E. G. Parrinder, *Religion in an African City*, pp. 128–9.
[12] Such as the Community of the Apostles at Aiyetoro in Nigeria, and the Musama Disco Christo in Ghana.

are still very numerous in the 'pagan' tribes of the semi-Sudanese areas. Yet it seems unlikely that the old traditional religions of West Africa can survive, at least in their old forms. They are tied too much to localities, and could hardly develop into universal or even inter-tribal religions. And in the life of modern towns and industry they appear increasingly out of place.

If the old cults collapse, then will not society and its morality disintegrate? The old gods and ancestors have been so closely entwined with moral sanctions that the decline of the old cults might be disastrous. This is the fear of the sociologist, who sees the unity of society and religion. But C. K. Meek, himself a sociologist, says that this is to ignore the fact that the new religions come with their own moral principles. 'Some of the old ethics will disappear with the old gods, but new gods will create new ethical values, and new ethical values in turn will create new conceptions of deity.'[13] So that both religious and moral ideas may be strengthened by change when the confusion of today is cleared and a longer view may be obtained.

J. S. Trimingham concludes that 'the majority will have the choice between Islam or Christianity or secularism forced upon them through the decay of their old religions and their manifest incompatibility for life in modern Africa'.[14] He sees Islam as having a great advantage because it has the field virtually to itself in many northern areas, and also because it appears indigenous though stagnant in many places. On the other hand Islam will be conditioned by the spread of Western secularism. Because of this 'Neo-Muslims today tend to manifest a Western attitude towards religion. African governments will have to remain neutral in matters of religion. This means that the absorption of secular ideas will limit the advance of Islam primarily to its religious aspects. . . . As in other parts of the world Christians and Muslims in West Africa have to adjust themselves to living and letting live side by side, and allowing their encounter to be one, not of competition for adherents, but an encounter of the things that pertain to the spirit.'[15]

This secularist attitude is an important factor in Africa today.

[13] *Law and Authority in a Nigerian Tribe*, p. 341.
[14] *Islam in West Africa*, pp. 224-5.   [15] Ibid.

In some ways it is disturbing, for it means that life may be divided into compartments, sacred and secular, instead of a religious influence being spread over the whole of life. On the other hand it may reduce the tensions of social and religious change, remove religious intolerance and give a deeper appreciation of what religion really is. Some old problems have been intractable because they were bound up with religion instead of being seen as social custom; such as female circumcision, dowry, and polygamy.

The new religions should be looked at for what they teach rather than for their foreign trappings, and considered in their religious aspects. With the disappearance of imperialism Christianity is being seen by the Islamic, as well as the African, world as a religious faith and a contribution to the needs of the world. The religious dialogue between Islam and Christianity is only now beginning, owing to their opposed empire-building in the past. But now they can meet, not in competition, but in 'an encounter of the things that pertain to the spirit'. African spirituality also has its part to play in this dialogue. The understanding of its own religious past is essential. But from there it must go forward to create, and contribute its own insights within the great new faiths.

Selected Bibliography

Basden, G. T., *Niger Ibos*, Seeley, 1938.

Bradbury, R. E., *The Benin Kingdom*, Ethnographic Survey, 1957.

Busia, K. A., *The Position of the Chief in the Modern Political System of Ashanti*, Oxford, 1951.

Cardinall, A. W., *Tales told in Togoland*, Oxford, 1931.

Danquah, J. B., *The Akan Doctrine of God*, Lutterworth, 1944.

Debrunner, H., *Witchcraft in Ghana*, Kumasi, 1959.

Farrow, S. S., *Faith, Fancies and Fetich*, S.P.C.K., 1926.

Field, M. J., *Religion and Medicine of the Gã People*, Oxford, 1937.
Search for Security, Faber, 1960.

Forde, D., *The Ibo and Ibibio-speaking Peoples*, Ethnographic Survey, 1950.
The Yoruba-speaking Peoples, Ethnographic Survey, 1951.
African Worlds, Oxford, 1954.

Hazoumé, P., *Le Pacte du Sang au Dahomey*, Paris, 1937.

Herskovits, M. J., *Dahomey, An Ancient West African Kingdom* (New York, 1938).

Idowu, E. B., *Olodumare, God in Yoruba Belief*, Longmans, 1961.

Johnson, S., *The History of the Yorubas*, Lagos, 1921.

Le Herissé, A., *L'Ancien Royaume du Dahomey*, Paris, 1911.

Little, K., *The Mende of Sierra Leone*, Routledge, 1951.

Lucas, J. O., *The Religion of the Yorubas*, Lagos, 1948.

Manoukian, M., *Akan and Ga-Adangme Peoples*, Ethnographic Survey, 1950.
The Ewe-speaking People, Ethnographic Survey, 1952.

Maupoil, B., *La Géomancie à l'ancienne Côte des Esclaves*, Paris, 1943.

Meek, C. K., *Tribal Studies in Northern Nigeria*, Kegan Paul, 1931.
A Sudanese Kingdom, Kegan Paul, 1931.
Law and Authority in a Nigerian Tribe, Oxford, 1937.

Meyerowitz, E. L. R., *The Sacred State of the Akan*, Faber, 1951.

Nadel, S. F., *A Black Byzantium*, Oxford, 1942.
Nupe Religion, Routledge, 1954.

Nketia, J. H., *Funeral Dirges of the Akan People*, Achimota, 1955.

Parrinder, E. G., *West African Psychology*, Lutterworth, 1951.
Religion in an African City, Oxford, 1953.
African Traditional Religion, Hutchinson, 1954.

SELECTED BIBLIOGRAPHY

The Story of Ketu, Ibadan, 1956.

Witchcraft, Penguin, 1958.

Rattray, R. S., *Ashanti*, Oxford, 1923.

Religion and Art in Ashanti, Oxford, 1927.

The Tribes of the Ashanti Hinterland, Oxford, 1932.

Smith, E. W., *The Golden Stool*, Edinburgh House, 1926.

African Ideas of God, Edinburgh House, 1950.

African Symbolism, Royal Anthropological Institute, 1952.

Spieth, J., *Die Religion der Eweer in Süd-Togo*, Göttingen, 1911.

Talbot, P. A., *Life in Southern Nigeria*, Macmillan, 1923.

The Peoples of Southern Nigeria, Oxford, 1926.

Tauxier, L., *Religion, Mœurs et Coutumes des Agnis de la Côte d'Ivoire*, Paris, 1932.

Tempels, P., *Bantu Philosophy*, Paris, 1960.

Trimingham, J. S., *Islam in the Sudan*, Oxford, 1949.

The Christian Church and Islam in West Africa, S.C.M., 1955.

Islam in West Africa, Oxford, 1959.

Verger, P., *Dieux d'Afrique*, Dakar, 1954.

Notes sur le Culte des Orisa et Vodun, Dakar, 1957.

Waterlot, E. G., *Les Bas-Reliefs des Bâtiments royaux d'Abomey*, Paris, 1926.

Westermann, D., *Die Glidyi-Ewe in Togo*, Berlin, 1935.

Index